The Hidden Key to

Harry Potter

Zossima Press titles may be purchased for business or promotional use or for special sales. For information, please write to: Zossima Press, 231 S. 7th Avenue, Port Hadlock, WA, 98339

First edition published December 2002
10 9 8 7 6 5 4 3 2 1

Edited by Stephen Schumacher
Designed by Colleen Schumacher

ISBN 0-9723221-0-8
Printed in the United States of America.

The Hidden Key to

Harry Potter

Understanding the Meaning, Genius, and Popularity of Joanne Rowling's Harry Potter Novels

John Granger

Zossima Press

"I believe in God, not magic."
In fact, Rowling initially was afraid
that if people were aware of her
Christian faith, she would give away too
much of what's coming in the series.
"If I talk too freely about that,"
she told a Canadian reporter,
"I think the intelligent reader — whether
ten [years old] or sixty — will be able to
guess what is coming in the books."

(Michael Nelson,
"Fantasia: The Gospel According to C. S. Lewis",
The American Prospect, vol. 13, no. 4,
February 25, 2002)

You will be both grieved and amused to
hear that out of about 60 reviews only 2
showed any knowledge that my idea of the
fall of the Bent One [in *Out of the Silent
Planet*] was anything but a private invention
of my own. But if there only was someone
with a richer talent and more leisure I think
that this great ignorance might be a help to
the evangelisation of England; any amount
of theology can now be smuggled into
people's minds under cover of romance
without their knowing it.

C. S. Lewis' letter to Sister Penelope,
July 9, 1939
(Letters of C. S. Lewis, p. 167)

Table of Contents

Maps & Charts

The *Iliad* is only great because
all life is a battle,
the *Odyssey* because all
life is a journey,
the *Book of Job* because
all life is a riddle.

G. K. Chesterton,
The Defendant, 1907

A very famous writer once said,
"A book is like a mirror.
If a fool looks in, you can't expect a genius
to look out."

J. K. Rowling
*on NBC's Today Show,
October 20, 2000*

Do you think I am trying to weave a spell?
Perhaps I am;
but remember your fairy tales.
Spells are used for breaking enchantments
as well as for inducing them.
And you and I have need of
the strongest spells that can be found
to wake us from
the evil enchantment of worldliness
which has been laid upon us
for nearly a hundred years.

C. S. Lewis,
"The Weight of Glory"

Introduction

I, Mr. John Granger, of Avenue Seven, Port Hadlock, am proud to say that I am perfectly normal, thank you very much. So I normally buy books that tell me the most on their outsides about what the author will explain in detail inside.

I hope very much this book's back cover has given away the heart of my argument already, but regardless I will spill the beans here, before the book proper begins, to be sure you have had fair warning.

Joanne Rowling's four **Harry Potter** novels and two fictitious textbooks (not to mention the first movie adaptations) have been the publishing and marketing events of the new century. At this writing, the books have sold almost 70 million copies in the United States alone and have been translated into close to 40 languages. However, there has been remarkably little discussion of the author's talent or the books' literary strengths or the reasons for their popularity. Criticism to date has been approached along either what I call the "Low Road" or the "Middle Road" rather than a "High Road".

Low Road criticism attempts to explain **Potter**'s success by pointing to how bad the books are or how stupid and unprotected their readers must be. Middle Road critics are charmed by the books, but do not see anything in them that sets them head and shoulders above other books. The Middle Road embraces **Harry Potter** with enthusiasm only because of his success. Neither answers the question most frequently asked Ms. Rowling: Why are the books so popular?

Whence this book! If the answer had to be made in one word, "Inkling" would be best and "Christian" would suffice. Ms. Rowling, a Classicist by training and Church of Scotland parishioner by confession, reveals in her books the traditionalist background and philosophy she shares with C. S. Lewis and J. R. R. Tolkien, the great Inkling novelists and Christian apologists.

She has said many times that her favorite authors are Jane Austen, Charles Dickens, and C. S. Lewis, so it should be little surprise that she is writing books along the same lines as these greats. We see Austen's shadow in Rowling's focus on "manners and morals" and human relationships; Dickens's critique of the institutions of his times (e.g., schools, debtor prisons, government, etc.) are evident in Rowling's treatment of modern institutions in the magical world; and the smuggled Christian theology of Lewis' **Chronicles of Narnia** and **Space Trilogy** give **Harry Potter** their larger meaning and biggest draw.

I spend very little time tracing the influence of Jane Austen and Charles Dickens in **Harry Potter**. Suffice it to say, these shadows are self-evident to fans of British 19th century fiction, and they amount in the end only to the conclusion that Rowling has good taste — and the good sense to write in imitation of the best. The watertight plotting, characterization, relationships, caste sensitivity, social concerns, and clever names (often with several meanings) reflect her enormous talent and her debt to Austen and Dickens.

Much less obvious, and certainly more controversial, is the link between Rowling, Lewis, and Tolkien. Despite the objections of certain Christian groups about Rowling's use of magic, *The Hidden Key* you are holding makes clear that by theme, by plot, and by design, the *Potter* books are meant to "baptize the imagination" in Christian imagery and doctrine, oftentimes as bald and bold as Lewis' Narnia and Tolkien's Middle Earth. Moreover, this initiation into what Lewis called the "Stock Responses" is the secret of Ms. Rowling's success.

Hidden Key, though, is really three books in one. First, it is most obviously a book about the *Harry Potter* novels and what they mean. Readers will find discussions of the themes that run through all four books and of the meanings of each novel in the series. But within this first book are two others.

The second book is explicitly about the Inkling world view, which some have called "neo-platonism", and others "Christian other-worldliness". These tags come with a lot of irrelevant baggage and irreverent pigeon-holing, so I prefer to call it "the symbolist outlook", a way of seeing which is common to the great religious traditions including Christianity.

The remarkable (to be honest, "unrivaled" is closer to the mark) popularity and literary power of Tolkien's, Lewis's and Rowling's fiction speaks to the possibility that this outlook is not just a perspective or another "ism". The human heart seems to respond to Inkling literature as it does to certainty in confusion, to light in darkness, and to learning the truth after being deceived. Clearly, the symbolist outlook is the anti-thesis of the naturalist and materialist world views that are the reigning paradigms of our day.

The third book is implicit to the **Harry Potter** exegesis, but is made explicit only in a brief epilogue. This "book" is about the usefulness of modern literary critical schools in evaluating traditional and anti-modern texts. I suggest that reductionist tools are of little value in explaining the success and meaning of works that argue, contrary to modern superstitions and scientism, that "lesser things can only come from the greater". Marxist, historicist, and personal arguments tell us as much about the meaning of such books as a chemical analysis of their pages, inks, and binding.

The Hidden Key to Harry Potter is organized in four parts in order to overcome the two principal obstacles to understanding Ms. Rowling's oeuvre. These obstacles are pervasive misconceptions both about Ms. Rowling and about Christianity.

Ms. Rowling, to her fans, critics, and even to many who have not read her books, is known as a woman who rose from "rags to riches" and inflamed the fundamentalist Christian groups opposed to the spiritual occult. In a nut-shell (or, better, pigeon-hole), she is considered a welfare mom who won the lottery and as an opponent of those who are truly devoted Christians.

Christianity, too, has been pigeon-holed by our media and popular culture. It is commonly portrayed as the sentimental refuge of the retarded, as an opiate for those who cannot think for themselves, and, most stridently in our schools and academies, as only one perspective among many — a perspective of value (if any) only in the limited, non-physical, subjective realms of ethics, emotions, morality, etc.

That Ms. Rowling has an intellectual pedigree of the first order is evident in her resume. That she is writing profoundly Christian books — drawing on classical philosophy, medieval and patristic theology, and the esoteric symbolist tradition of East and West — is the thesis and argument of this book. That Christianity may hold the truth about the world and the answer to the largest questions about human life and death — I offer it as a possibility, at least, that this may be why Inkling books which "smuggle Christian theology" (*Narnia*, *The Lord of the Rings*, and *Harry Potter*) are the best selling books of modern times. Believers and de facto atheists thrill to their veiled Christian message, with which their hearts resonate.

Hidden Key is organized to help the reader over these obstacles gently. The first part introduces the seriousness of the books without mentioning theology, smuggled or otherwise, to clue in the reader (who may think *Harry Potter* books are overly long "Goosebumps" novels) about their depth and structure. Not until the last chapters of the second part and the "meaning" chapters of the third are the books' Christian meaning discussed or even mentioned. It is hoped that by the end of *Hidden Key* even the angriest fundamentalist or dismissive critic will have come to an appreciation of Ms. Rowling as a Christian and as an author of the highest ranks.

The first part, "Taking Harry Seriously", explores the spectrum of critical responses to *Harry Potter* and why they do not and cannot explain the popularity of the books. A look at the structure of the books, their formula, and their two most obvious themes ("Prejudice" and "Death and Grief") begins the High Road walk to understanding Ms. Rowling's special genius as a writer, and her popularity with readers around the world and of all ages.

The second part, "The Secret of Harry Potter", opens up two more themes of the books ("Choice" and "Change") before discussing the symbolism of the major characters, the story, and the magical creatures. The Christian quality common to both Ms. Rowling's themes and symbolism presented throughout her books force the conclusion that she is an "Inkling Wanna-be".

The third part, "The Meaning of Harry Potter", is a book-by-book look at the series, plumbing the depths and explicit Christian truths she offers in each. This part concludes with chapters explaining the meaning of the books' titles and the name "Harry Potter" itself.

The fourth part, "What Will Happen With Harry?", offers predictions which answer the many questions the last three *Potter* books must address (most notably, "Who is Harry Potter?" and "Why does Lord Voldemort want him dead?"). The *Key* shows no fear or prudence in spelling out probable events and nominating a good title (!) for each remaining book, in light of the themes and plot lines developed in the first four books.

The *Key* closes with a discussion of schools of criticism and their utility in examining Christian or traditional literature. As mentioned above, I try in this epilogue to make the point that modern tools of analysis have a limited value in unwrapping works failing to share (or which actively oppose) modern conventions and superstitions.

Some warnings for you, gentle reader (caveat lector!). C. S. Lewis in **Perelandra** has his stand-in narrator muse:

> I realised that I was afraid of two things — afraid that sooner or later I myself might meet an eldil [an angel-like creature], and afraid that I might get "drawn in". I suppose every one knows this fear of getting "drawn in" — the moment at which a man realises that what had seemed mere speculations are on the point of landing him in the Communist Party or the Christian Church — the sense that a door has just slammed and left him on the inside. (*Perelandra*, **p. 10**)

I recalled this passage when introduced last week to the works of Zecharia Sitchin by a thoughtful friend, and experienced this fear of being "drawn in" to a cultish ideology. Sitchin and his devotees believe that space travelers created *homo sapiens* from ape-like creatures by genetic manipulation. They explain a host of mysteries from the yeti and pyramids to birth defects and racial differences via this core belief. I marveled at my friend's engagement with this alternate cosmology and world history — and I found myself wrestling with the fear that he might be right. (He isn't.)

The idea that Harry Potter is actually a Christian hero seems to generate a similar fear in readers of this book. So deeply held is the conviction that Ms. Rowling is not that bright (a "welfare mom") and anti-Christian, because of the media harping on these two themes, that even the possibility that she is brilliant and profoundly Christian creates concern of being "drawn in" to a nutty theory.

I hope, of course, that you will be drawn in, if only to consider the overwhelming textual evidence drawn directly from Rowling's books, demonstrating that what seems so unlikely is indeed the case. The mind being its own place, we too often cast what is heavenly into hell lest we seem out of step with popular misconceptions. Lewis' Aslan marvels at the dwarves who, for fear of being "taken in", cannot be "taken out" of their stubbornly-held blindness to the heavenly reality of the world (*The Last Battle*, Chapter 13). If **The Hidden Key** draws any one modern person out of blindness to the meaning of **Harry Potter**, it will have been worth the writing.

I am grateful to those friends who encouraged me to write this book and supported it from conception to publication:

- Thank you's to my several friends in the Port Townsend C. S. Lewis Society, especially Richard, Raphael and Stephen, for the discussions that forged my thinking about Lewis, Tolkien, and Rowling;

- I am grateful to Jean and Beth at the Port Townsend Carnegie Library for their invitation to deliver the lecture series that became this book;

- Without the kind words and generous help — almost daily and over a great distance! — of James Devine, Elaine and Douglas John Trainor, this project would have died at conception;

- Robert Trexler's thoughtful advice and last-minute corrections played a large role in the existence and quality of the book you are holding;

- Presbytera Frederica Matthewes-Green was nothing but kindness and generosity in answering my unending electronic appeals for guidance; and

- Stephen and Colleen Schumacher gave the book its readability and professional appearance, what beauty it has — their charity and sacrificial kindness in this is an edifying example of friendship I hope someday to emulate.

This book is dedicated to my wife and children as a token of my wish and meager efforts to become the man they think I am — and to my Father in gratitude for both his support and courageous example of living and thinking "outside the box".

Gratefully,
John Granger

Part
One

Taking Harry
Seriously

Part One

Taking Harry
Seriously

This is an unusual book in that it is about other books — namely the four **Harry Potter** novels by Joanne Rowling. I will assume you have read all four books in much of what follows.

What is important about them is that, more than any other book of the last fifty years (and perhaps ever), the **Harry Potter** books have captured the imagination of the reading public worldwide. What is interesting about them is that, though wildly successful, no one to date has been able to explain their popularity. This book is the missing explanation or **Hidden Key** to understanding Joanne Rowling's **Harry Potter**.

Very quickly, let's review the story behind the story: how Ms. Rowling came to write the **Harry Potter** books. She claims that Harry came to her imagination fully formed (including the scar!) one afternoon in 1990 while riding a train. She felt her task was to tell this young wizard's story, to explain how he got the scar.

Rowling didn't get off the train and start writing! In fact, she spent five years outlining the seven novels and creating (or learning) the details of Harry's world and Hogwart's School of Witchcraft and Wizardry. In the three years after meeting Harry, she held various jobs, got married in Portugal, had a baby daughter, divorced her husband, and returned to Scotland. Unable to afford child care so she could return to work, Ms. Rowling went on welfare and at last began to write down what became **Harry Potter and the Philosopher's Stone.** Legend has it that she was so poor, she was unable to afford having the book copied to send to an agent. So, the story goes, she typed the book out again by hand!

She eventually received a grant from the Scottish Arts Council to finish the book. It was turned down by a publisher, but was picked up by an agent after he read part of the unsolicited manuscript, filling time while waiting for a late client. Even though it is the shortest book of the series, **Philosopher's Stone** was turned down by Penguin and Harper Collins as being too long for a children's book.

The agent at last sold the British rights to Bloomsbury Publishing before the end of 1996. Rowling's token advance from Bloomsbury and the Arts Council grant allowed her to leave her day job as a French teacher at a local high school and write about Harry full time. Bloomsbury published **Philosopher's Stone** in June of 1997 and **Chamber of Secrets** in July of 1998.

Scholastic Press brought out the American edition that fall, renaming it **Sorcerer's Stone**. Fans unable to wait for the Scholastic version of **Chamber** caused something of an international crisis by ordering the earlier Bloomsbury edition via the UK branch of Amazon.com! With the publication of **Prisoner of Azkaban** in 1999 and **Goblet of Fire** in 2000, the Pottermania phenomenon went global. A recent delay in the publication of Book 5 when announced was worthy of a front page article in the Sunday New York Times.

To date, in Scholastic editions alone, the books have sold almost 70 million copies and worldwide sales are said to be well over 100 million. Editions have appeared in 37 languages, including one in Latin commissioned by Ms. Rowling. (Can you name 37 languages? Sure you can!) And the hunger for Harry Potter has spawned a movie, which when released the week of Thanksgiving in 2001, broke single day, weekend, first week and month records at the box office. Warner Brothers has promised nearly a movie a year until series end and has marketed innumerable Harry Potter products from stuffed animals and action figures to Harry blankets, Nimbus 2000 broomsticks, and Gryffyndor House clothing accessories. I am fairly certain Amish children play with Gryffyndor action figures, and would not be surprised if Osama bin Laden has an Arabic translation he reads on the sly.

The books, if you have been living on the Planet Zeno since 1997 or have recently come out of a coma, recount the adventures of an English schoolboy as he advances from grade to grade at Hogwarts School. However, Hogwarts is no ordinary boarding school and Harry Potter is not your typical student — the former is a school for Witchcraft and Wizardry and Harry is not only a wizard in training but the target of attack by the worst of evil wizards, Lord Voldemort, and his followers, the Death Eaters. Each book ends with a life or death battle with Voldemort or his servants and enough plot twists to make you dream of salt water taffy.

With these background essentials in place, let's begin our search for why Rowling's books are so popular with a review of what fans and experts have suggested as the source of their success.

Chapter 1

The Critical Response to Harry Potter

*The High Road Approach
to Understanding Pottermania*

Why are the *Harry Potter* books so popular? When asked, Rowling has explained in several interviews that this is the question she is always asked. She refuses to answer it lest her readers believe there is a magic formula or element to her writing that she must include in the next book for success. (She won't answer the question, but **Hidden Key** will.) A quick survey of popular and critical response to the novels over the past five years yields a variety of opinions and no consensus as to why the *Harry Potter* books have enchanted the world.

There have been four categories of response to Harry:

- Delight,
- Gratitude,
- Caution, and
- Disdain.

Delight

The delighted response has been from the legion of fans (some truly fanatical) who have read the novels and seen the movie. However, the few members of this group who have tried to explain their enjoyment in terms of what Harry means, either do not attempt or fail to answer the question of why the books have been so successful. **(See Appendix B for a description of the eight _Potter_ guidebooks published thus far.)** For an example of how delighted readers and critics fail to grasp what sets Ms. Rowling's work apart, here is a longish excerpt from one of the reviews of **Goblet of Fire,** this one from _The New Yorker:_

> "I would love to tell you that the book is a big nothing. In fact, it's wonderful, just like its predecessors....
>
> The great beauty of the Potter books is their wealth of imagination, their sheer shining fullness.... [T]he main virtue of these books [is] their philosophic seriousness. Rowlings is a good psychotherapist, and she teaches excellent morals. (Those parents who have objected to the Potter series on the ground that it promotes unchristian values should give it another read.).... [H]er great glory, and the thing that may place her in the Pantheon, is that she asks her pre-teen readers to face the hardest questions of life, and does not shy away from the possibility that the

answers may be sad: that loss may be permanent, evil ever present, good exhaustible." **(Joan Acocella, "Under the Spell",** *New Yorker,* **July 31, 2000)**

Ms. Acocella lists the many influences she sees in *Harry Potter* and discusses cogently her belief that the books are an exploration from various perspectives of power. But asking hard questions and exploring challenging themes in a literary style, even in the context of a great story, don't add up to the sales and mania that have made the *Potter* books a cultural event and landmark. As children's librarians love to point out to me, Philip Pullman's *Dark Materials* trilogy is better written than *Harry Potter*, more challenging, and as good if not better in terms of story. More on Pullman later, but would you have bought this book if it were about his *Dark Materials* trilogy? Have you ever heard of Philip Pullman?

From the delighted corner, Ms. Rowling's admirers give us their admiration of her cleverness and no little wonder and marveling at their own enjoyment of the books — but no satisfactory explanation of their popularity, what makes them different.

Gratitude

Another type of critical response comes from those who admire the *Harry Potter* books because of their usefulness. I am thinking here of child psychiatrists and those concerned about children's literacy. In a report on the American Psychiatric Association's four-day annual meeting in May, 2001, for example there was a symposium on the uses of *Harry Potter* and "why Harry Potter is so wildly popular".

Panel members noted that not only are the **Potter** books… great fun, but they also can help both young readers and psychiatrists.

Dr. Elissa P. Benedek, a forensic and child psychiatrist, said she regularly asks patients and their parents what TV shows and videos they watch and what books they read.

"Now I ask if they read Harry Potter. Who do they like? Who do they not like? What are their favorite scenes?"

It helps establish rapport and gives her an idea of what the children think and feel. One thing is consistent, Benedek said. None of her young patients — not even those who idolize the rapper Eminem and quote his violent lyrics — identifies with the character of Harry's archenemy Voldemort, a dark wizard driven by his lust for power into a life of evil.

"And I see some pretty bad kids," Benedek said.

The books are "not merely escapes, but tools for children and adults to work through their daily struggles," said Dr. Daniel P. Dickstein, a pediatrician and resident in child psychology. **(Janet McConnaughey, *Harry Potter and the Shrinks*, Associated Press, May 8, 2001)**

Some therapists appreciate Harry Potter because he can be used both as a diagnostic tool and as something of a therapy to recommend to others. We are left to suppose Harry's popularity springs from his Ritalin-like effects on the young and their stressed-out parents. But why does Harry act as a narcotic or sedative? No answer.

A group more vocal in their gratitude for **Harry Potter** are the various promoters of children's literacy. These groups, from children's librarians to the President's mom, have been Harry's most ardent advocates in the face of objections to Harry's occult paraphernalia from certain Christian critics. Jim Trelease, author of the best selling **The Read Aloud Handbook** (Penguin, 2002), cites Harry as one of the primary reasons Americans are buying and reading books now more than ever before.

> If you think the adults [in the 50's] were all home reading books when TV arrived, a Gallup poll in 1952 reported only 18 percent of the adults were reading a novel when surveyed, and in 1963 less than half the adults had finished a book in the last year. By contrast, in 1999 that figure had climbed to 84%. ... They really weren't reading all that much in the good old days (but they sure are now, thanks to Harry, Oprah, and user-friendly bookstores).
>
> Before someone exclaims, "I've read Heidi and Harry's no Heidi," I'm not talking about the book's literary style or imagery, not even its emotional levels — just the number of words a child must traverse in order to reach the end. Here's a word count I did on some books, including a few classics:
>
> - *Goosebumps*: 8 words per sentence, 22,450 words in book
>
> - *Heidi*: 19.6 words per sentence, 93,600 words in book
>
> - *The Hobbit*: 18 words per sentence, 97,470 words in book
>
> - *The Hunchback of Notre Dame*: 15 words per sentence, 126,00 words in book
>
> - *Harry Potter and the Goblet of Fire*: 13 words per sentence, 181,000 words in book
>
> Harry Potter has children willingly reading books that are eight times longer than Goosebumps and twice as long as Heidi. (Jim Trelease, *The Read Aloud Handbook*, Penguin Books, 2002, 5th edition, pp. 182, 177).

Trelease loves **Harry Potter** because children love **Harry Potter**. That **Harry Potter** is a series book, easily lumped with the production-line series (**The Baby Sitters Club**, **Goosebumps**, **Nancy Drew**, etc.) ground out by American publishers, doesn't bother Trelease. His judgment: "Series books are avidly read by the best readers, without impeding skills" **(p.184)**. He defends Rowling from her occult-focused detractors with a short history of objections to Baum's **Oz** books among others, but Trelease's concern is not really with whether the **Potter** books are especially good or safe; he and literacy advocates everywhere love the books because children love them and read them. No clues here or even much of a care about why the books are so popular. Let's see what the cautious have to offer.

Caution

The **Harry Potter** books are ofttimes hilarious, but as the series progresses, the books get longer, more melodramatic, and in spots even downright frightening. Some parents think they may be a little much for young readers — and Joanne Rowling agrees with them. About reading to her own daughter, she commented in an interview with *Newsweek* at the publication of **Goblet of Fire:**

> I had told her, "Not until you're seven," because I think a bright 6 year old can definitely manage it in terms of language, but in terms of themes, things get increasingly scary and dark, and some six year olds are going to be disturbed by that. So for my own daughter, I said, "We're going to wait till you're seven." ... I never thought of writing for

children, ironically. I always thought I'd write for adults."
(*Newsweek*, July 10, 2000, pp. 59-60)

It has been estimated that up to a third of Rowling's readers are adults who do not buy the books to read to children. Bloomsbury even put out a special edition of **Philosopher's Stone** with a conservative dust jacket (a plain brown wrapper?) so adults could read it on the train without embarrassment. As we will see, a major theme, perhaps the overriding theme, of the **Harry Potter** books is death and bereavement, and some critics urge caution in adults buying them for or even reading them to younger children.

My concern was less about scaring my children than it was about exposing them to occult elements and forces. I grew up in a time when Dungeons and Dragons was a rage and knew a few people whose lives turned around the game for years (and in anything but a healthy way). I also have convictions that, just as there are beneficent spiritual beings, there are malevolent spirits as well. Pretending there is no devil is as naïve and perhaps as dangerous, if not more so, than seeing demons behind every door. Not being gifted with discernment of spirits, I choose to avoid exposure to anything hinting of the supernatural that is not from a traditional, revealed spiritual path. I observe this simple rule when I buy books for myself and when I choose books for my children.

You should know that I live on one of the moons orbiting the Planet Zeno, for I did not hear of Harry Potter until a few months before **Goblet of Fire** was published. A co-worker and good friend — who was lesbian, tattooed, and complete with facial piercings — told me in a conversation over lunch about these great books about a boy wizard I should read to my children. I was unaware of the controversy involving Christian objections to the books, but I didn't need guidance from "Focus on the Family"; I assumed my friend was something of a Wiccan or Goddess worshipper, and made a mental note to keep clear of anything to do with Harry Potter.

Oh, well. My oldest daughter was given a paperback copy of **Sorcerer's Stone** by our pediatrician, who happens to be a thoughtful mother and Evangelical Christian to boot. Now that Harry was in my house, I elected to read one of the books, if only to explain to my daughter why she wasn't allowed to read it. I read through the night and, ashamed of my judging a book by its readers, bought the other two books then available early the next morning (and apologized to my co-worker! Turns out she is a Unitarian).

I tell my story only because I hope you will remember that Caution was my first response to *Harry Potter* as a parent and reader. I am a great admirer of the books and maintain that caution or care in book selection is not ignorance or closed-mindedness. People — and especially those responsible for the shaping of young minds and hearts — are properly careful about what books their charges read, in the same way they should be discriminating in what they eat for snacks or what they watch on the teevee (if they choose to watch it at all). Only the careless or fools equate such prudence with prurience and prejudice.

The most widely reported response to the *Harry Potter* books has been the criticism and warnings from some

Christian readers. I say "some" because (though it is not widely reported) the community of Christian believers in America is not a monolith but a kaleidoscope; the response to **Harry Potter** from this kaleidoscope covers the spectrum of opinions rather than the simple "for" and "against" (mostly the latter) noted in newspaper articles and broadcast sound bites. Articles from *First Things*, *Christianity Today*, and the Vatican newspaper lauding the **Potter** books for their morality and Harry as "Christian Hero" could have been cited in the Delight section of this review of reviews.

Criticism emphasizing Caution ranges from recommendations of care for the youngest readers and warnings about exposure to witchcraft, to condemnation of the books as gateways to the occult and of Christians who read them for their disobeying Holy Writ. A sober explanation of Christian caution as concerns **Harry Potter** comes from Kimbra Gish, a member of the Assemblies of God Church and a librarian at Vanderbilt University.

> The foundation of my church is the Holy Bible....This book forms the underlying basis for all our beliefs. Two very important beliefs concern children and the occult. In our faith, the spiritual education of children is considered crucial. This stems largely from attention to Proverbs 22:6: "Train up a child in the way he should go: and when he is old he will not depart from it." Because those of my faith believe that casual exposure to the occult ... can desensitize a Christian to the sinful nature of such beliefs and practices, any exposure is commonly prohibited. This includes reading books that portray the occult in a positive light.

Most criticisms for the occult in fiction have their basis in
Deuteronomy 18:9-12: "When thou art come into a land
which the Lord thy God hath given thee, thou shalt not
learn to do after the abominations of those nations. There
shall not be found among you any one that maketh his
son or his daughter to pass through the fire, or that useth
divination, or an observer of times, or an enchanter, or a
witch, or a charmer, or a consulter with familiar spirits, or
a wizard or a necromancer. For all that do these things are
an abomination unto the Lord: and because of these
abominations the Lord thy God doth drive them out from
before thee."…. This is the primary reason parents might
challenge a book with any hint of occult or satanic practices
— they are concerned that their children may learn to see
them as acceptable…**(Kimbra Gish,** *Hunting Down Harry Potter:*
An Exploration of Religious Concerns about Children's Literature,
Horn Book, 5-6/2000, pp. 264-265).

Ms. Gish concludes with a plea for tolerance from and for
Christians who enjoy or disapprove of Harry. She affirms both
her right not to want "door-openers" to the occult in her home
and the rights of others of more secular beliefs to make their
own decisions.

Less generous is Richard Abanes, author of ***Harry Potter and***
the Bible: The Menace behind the Magick. Mr. Abanes has written
widely on cults and the occult for many Christian magazines and
believes that Christians who allow their children to be exposed to
the ***Potter*** books are failing in their responsibilities as parents and
disciples of Christ. Responding to Christian commentator Chuck
Colson's approval of ***Harry Potter***, Abanes writes:

God's Word does not forbid "involvement with
supernatural evil." The Bible condemns all forms of

communication with the spirit world, except communication with God, through the Holy Spirit, in the name of the Son. In other words, all interaction with the spirit world, if it takes place apart from God, is prohibited by Scripture. Yet unbiblical spiritual involvement takes place all through the Potter books, which is why they are so dangerous for young children. **(Richard Abanes, *Harry Potter and the Bible: The Menace behind the Magick*, Horizon Books, 2001, pp. 62-63)**

He condemns Rowling (not one kind word for her work in 275 pages) for not only the "unbiblical spiritual involvement" of her books but for their occult symbolism, moral ambiguity, ethical confusion, bad language ("git" and "damn"), gruesomeness, and poor writing. Not much to like there. He attributes their popularity to savvy marketing, poor taste, peer pressure, a tremendous and unguided spiritual hunger amongst the unchurched, and, perhaps, he hints, a little help from the Dark Side.

Abanes' critique of the books is unsympathetic at best (with some whopping mistakes a less jaundiced reading eye may not have made) and his interpretations of other Christian children's books he says are not like **Harry Potter** will surprise admirers of Tolkien and Lewis (see Appendix A). It would be careless, though, to dismiss Abanes' concerns; right or wrong about **Harry Potter**, he is not hysterical or loony to think there are dangers in careless spirituality.

My disappointment with Abanes' book is with its reasoning. Arguing from the premises that the books are popular and the books are bad on several levels, it concludes in a failed syllogism that they are popular because they are bad. The truth of the premises is not well established (though argued at length, Abanes makes no greater link between Rowling and the occult than look-alike association, and he is unable to cite a soul lost to the occult caused by reading *Harry Potter*) and the premises do not support the conclusion.

Disdain

The Low Road explanation of *Harry Potter*'s success (that they are popular because they are no good) is not limited to those who argue from spiritual prudence — it is the touchstone of literary critics and sociologists who despise the Rowling oeuvre. Here are a few of their pronouncements on the intellectual worth of *Harry Potter*:

- Roger Sutton, editor of the Horn Book: a "critically insignificant" series, "nothing to get excited about."

- Pierre Bruno, Liberation: "Harry Potter is a sexist neo-conservative autocrat."

- Anthony Holden, *The Observer*: "These are one dimensional children's books. Disney cartoons written in words, no more."

- Andrew Blake, Head of Cultural Studies, King Alfred's College, *The Irresistible Rise of Harry Potter: Kid-Lit in a Globalized World*: "[The Harry Potter books] are the literary equivalent of fast food."

- William Safire, columnist: Harry Potter reading is not "prizeworthy culture" but a "a waste of adult reading time."

- Harold Bloom, Yale Professor: "not well written", not a classic of imaginative literature because it "lacks an authentic imaginative vision." "Her prose style, heavy on cliché, makes no demands on its readers." "Why read it?

Presumably, if you cannot be persuaded to read anything better, Rowling will have to do."

• Jack Zipes, University of Minnesota Professor, **Sticks and Stones**: "for anything to become a phenomenon in western society, it must become conventional.... [The Potter books] sell extraordinarily well because they are so cute and ordinary."

• Elvis Mitchell, *New York Times*: "Ms. Rowling's books cannibalize and synthesize pop culture mythology, proof of the nothing-will-ever-go-away ethic. She has come up with something like 'Star Wars'... but this is 'Young Sherlock Holmes' as written by C. S. Lewis from a story by Roald Dahl."

• Margo Jefferson, *New York Times*: "J. K. Rowling can plot as well as any thriller or television drama writer" but eventually "you see how the thing is done, and even if you can't predict what will happen next, you can anticipate how it will happen, within what limits..., and what the effect on you will be. So you start to register all the tricks of characterization, of style, of ambition. You yawn, you get irritable, you turn away."

• Deidre Donahue, *USA Today*: "[**Goblet of Fire**] has the telltale lopping pace and paper chewing verbosity that best-selling authors develop when they try to write a book a year...Rowling seems to be getting more like a Gothic Dean Koontz and less like C. S. Lewis with every book."

• Harold Bloom, Yale Professor (a second helping!): "There's nothing there to read. They're just an endless string of cliches. I cannot think that does anyone any good. That's not **Wind in the Willows**. That's not **Through the Looking Glass**.... It's really just slop."

This disdain for Rowling and **Harry Potter** is really just another ripple from the self-important circle of literati who must deride all things popular to justify their positions as arbiters of taste. Don't think so? Here are a few reviews of Tolkien's **Lord of the Rings** as gathered by Tom Shippey for his recent best seller, *J. R. R. Tolkien: Author of the Century:*

- Alfred Duggan, *Times Literary Supplement*, 1954: "This is not a work which many adults will read through more than once."

- Philip Toynbee, *Observer*, 1961: Tolkien's supporters are beginning to "sell out their shares" and the whole **Lord of the Rings** craze is passing into a "merciful oblivion".

- Edmund Wilson, Nation, 1956: **Lord of the Rings** is "balderdash", "Juvenile Trash" and an isolated British taste.

- Mark Roberts, **Essays in Criticism**, 1956: "It doesn't issue from an understanding of reality which is not to be denied, it is not moulded by some controlling vision of things which is at the same time its raison d'être."

Roberts' comment about the absence of "an understanding of reality" or "some controlling vision of things" wins Shippey's prize for "having made the least perceptive comment on Tolkien" **(p. 156)**. As Shippey demonstrates in his detailed exegesis of Tolkien's fiction, it is precisely Tolkien's understanding of reality and vision that has made the **Lord of the Rings** a perennial best seller and the consensus choice of critics and readers a generation after the author's demise as the best book of the twentieth century. If dismissal at the time of publication by the critics is a sign of lasting value, **Harry Potter** is a classic our great grandchildren will be loving.

Harold Bloom has to be considered the leader thus far in the race to make the least perceptive comment about Rowling;

his denial of her having "an authentic imaginative vision" and assertion that her books are "just slop" are clearly over the top. It should be noted that both Professor Bloom and William Safire have read only the first book of the series and only enough of it to pass or confirm judgment. But it is not only disdainful snobs and properly cautious Christians who neglect to read Ms. Rowling. Her delighted admirers and fans among the literary advocates often have not read the books either.

For example, many school teachers, parents, and librarians I have met, while professing a great admiration of Ms. Rowling's success, hold it as a point of pride not to have read her books — for the same reasons they do not read the **Hardy Boys**, **Nancy Drew**, or **Baby Sitters Club** serials. They do not consider them serious reading or literature with a capital "L". Consequently, I only nodded my head when I read about a Reading Conference in 2000 where a presenter asked a group of 42 teachers and school librarians how many had read at least one **Harry Potter** novel — and only two people raised their hands! This group did not think there was any more meaning in **Harry Potter** than in an "I Love Lucy" episode.

My point? Everyone agrees Ms. Rowling has written books of never-before-reached heights of popularity. Those who admire them point to their humor, strong characters, and water tight plotting, and the more literate make reference to various themes and "influences" in the books. Those who dislike them call them a variety of clever (and not so insightful) disparaging names or attempt to link them with more and less believable associations in the occult periphery of our culture.

What these critics on the Low and Middle Roads of criticism have in common is their failure to explain why these books have earned a response from adult and children readers which is an order of magnitude greater than any book in modern publishing history. No one has dared take the high road to suggest the books are selling so well not because of marketing, our collective bad taste and herd reflexes, or because of a demonic assist; no one wants to say the obvious, namely, that the *Harry Potter* books are setting sales records *because they are so much better than other books.*

The Hidden Key to Harry Potter argues from just this high point: the *Harry Potter* books are significantly different in the way they have been written and in their choice of subject. This difference affects the reader, child or adult, more powerfully than most fiction and certainly more so than any releases of recent vintage. *The Hidden Key* will discuss the various themes, symbols, and plot events of the first four books to illumine the meaning of the *Harry Potter* series and of individual books, throwing light on Ms. Rowling's genius in delivering these meanings in what I will call a "three-dimensional, one-two punch".

Chapter 2

Harry Potter 101

or

The Map and Influences Chapter

Before we rush to the meat of this argument, let's drink some milk and eat some cookies. To take **Harry Potter** seriously and plumb his depths, it is necessary to do the groundwork of understanding its internal structure and place in the history of fiction (the dreaded "influences" of literary criticism). This will require drawing a couple of maps we will use throughout our look at the series, but especially when guessing what will happen in the last three **Potter** books (which we'll do in Part Four of this book).

The Ring of Relationships Map *(see Map 1)*

One of the novelties of the *Harry Potter* books is that, while each book is an exciting story in itself, whose ending rewards its reader with some sense of resolution, there is a larger story which is the context of these separate adventures. Every book lets the reader in on another part of the puzzle that clarifies the relationships of the major players. The quickest way to get a mental grip on these adventures is with a map of the various relationships that join the characters as they have been revealed so far. This snapshot overview allows the reader to understand at a glance who is on whose side, who opposes whom, and who does not fit neatly into a relationship slot.

The Ring Map begins on its periphery with the founders of Hogwarts School: Salazar Slytherin, Godric Gryffyndor, Rowena Ravenclaw, and Helga Hufflepuff. The two defining figures of this quartet are Slytherin and Gryffyndor whose disagreements and characters bleed into the remaining rings. Place Gryffyndor at the top and Slytherin at the bottom just as their respective houses are in a tower and dungeon.

The next ring in, we find Albus Dumbledore and the Order of the Phoenix on the Gryffyndor end of the ring and Lord Voldemort and his Death Eaters. Voldemort we learn in *Chamber of Secrets* is Slytherin's heir and he and his Death Eaters labor to create a world ruled by pure-blooded wizards after the founder's vision. Hagrid mentions in the first book that nearly all the wizards who joined with Voldemort were from Slytherin house.

Dumbledore is linked with Gryffyndor by artifacts and personal history. He "owns" the sorting hat which belonged to Godric Gryffyndor and the sword of Godric Gryffyndor which

Harry pulls from it in **Chamber** ("sword-in-hat", get it?). His office has a griffin door knocker and, more importantly, his life has been spent resisting evil wizards, from the dark wizard Grindewald in 1945 to Lord Voldemort in the present.

I assume that the Order of the Phoenix will be a counterbalancing collection of wizards under Dumbledore's influence (the "old crowd" he tells Black to bring together at the end of **Goblet**, such as Figg, Fletcher, and Gudgeon), offsetting the Death Eaters under Lord Voldemort. Dumbledore's glorious pet phoenix, Fawkes, is mirrored in a horrible contrast on the dark side by Voldemort's giant black snake, Nagini.

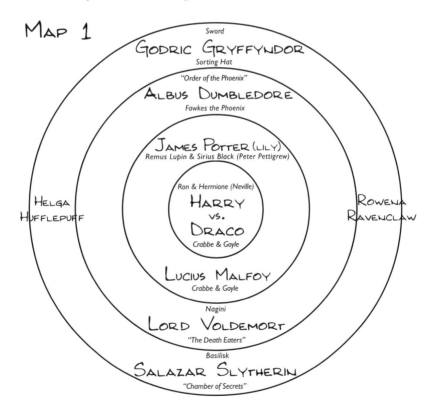

MAP 1

Sword
GODRIC GRYFFYNDOR
Sorting Hat

"Order of the Phoenix"
ALBUS DUMBLEDORE
Fawkes the Phoenix

JAMES POTTER (LILY)
Remus Lupin & Sirius Black (Peter Pettigrew)

Ron & Hermione (Neville)
HARRY
vs.
DRACO
Crabbe & Goyle

LUCIUS MALFOY
Crabbe & Goyle

Nagini
LORD VOLDEMORT
"The Death Eaters"

Basilisk
SALAZAR SLYTHERIN
"Chamber of Secrets"

HELGA HUFFLEPUFF

ROWENA RAVENCLAW

Moving towards the center, one ring in we meet the parents of Harry Potter and Draco Malfoy. Lucius Malfoy, a loyal Death

Eater and former member of Slytherin House, lines up, of course, on the Slytherin side of the map. I put Crabbe and Goyle's name here if only for symmetry with the center (where their sons are inseparable from the son of Lucius and Narcissa).

Harry's father, James, aligns with Gryffyndor and Dumbledore; James was in Gryffyndor House, lived in Godric Place before his death, had a close relationship with Dumbledore (close enough that Dumbledore acts as his executor at his death and protector of his son), and his opposition to Voldemort, his murderer, is total.

James' two close friends from school, Remus Lupin, and Sirius Black, join him in the ring with parenthetic inclusion of their sidekick, hanger-on, Peter Pettigrew. They balance Crabbe and Goyle opposite them and are foreshadowing of Harry's close friends Ron and Hermione — with Neville Longbottom as their hanger-on, similar to Pettigrew (whom he resembles; compare *Prisoner*, p. 213).

In the center we find Harry Potter and his opposite number and great rival, Draco Malfoy. Each lines up with their parents, patron, and respective House founder. Each has friends who echo in number and character the friends of their parents. Each despises the other and lives for the pleasure of seeing the other fail.

The major characters, then, fall into place on the Gryffyndor/Slytherin axis. Look for Hagrid, the Weasleys, and Professor McGonagal in the Order of the Phoenix and Ludo Bagman, the Minister of Magic, and Rita Skeeter (among others) to be collaborators at least with Lord Voldemort. Other characters — Argus Filch, say, or Stan Shunpike — are either not important enough to include on the map or are obvious placements (look for the La Stranges and the Dementors, for example, on the Slytherin side).

But there are a few question marks. Most importantly, on whose side is Professor Severus Snape? As the Master of Slytherin House and an alumnus, an open enemy of Harry Potter, his father, and his father's friends, and a Death Eater with the Dark Mark tattooed on his arm, isn't it obvious? No, not really. Snape haunts Professor Quirrell in **Philosopher's Stone** and does everything he can to keep him from winning the stone for Lord Voldemort. He saves Harry's life in the same book and has Dumbledore's trust because he acted as a double-agent for the Gryffyndor side in the last war with Voldemort. At the end of **Goblet**, Snape returns to Lord Voldemort at Dumbledore's request and at obvious risk of his life. Whose side is he on? He is on Snape's side or both sides of the map **(skip to Part Four for my guess as to Snape's final loyalty)**. By not being able to place Snape, the map highlights his role as a critical or swing character.

Besides Snape, don't rush to pin down Peter Pettigrew ("Wormtail") or Percy Weasley. Wormtail is in debt to Harry for sparing him at the end of **Prisoner** and he shows some signs of being in unwilling service to Voldemort in **Goblet**. Nonetheless, he bears the responsibility not only for the death of the Potters but also for the most recent return of Voldemort to physical form. Peter/Wormtail is an echo of two schizophrenic Tolkien characters (Smeagol/Gollum and Grima/Wormtongue); only his end will reveal his true quality and fealty.

Percy Weasley, as a "Percival" figure and son of Arthur, seems a born good guy; Gryffyndor prefect and Head boy, Order of the Phoenix family, rising star at the Ministry of Magic — what is the problem? Well, Rowling has made it very clear in each book that Percy Weasley is dangerously ambitious, focused on status, and hysterically concerned about rules. The only sympathetic moments he has in the series are when his girlfriend is attacked by the Basilisk in **Chamber**, and his emotional rush into the lake to help Harry with brother Ron at the end of the second TriWizard task in **Goblet**. Look for Percy to break with the family in Book 5, if only for a book or two.

But this is the work of Part Four, in which we'll use this map and the next one to guess what happens next ("Will the Magic Car return?", "Does Dobby marry Winky?"- you get the idea). Let's look at the second map.

The Formula Map of the Journey *(see Map 2)*

The **Potter** books, individually and perhaps as a series, are laid out according to a formula. David Colbert, author of

The Magical Worlds of Harry Potter, thinks the formula is the Universal Hero pattern described by Joseph Campbell in his *Hero With a Thousand Faces*. Joan Acocella traces the pattern to Vladimir Propp's 1928 book *Morphology of the Folk Tale*. Elizabeth Schafer believes Rowling is a fan of Carl Jung; she cites Lord Ragland's work on archetypal heroes, *The Hero: A Study in Tradition, Myth, and Drama* as a guide to the formula Rowling follows.

All of these writers are correct in so far as Ms. Rowling does have a pattern she follows in each book and Harry is an "archetypal hero". None of the patterns mentioned above are an exact fit, however, so for our purpose (understanding Harry) it is best just to describe the formula she follows in drawing our second map. All four books begin and end in the same place and pass a series of landmarks that differ only in details. Here is a rough chart of the pattern as it appears in each book:

	Stone	Chamber	Prisoner	Goblet
Start	Privet Drive	Privet Drive	Privet Drive	Privet Drive
Escape	Admission letters and Hagrid visit	Flying Ford Anglia	Knight bus	Flu powder
Mystery	Stone's seeker and location	Chamber opening and Slytherin heir	Sirius Black's escape	TriWizard tournament entry
Crisis	Albus leaves	Ginny taken	Ron taken	Third trial
Descent	Trapdoor	Bathroom chute	Under willow	Graveyard
Combat	Quirrell	Riddle	Black/ Dementors	Voldemort
Return	Albus, 3 days	Fawkes	Hippogriff	Portkey
Revelation	Snape OK, Quirrell = Voldemort	Dobby OK, Riddle = Voldemort	Black OK, Scabbers = Wormtail	Snape a hero, Moody = Death Eater
Finish	Station 9¾	Station 9¾	Station 9¾	Station 9¾

The Harry/Hero Journey as drawn on Map 2 is a picture of the generic sequence of each adventure Harry has taken so far.

- He begins at home on Privet Drive with his muggle family, the Dursleys.

- He escapes to Hogwarts from this living death via the intrusion of extraordinary magic (Hagrid's birthday arrival, the flying Ford Anglia, etc.).

- Harry arrives at Hogwarts to find something mysterious going on ....

- With help from Hermione and Ron, Harry tries to solve the mystery, which, inevitably, comes to a crisis demanding his immediate action (with or without his friends).

- He descends into the earth to face this crisis (except in *Goblet* in which story he portkeys to a graveyard which earthy surroundings have a resonant meaning).

- Harry fights Voldemort or a servant of the Dark Lord and triumphs against impossible odds (in Books 3 and 4 merely by escaping alive).

- He rises from the battlefield miraculously and returns to the land of the living.

- Harry learns from Professor Dumbledore that a good guy is really a bad guy and a bad guy is really a good guy (along with the meaning and lesson of his adventure).

- Harry leaves us at Station 9¾ to go home with the Dursleys.

Perhaps seeing the pattern of the books is a disappointment. Some friends have told me when I have shown them the second map that they feel Ms. Rowling is cheating somehow. If this were just a mechanical formula to make her job easier, disappointment would make sense, as in the scripting of teevee action dramas. (Remember "The A Team"? Same show every week with a different machine at the end to save the day?)

This is not the case, however, with the **Harry Potter** books. Her formula is anything but a scripting cookie cutter. As we will see soon, the structure common to all four of the books is an important part of the unique, three dimensional, one-two punch with which Ms. Rowling delivers her meaning. Really. Turn down a corner of the page with Map 2 (tell me you bought this book!) so you can find it again in a little while. Onto "Literary Influences".

Literary Influences

I had a teacher my first year of High School named Mrs. Smith who changed my life. One, she taught me some Latin (a small miracle given my attitude). Two, she taught me how to write a passing expository composition — thesis, major supporting reasons, conclusion. And, three, she taught me that the way to an English teacher's heart is citing an "influence" or allusion to a previous work. In Mrs. Smith's class, everything was tied back to Homer's **Odyssey**; from Shakespeare and Chaucer to Lennon and McCartney, it all came from the **Odyssey**.

Why was this such a great lesson? Well, I passed her English course with high marks (unlike the Latin...) and I learned not to take literary courses that are mainly allusion/influence tracking seminars too seriously. "Strawberry Fields Forever" may share some meaning with Homer's Lotus

Eaters, but that connection is a waste of time unless it affects my grasp of their common meaning. Right? The idea itself and how I use or neglect it in daily life is more important than where the idea came from or who used it first.

I write out a list of the more important influences, then, with just this hope: throwing some light on what the *Harry Potter* books are about. I am not an English Lit grad student in search of a thesis; I believe understanding where Harry Potter was born ("in the mental compost of Books [she'd] read," Rowling says in one interview) is a big help to comprehending her intention and power as a writer. Come back to this list and judge for yourself after reading what the books mean in Part Three of this book. If I'm wrong, just consider this an overdue thank you letter to Mrs. Smith. The *Odyssey* is in there.

Much of what follows will refer back to the influence chart. I don't have enough academic training or hubris even to imply Ms. Rowling's genius is a matter of "cutting and pasting" literature themes patchwork style into a charming children's story; all the influence chart tells us is that she is very well read and her intellectual compost (to use her phrase) is of only the best authors, dramatists, philosophers, and theologians.

If you needed to identify the most telling influences from this oversized compost heap, you'd do well to choose Austen, Dickens, and the Inklings. Much of this book is about the link between Rowling and Sayers, Lewis, and Tolkien, so I won't belabor that here. Something needs to be said, however, about Jane Austen and Charles Dickens.

Type	Author & Books	Reflection In Harry Potter
Children's Fantasy	C. S. Lewis' *Narnia* series; J. R. R. Tolkien's *The Lord of the Rings*	Seven book format; Magical setting sans religion; Inkling worldview and morality; disdain for schools and "good" food; heroic adventure
	Roald Dahl's works; Norton Juster's *Phantom Tollbooth*; Lewis Carroll's *Alice* fantasies	Hilarious, meaningful, satirical fantasy literature (for children?)
Bildungs Roman	Thomas Hughes' *Tom Brown's Schooldays* novels	"Coming of Age" fiction; English Public School setting; importance of sports and Houses
Serial Novels (1)	Charles Dickens; Leo Tolstoy; Fyodor Dostoevsky	Publishing work while writing; meaningful character names; Love and Death themes; three character lead (a la *Brothers Karamazov*)
Serial Novels (2)	Franklin W. Dixon's *Hardy Boys*; Carolyn Keene's *Nancy Drew* mysteries	Children detectives on the job: brilliant girl, determined boys
Morals and Manners Realism	Jane Austen; Charles Dickens	Believable, engaging depiction of "money and position and trying to keep your head up if you have neither"
Epic	Homer's *The Odyssey*; Virgil's *The Aeneid*; Dante's *Divine Comedy*	Hero's journey; return of the king; "to hell and back" theme; guide leading progress
Myth	King Arthur	Wizard guardian; concealed childhood; sword revealing bloodline; evil wizard enemy
Fairy Tale	Cinderella	"Rags to Royalty" theme; wicked step-family
Cathartic Finish	Sophocles; Shakespeare; O.Henry; Agatha Christie	Surprise ending; audience engagement; mystery drama; meaning in resolution
Traditional	Christian Scripture; Aristotle; Plato; Church Fathers	Moses/Christ life path; resurrection formula; doctrine of Soul; Heaven and Hell as Love & Glory of God
Traditionalists	Titus Burckhardt; Rene Guenon; Fritjof Schuon	Understanding of alchemy; symbolist outlook; "Contra Modernity" worldview

These are the two influences Ms. Rowling always mentions when asked, and Jane Austen is Rowling's answer to the inevitable "favorite author" question. Joan Acocella in *The New Yorker* put her finger on the telling mark of these two authors on Rowling when she wrote:

> Rowling's favorite writer, she has told interviewers, is Jane Austen. She also loves Dickens. And it is in their bailiwick — English morals-and-manners realism, the world of Pip and Miss Bates, of money and position and trying to keep your head up if you have neither — that she scores her greatest victories. **(Joan Acocella, "Under the Spell", New Yorker, July 31, 2000, p. 76)**

Our great sympathy with Ron as he comes to terms with being poor, with Harry and Neville as orphans, with all the students away from home struggling with their friends and teachers — these are a much larger part of *Harry Potter*'s popularity than the magic. Magic may be a fascinating backdrop, but the echoes of *Pride and Prejudice* (a theme we will explore in a moment) and *David Copperfield* are what engage and delight the reader.

Rowling's humorous dialogue and believable characters can be traced to her affection for Austen novels. The melodramatic and caricature-like folk of the *Potter* books (think of the Potions Master, Severus Snape) may be best described as "Dickenesque". Rowling's magnificently meaningful and clever names, too, are a tip of the hat to Dickens, the first master of the serial novel.

Rowling's critique of conventional institutions and human failings, from prisons and prejudice to schools and self-serving cowardice, also place her firmly in the Austen/Dickens school of activist authors. As we shall see, her criticisms of modern conventions are simultaneously lighter and more profound than either of her favorites, but there is no denying that her great talent in story-telling is only equalled by her great good sense in following the masters of her medium.

No doubt these influences will become the subject of innumerable Ph. D. dissertations in the years to come. The four themes in **Harry Potter** we will explore (Prejudice or "Snobbery", Death, Choice, and Change) are all Austen and Dickens themes, and her answers to these human questions are remarkably similar to those of her favorites.

Consequently, when I am asked the pointed question, "why are the books so popular?", my short answer is: "Rowling writes books like the ones she loves to read; she is a curious throwback to and combination of Austen, Dickens, and Lewis." This book only nods to the influence of the 19th Century novelists but dwells on that of the Inklings, because the latter influence is more difficult for most people to see and much more controversial. By contrast, any reader of Austen or Dickens recognizes Rowling's brilliant borrowings from and debts to these authors.

Enough of the "influences tracing", and on to "meaning"! Drawing maps and posting influences helps folks "take Harry seriously", but without getting into the books' themes and meaning, we have only a laundry list and a couple of drawings.

It's time to begin unpeeling the onion to get at its power; only then will we understand why **Harry Potter** has captured the world's heart and imagination. So, what does Ms. Rowling herself say the books are about?

Chapter 3

Prejudice
in
Harry Potter

In my (admittedly anything but comprehensive) survey of her interviews, Ms. Rowling has been hesitant to lay out the various themes and meanings of **Harry Potter** as would (say) a Literature Professor. This is understandable and commendable because hers is a work in progress, something she is still bringing to life. That she would or could dissect Harry as a cadaver at the same time is asking a bit much. She has, however, acknowledged the two most obvious themes when they have been brought up by her interviewers. Our job here is to look at these themes and then try to explain why her treatment of them has had the effect it has on the reading public. First prejudice and then death and bereavement.

Prejudice

Rowling has special sympathy for the victims of prejudice and ill treatment. Her favorite writers are Jane Austen and Charles Dickens, who champion the downtrodden and underdogs in every one of their books. Before her writing career took off, Rowling worked professionally on behalf of the helpless at Amnesty International, the worldwide advocacy arm and voice of political prisoners and the unjustly persecuted and tortured everywhere. Closer to home, Rowling experienced the agonies of losing friends who avoided her during the degenerative illness of her mother and the public shaming of single mothers during the Thatcher/Major years. Since her success, her largest public gifts have been to causes supporting single mothers and those with AIDS. Her heart and her money go to underdogs on the periphery or forced to the periphery of our society. No surprise,

Book	Prejudice Against	Origin	Object
Philosopher's Stone	Abnormal or magical folk Non-magical folk (Muggles) Poor Clumsy, awkward, stupid	Dursleys Slytherins Malfoys Draco	Harry & Hagrid Muggles Weasleys Neville
Chamber of Secrets	Mudbloods (muggle parent) Squibs (magic-born muggle) Ugly, unpopular The Nearly Headless	Slytherins Magic folk Olive Hornby Headless Ghosts	Hermione & others Argus Filch Moaning Myrtle Nick
Prisoner of Azkaban	Prisoners Werewolves Hippogriffs Intelligent women	Everyone Almost everyone Ministry Boys & teachers	Sirius Black Remus Lupin Buckbeak Hermione
Goblet of Fire	Young people Giants Foreigners Non-prejudiced	Fleur Magic folk Hagrid Death Eaters	Harry Hagrid & Maxime TriWizard guests Albus & Weasleys

then, to find that prejudice, its cause, effect on believer and victim, and cure, is a primary focus in her **Harry Potter** novels.

As you can see by just glancing at the chart, every one of the **Harry Potter** books reveals another prejudice against another downtrodden group of people who are different from "normal" wizards or muggles in big ways and small. And, no, I didn't forget house elves. The books are so much about prejudice that Rowling includes a satirical look at people consumed by "the cause" of standing up for the injured and persecuted. We know this is self-satire because, while the house elves are nominally slaves, they are delighted in that condition congenitally. (One critic, missing the cue on this, lambasted Rowling for writing "the first book since Little Black Sambo to lionize slavery".)

Rowling doesn't just lay out a black and white world of "the characters I like aren't racist and the characters I hate are". Only Dumbledore seems free of prejudice. Hagrid doesn't trust foreigners or muggles though he is hated because he is a half giant. Ron, despite his insecurities about being poor, has a host of wizarding prejudices from giants to werewolves (though he only knows — and likes — one of each) and is always the first to point his finger at someone he doesn't like. Ron has been wrong so many times in this it's almost a given that his guess is the wrong one. And Rowling makes the prisoners of prejudice, mostly the Slytherins, seem so unhappy in their sarcasm and meanness that they are more to be pitied than despised.

What is remarkable about the Magical World of Harry Potter visible in the chart, then, is less the incredible creatures and structures and enchantments found there than it is how much the Wizards and Witches are as unloving and self-important as the muggles many of them despise (and all patronize). If anything, the number of downtrodden folk make it seem that Harry's World has more "niggers" than our own. Good thing the Magic folk have an enlightened government and a free press to stand up for the oppressed!

Ha! Pardon my sarcasm. *The Daily Prophet* is the teevee news and newspaper media conglomerate for Wizards and Witches. In every book it spreads half truths and misinformation as Gospel wisdom 'hot off the presses'. In **The Goblet of Fire**, though, we learn these are not just the mistakes inevitable in rushing news to print. Meeting Rita Skeeter, star reporter for the *Prophet* and other Wizarding publications (*Witch Weekly*, etc.), errors that might have been incompetence or negligence are revealed to be plain and simple wickedness.

Take a look at Rita's name for a clue as to what she's about: *Rita* = "Read-a", *Skeeter* = "Squito, Mosquito, or Blood-sucking-disease-carrying-parasitical-bug". And Rita is equal to her name. Rather than exposing the unjust and prejudiced in defense of the downtrodden, Ms. Skeeter, an illegal "beetle bug" animagus, does everything she can to make life miserable for those in positions of responsibility or who are somehow different. She loves to create hardship for the Ministry, of course, but saves her special venom for individuals she dislikes. In **Goblet** she writes unflattering, unkind, and rude pieces, several of which she makes up whole cloth, about Albus Dumbledore, Hagrid, Hermione, and Harry, who is misrepresented once and crucified another time on the morning of the last TriWizard task.

Thus the media in the magical world (I think we are meant to ask, "Unlike our own?") is not about the life-supporting mission of exposing prejudice and uplifting those beaten down by it. The newspaper instead actively and with intention creates or fosters prejudice against individuals and groups. Giants, mudbloods, generous souls like Albus Dumbledore, and the innocent are held up for public ridicule and suspicion.

The reading public acts on cue from the shadow casters and either attacks or passively agrees to thinking less of the misrepresented. Remember how Hermione is treated by Mrs. Weasley after the Witch Weekly article portrayed her as a scarlet woman? And Cornelius Fudge's inability to trust Harry's eyewitness testimony about Voldemort after the second Skeeter piece cast Harry as a mental defective? Even the good and wise have their opinions made to order and prejudices confirmed by the popular media.

The Ministry of Magic (MOM), one assumes from its initials, is supposed to be the protector of the helpless and a force for good against evil in the world. However, the Ministry (I think we are again meant to ask, "Unlike our own?") is anything but maternal or heroic. Rowling consistently represents them as a gaggle of self-important airheads busying themselves with laughable trivia ("cauldron bottom reports") or international bread-and-circus functions like the Quidditch World Cup, while neglecting even to take care of their own. Just how long was Bertha Jorkins missing before the Ministry sent out a search party?

But the Ministry is worse than bumbling and distracted. In **Chamber**, in response to pressure and the need to appear to be acting, Cornelius Fudge, the Minister of Magic, has Hagrid imprisoned in Azkaban though he knows Hagrid is innocent. In **Goblet**, Sirius Black reveals that he was given a life sentence in

Azkaban by a Ministry official without a trial, again, just for the appearance of acting with strength. We meet the Azkaban guards in *Prisoner* because they come to Hogwarts to look for Black; the Ministry, it turns out, is torturing those imprisoned in Azkaban because their guards, the Dementors, live by sucking everything good and beautiful from their souls. Azkaban is a psychic concentration camp few survive. The name of the prison itself is a magical turn on Alcatraz and gulag-rich Soviet republics like Uzbekhistan.

The Ministry has its comic front, then, but a Gulag back. Ambitious ministers fiddle with inconsequential matters and act in response to pressure generated by the rich and publishing. It is incapable of passing "The Muggle Protection Act" or of policing Wizards practicing Dark Magic and muggle baiting. Those who press for this sort of social good legislation are demoted for lacking "real Wizard pride". And, beyond its failure to protect the innocent, in its nightmarish prison and zeal to incarcerate the innocent, the Ministry becomes the agent of discrimination and persecution of the defenseless. The modern, Orwellian regime with MOM's face!

It is a great disappointment but little surprise, consequently, when the Minister of Magic, in the dark hour at the end of *Goblet of Fire* requiring decisiveness and courage to combat the risen Lord Voldemort, shows himself an impotent coward and fool. In a world (unlike our own?) ruled by prejudices and stereotypes, whose thoughts and feelings are guided by a self-serving media, and whose government maintains order by fear of tortuous imprisonment, don't look for public figures of the stature of a Churchill or even a Coolidge; look for Chamberlain-like appeasement in *Order of the Phoenix*. Sadly, the "good guys" or "white hats" have black hearts; the Dark Lord is ready to take his place as rightful ruler of this nightmare world.

This is a kid's book? Hardly. Another irony of the critical response to the books has been that those having only disdain for them dismiss the series as "Disney cartoons in words, no more" and "the literary equivalent of fast food". Harry Potter, one pundit proclaims, is a "sexist, neo-conservative autocrat". Harry Potter is no autocrat or neo-conservative; he is a force for the truth *contra mundum* (and look for the world to turn on him with a vengeance in the next few books). The critics see her commercial success and overlook Rowling's loud, subversive message: poisonous prejudice is everywhere and only constant vigilance and resistance to the regime of ideas (whose government and media authorities foster and codify this hatred) will free us of it.

Now that's a powerful meaning delivered in an exciting story. Is this the secret reason Rowling's books are so popular? I doubt it — if anything it only explains the discomfort of the self-righteous and self-justifying with Harry's message. Roald Dahl in several of his books, all of which are as funny and clever as anything in Harry Potter, presents a similar contra-regime message about schools, business, poverty, you name it. But can you name three books by Mr. Dahl? I'm a big fan of his and I struggle to remember three titles.

If the prejudice theme itself were responsible for its popularity it could only be because we readers get a warm fuzzy reading about other people's ignorance and meanness — with the warm self-congratulations of knowing we're not like them! This would makes us choir members nodding our heads in agreement with the Reverend Rowling's sermon on social injustice. That may be part of what charms some readers but the majority are moved, I think, by Rowling's ability to force us *to confront ourselves as prejudiced and unkind.* Understanding her ability to turn a mirror on her reader's own rush to judge others is the first step to grasping her popularity.

Prejudice in Us — the Pop-Up Book!

How does she do that? First, let's be clear she *does* shock her readers into self-reflection about hurried judgments. If you concur that Rowling's trademark in the writing game is not flying school-aged wizards but water tight plotting and stunning "wait-a-minute, who would believe it?!?" endings, then you see where I'm going. Rowling's surprise endings make the dullest reader slap himself in the forehead and say, "Duh! What was I thinking? I should have known that bad guy was a good guy! Why was I so sure he was a bad apple?"

This punishing self-reflection adds a third dimension to her discourse on prejudices, a follow-up punch, if you will, creating a powerful one-two cathartic combination. But I'm ahead of myself. Let's take a look at the surprises we have in each book.

Harry Potter readers are taught to sympathize with the downtrodden and victims of blind prejudice by Rowling's thematic repetition of their sufferings. Think of Hagrid locked in his hut, wanting to resign because of the backlash against him after he is exposed as a half-giant. Remember Harry imprisoned under the stairs and hated by his Aunt and Uncle for a reason he does not know. And what of Sirius Black, kept in Azkaban for twelve years for a crime he did not commit and without a trial?

Book	Character	Surprise!
Philosopher's Stone	Harry Potter Severus Snape Professor Quirrell The World	A Wizard! A Seeker! A Hero! Harry's defender Voldemort's host Magical and Mundane
Chamber of Secrets	Draco Malfoy Tom Marvolo Riddle Ginny Weasley Gilderoy Lockhart Riddle's Diary Harry Potter Dobby	Not Heir of Slytherin "I am Lord Voldemort" Servant of Voldemort Coward and fraud Malfoy attack on Weasleys Heir of Gryffyndor Malfoy House Elf & White Hat!
Prisoner of Azkaban	Scabbers Grim Peter Pettigrew Remus Lupin Hermione Granger Sirius Black Harry Potter	An Animagus! Another Animagus! Alive and a rat Werewolf! Time traveling scholar Innocent! Hero! Defender! Patronus Proficient
Goblet of Fire	Mad Eye Moody Barty Crouch, Jr. House Elves Ludo Bagman Severus Snape Rubeus Hagrid Hermione Granger Harry Potter	Death Eater helping Harry Alive and a patricidal ghoul Delighted to be of service Dark Wizard Heroic double-agent Half-Giant Victor's date - a knock-out! Voldemort's equal in battle

Readers also learn the cause and cure of prejudicial treatment. Hermione, a mudblood assaulted in print by Rita's lies, teaches Hagrid (with an assist from Dumbledore) that self-pity is no answer — ignore the spiteful and ignorant, she tells her friends again and again. From Ron, we saw the genesis of prejudice in cultural mores; he has all the usual wizard's preconceptions. He also, however, transcends them after meeting with and learning to like those he was taught to hate.

All this is well and good but, without the surprise endings, the books would probably have sold as well as updates of

Uncle Tom's Cabin or ***The Jungle***. The in-your-face twist that concludes each volume of the series is what compels the reader to take the prejudice theme home; she learns, "Hey, this is not just Draco Malfoy's problem, I have this problem, too." The "A-ha" moment in every book when the reader learns he was wrong (the good guy was bad! The bad guy was good!) is the moment Rowling's thematic lessons slip inside the reader's heart.

What's more, the reader is delighted by this three-dimensional, one-two punch and can't wait for the next volume and a similar catharsis. This "trick" — creating for us an experience of our own inclination to prejudge others, via characters who turn out not to belong in the boxes we've pigeonholed them — makes the ***Harry Potter*** books as different from most fiction as a Pop-Up book is to the usual picture story. The look of delight on a child's face when the covers open and the book pops up in three dimensions — that's also the look of a delighted ***Harry Potter*** reader after peering into the prejudice mirror (and slapping one's own forehead!).

Chapter 4

Death & Bereavement
in
Harry Potter

If after reading all the above about **Harry Potter** and prejudice, you're feeling like you know what **Harry Potter** is about, whoops, you're in for another surprise. The big theme in **Harry Potter** is "Death and Bereavement". How am I so sure of that? Because Ms. Rowling tells us that's what the books are about. Take, for instance, this excerpt from *Newsweek*'s coverage of the publication of **Goblet of Fire**:

> In the first book the orphaned Harry stares into the Mirror
> of Erised, which shows the viewer his or her utmost
> desires. Harry sees his dead parents. "Not until I re-read

what I'd written did I realize that that had been taken entirely — entirely — from how I felt about my mother's death," Rowling said. "In fact, death and bereavement and what death means, I would say, is one of the central themes in all seven books. **(Malcolm Jones, "Harry's Hot",** *Newsweek,* **July, 17, 2000, p. 56)**

Can't be much plainer than that. Why would a young woman in the bloom of life write a series of books about death and bereavement? The best guess I've read is the common-sense one; she has experienced death of loved ones and grief and has something to say. Here is an article from *Entertainment Weekly*, also at the publication of *Goblet of Fire*:

Death is a major theme. The villain wants to live forever, by whatever means it takes, and the hero is the child of murdered parents, whose mother died to preserve his life. Death and family are inextricably linked for Rowling. "I'm fascinated with big families in the stories I like, probably because I'm from such a small one," she says. "My parents were so young when they married — my mother was only 20 when she had me, 23 for my sister Di — that we had four living grandparents and lots of great aunts and uncles. But they soon began to die, including my mother from multiple sclerosis when I was 25, so now there's only me, my sister, my daughter, Jessica, my father and one aunt."

Perhaps it's Rowling's family history that has given her the "handle on dying" that Toronto bookseller Jessy Kahn, owner of the Constant Reader, sees in her books. "She deals with death very sensitively. I didn't think of it until customers began to return for additional Harry Potter copies to give to friends who had suffered a loss. And those people found them comforting." A pleased

Rowling responds: "If that's the case, then I'm very gratified."**(Brian Bethune, "The Rowling Connection",** *Entertainment Weekly,* **July 2000)**

Even people who have read the books have balked at the possibility that the *Harry Potter* series is about death and grieving. Perhaps because they are marketed as children's books, the association with the young and innocent makes it an unlikely match. Perhaps that people like them so much suggests that they could not be about something as discomforting as, egad, mortality and the loss of a friend or relative. Whatever the reason, it's just not true; the phenomenally successful *Harry Potter* books *can* be about death and they are. Let's take a look, one book at a time.

Death in *Harry Potter and the Philosopher's Stone*

Albus Dumbledore, the greatest wizard of the age and Headmaster of Hogwarts, has two heart-to-heart talks with Harry his first year at Hogwarts. The first is after Harry has discovered the Mirror of Erised ("Desire" in mirror writing). This mirror has the property of revealing the heart's desire of whoever looks into it. Harry sees his dead family, all alive and delighted to see him, and he returns again and again at night to look into it. Dumbledore surprises him there one night and explains what the mirror is and does. He concludes:

> "The Mirror will be moved to a new home tomorrow, and I ask you not to go looking for it again. If you ever do run across it, you will be prepared. It does not do to dwell on dreams and forget to live, remember that. Now, why don't you put that admirable cloak back on and get off to bed?" **(p. 214)**

This passage has importance to the larger meaning of **Stone** (discussed in **Part Three**), but here we hear at least Joanne Rowling's final words on her experience at her mother's death: "It does not do to dwell on dreams and forget to live, remember that." Death will come and grief follows, but grief must come to some sort of end in order to "have a life". Dumbledore clearly worries about Harry and his coming to terms with his parents' death (and the Mirror) because he congratulates Harry after his next Quidditch match with a "Well done" and then "Nice to see you haven't been brooding about that mirror... been keeping busy... excellent..."(p. 224).

Harry has another tete-e-tete with Headmaster at book's end after he defeats Professor Quirrell in front of the Mirror of Erised. Dumbledore explains to Harry that he has destroyed the Philosopher's Stone. This shocks Harry because he knows that Dumbledore's friends, Nicholas Flamel and his wife, are only alive because of the Elixir of life they get from the Stone. Dumbledore explains:

> "They have enough Elixir stored to set their affairs in order and, then, yes, they will die." Dumbledore smiled at the look of amazement on Harry's face.
>
> "To one as young as you, I'm sure it seems incredible, but to Nicolas and Perenelle, it really is like going to bed after a very, *very* long day. After all, to the well organized mind, death is but the next great adventure." **(p. 297, and again on p. 302)**

This definition of death, how to think of it rather than fear it, is the only part of this conversation repeated word for word in Harry's account to Ron and Hermione later. Harry then asks how it was possible for him to defeat Professor Quirrell whose hands burned at the touch of Harry's skin.

"But why couldn't Quirrell touch me?"

"Your mother died to save you. If there is one thing Voldemort cannot understand, it is love. He didn't realize that love as powerful as your mother's for you leaves its own mark. Not a scar, no visible sign... to have been loved so deeply, even though the person who loved us is gone, will give us some protection forever. It is in your very skin. Quirrell, full of hatred, greed and ambition, sharing his soul with Voldemort, could not touch you for this reason. It was agony to touch a person marked by something so good." **(p. 299)**

In the opening book of the seven book series, then, Rowling offers explicit teaching of what death is, the importance of closure in grief, and the as great importance of recalling in gratitude the love of those departed whose love continues to protect us even in their absence.

Death in *Harry Potter and the Chamber of Secrets*

Harry's meetings with Dumbledore in the next book are a short discussion in the Headmaster's office and, again, after Harry fights the young Voldemort and his pet basilisk. Neither talk is about death. Harry does have a near-death scene, however, in the Chamber of Secrets. He was wounded by the basilisk as he killed it and Voldemort/Riddle taunts him as he "dies":

"So ends the famous Harry Potter," said Riddle's distant voice. "alone in the Chamber of Secrets, forsaken by his friends, defeated at last by the Dark Lord he so unwisely challenged. You'll be back with your dear Mudblood mother soon, Harry... She bought you twelve years of borrowed time... but Lord Voldemort got you in the end as you knew he must..."

If this is dying, thought Harry, it's not so bad. Even the pain was leaving him... **(p. 321)**

As it turns out Harry has been saved by the healing tears of the Phoenix. Harry, facing certain death in combat with an older and wiser wizard, not to mention his giant, poisonous pet basilisk, triumphs through loyalty to Dumbledore and the graceful help of his pet phoenix, Fawkes. Believe it or not, this is Rowling's implicit, symbolic teaching on how to escape death, which I'll discuss at some length in Part Three.

Death in *Harry Potter and the Prisoner of Azkaban*

The title of Book Three is meaningful (see the discussion of book titles at the end of, you guessed it, Part Three), but it might have been titled *Harry Potter and the Dementors* because so much of it turns on Harry's meeting with these soul-sucking monsters. As if they were not horrible enough, raising in their victims their most painful memories to sap them of joy and hope, for Harry that memory is a reliving of his parents' murder at the wand of Lord Voldemort. Harry fears this replayed experience more than he does Lord Voldemort; the pain of seeing his parents die again is worse than facing his own death.

Harry spends much of the book, consequently, with his teacher/analyst Professor Lupin, learning how to conjure a Patronus charm that will protect him from the Dementors (the Patronus charm is discussed in, of course, Part Three). Not surprisingly, given the meaning of *patronus* and the moral Dumbledore draws for Harry at book's end, Harry's Patronus is very much about his late father.

His meeting with Dumbledore after the bizarre ending of **Prisoner** is a return to the discussion in **Philosopher's Stone** of death and our relationship with those dead who loved us. Harry admits to Dumbledore that he thought he saw his dead father save him from the Dementor's kiss.

> "It was stupid, thinking it was [my Dad]," he muttered. "I mean, I knew he was dead."
>
> "You think the dead we loved ever truly leave us? [Dumbledore responds] You think that we don't recall them more clearly than ever in times of great trouble? Your father is alive in you, Harry, and shows himself most plainly when you have need of him. How else could you produce that particular Patronus? Prongs rode again last night. ….You know, Harry, in a way, you did see your father last night…. You found him inside yourself."
> **(pp. 427-428)**

Rowling here returns to her conviction about love and death we learned through Dumbledore at the end of the first book: that the love of the departed lives on in us as a protecting grace and, in this, the dead are never truly "departed".

Death in *Harry Potter and the Goblet of Fire*

Rowling gives us a picture of this thought again in Harry's combat with Lord Voldemort at the end of Book Four. Lily and James Potter, via the "Priori Incantantem" effect consequent to twin-cored wands doing battle, appear as shadowy echoes out of Voldemort's wand (in the company of his other victims).

Harry's Dad coaches him and comforts him and, after explaining to Harry how to escape, gives him the cue to go and attacks Voldemort with the other shadows to buy Harry the time he needs to get away. Not bad for a dead man who is not even a ghost.

Harry is traumatized by this experience of meeting his parents even in this form and by the murder of his classmate Cedric, but Dumbledore makes him talk about his ordeal right away.

> "If I thought I could help you," Dumbledore said gently, "by putting you into an enchanted sleep and allowing you to postpone the moment when you would have to think about what has happened tonight, I would do it. But I know better. Numbing the pain for a while will make it worse when you finally feel it."...
>
> Once or twice, Sirius made a noise as though to say something, his hand still tight on Harry's shoulder, but Dumbledore raised his hand to stop him, and Harry was glad of this, because it was easier to keep going now he had started. It was even a relief; he felt almost as though something poisonous were being extracted from him. It was costing him every bit of determination he had to keep talking, yet he sensed that once he was finished, he would feel better. (p. 695)

Rowling in *Goblet of Fire* tries to show us how to grieve well for closure. First, talk out the poison. It won't be easy but as Dumbledore tells Minerva McGonagal (who tries to take Harry to the hospital wing), you have to have the facts in the open before you can recover from a blow:

> "He will stay, Minerva, because he needs to understand," said Dumbledore curtly. "Understanding is the first step

to acceptance, and only with acceptance can there be recovery. He needs to know who has put him through the ordeal he has suffered tonight, and why." **(p. 680)**

Professor Kubler-Ross? The next step to grieving well is public ritual to honor the dead and the meaning of their life and death. Dumbledore does this duty for Cedric and Hogwarts at the Leaving Feast. In front of the whole school, he speaks frankly about Voldemort's murder of Cedric Diggory.

> "His death has affected you all, whether you knew him well or not. I think that you have the right, therefore, to know exactly how it came about."
>
> Harry raised his head and stared at Dumbledore.
>
> "Cedric Diggory was murdered by Lord Voldemort."
>
> A panicked whisper swept the Great Hall. People were staring at Dumbledore in disbelief, in horror. He looked perfectly calm as he watched them mutter themselves into silence.
>
> "The Ministry of Magic," Dumbledore continued, "does not wish me to tell you this. It is possible that some of your parents will be horrified that I have done so — either because they will not believe that Lord Voldemort has returned, or because they think I should not tell you so, young as you are. It is my belief, however, that the truth is generally preferable to lies, and that any attempt to pretend that Cedric died as the result of an accident, or some sort of blunder of his own, is an insult to his memory." **(p. 722)**

This memorial, with toasts to Cedric's memory and the injunction to recall him in times of difficulty, completes Harry's digestion, if you will, of the trauma of Cedric's death.

"Harry, Ron, and Hermione talked more fully and freely than they had all week as the train sped them southward. Harry felt as though Dumbledore's speech at the Leaving Feast had unblocked him, somehow. It was less painful to discuss what happened now. They broke off their conversation about what action Dumbledore might be taking, even now, to stop Voldemort only when the lunch trolley arrived." **(p. 726)**

Goblet of Fire is full of deaths. It opens with the murder of Frank Bryce and ends with the death of Cedric Diggory but off stage we learn of two other murders (Bertha Jorkins, Bartimeus Crouch, Sr.) and the worse-than-death execution of Barty Crouch, Jr. Book Five of the series promises more of the same. From the *New York Times*:

"There are deaths, more deaths coming," she said in an interview with the British Broadcasting Corporation in December, adding that one character's end "will be horrible to write."(David Kirkpatrick, **"Harry Potter and the Quest for the Unfinished Volume"**, *New York Times*, **May 5, 2002)**

Rowling thinks by this point, it seems, that her readers should have learned what death is and isn't, how to grieve and mistakes to avoid in grief. Let's review what she has to tell us.

Death: What It Is and Isn't
— *It is final.*
Rumor has it that Rowling has been besieged by letters from young fans begging her not to kill Ron and to please raise Harry's parents from the dead. Ron's life may be in jeopardy, but Rowling responds in *Goblet* to the plea for Lily and James'

resurrection via Dumbledore heavily saying, "No spell can reawaken the dead" (p. 697). Death is no joke in *Harry Potter*; there's no coming back.

— *Death is human and isn't "the end".*

Ron's response to learning the Stone has been destroyed is instructive.

> "So the Stone's gone?" said Ron finally. "Flamel's just going to *die*?"
>
> "That's what I said, but Dumbledore thinks that — what was it? — 'to the well organized mind, death is but the next great adventure.'"
>
> "I always said he was off his rocker," said Ron, looking quite impressed at how crazy his hero was. (*Stone*, pp. 301-302)

Though this teaching is counter-intuitive and seemingly superhuman, death, if rightly understood, is a part of life. Not like this life, certainly, but another adventure. It seems Dumbledore (and Rowling) believe there is a next life that makes death anything but the end. Rowling is not contradicting herself here. Death is final in the sense that the dead will not come back to this life. They have another adventure elsewhere.

— *The dead live on in those they love.*

His mother's sacrificial love saves Harry from Lord Voldemort as an infant and again before the Mirror of Erised in combat with Quirrell and Voldemort. Dumbledore explains: "to have been loved so deeply, even though the person who loved us is gone, will give us some protection forever" (*Stone*, p. 299).

Harry's father, too, lives on. As Dumbledore explains at the end of **Prisoner**:

> "You think the dead we loved ever truly leave us? You think we don't recall them more clearly than ever in times of great trouble? Your father is alive in you, Harry, and shows himself most plainly when you have need of him…. You know, Harry, in a way you did see your father last night…. You found him inside yourself." **(pp. 427-428)**

Death, then, is not even final in this world. Though the dead cannot have a physical life again, they can live on in those they have loved. Love is the only path to immortality.

—— Death is not the greatest evil.

If there is one single difference between Harry Potter and He-Who-Must-Not-Be-Named, it is that Harry thinks there are worse things than dying. Voldemort reminds his supporters at his re-birthing party at the end of **Goblet**: "You know my goal — to conquer death" **(p. 653)**. He claims to have taken "the steps" to "guard [himself] against mortal death" **(p. 648)** and "to have gone further than anybody along the path that leads to immortality" **(p. 653)**.

But this path is not the way of love. As Hagrid says to Harry in **Philosopher's Stone** when relating what happened to Voldemort after he attacked Harry: "Some say he died. Codswallup, in my opinion. Dunno if he had enough human left in him to die" **(p. 37)**. Dumbledore echoes this point in **Goblet** when he explains that Voldemort could not die because he was not truly alive. Voldemort, fearing death, pursues a personal immortality; such a self-focused, unloving existence ironically separates him from the love of others which is life and, Rowling suggests, our hope of immortality. Fleeing death, Voldemort becomes its non-living incarnation.

On the other hand, when given Dumbledore's "choice between what is good and what is easy", Harry always chooses the good — even though it means the probably loss of his life. He does so in every book at the moment of crisis. My favorite is in *Philosopher's Stone*:

> "I'm going out of here tonight and I'm going to try and get to the Stone first."
>
> "You're mad!" said Ron.
>
> "You can't!" said Hermione. "After what McGonagall and Snape have said? You'll be expelled!"
>
> "SO WHAT?" Harry shouted. "Don't you understand? If Snape gets hold of the Stone, Voldemort's coming back! Haven't you heard what it was like when he was trying to take over? There won't be any Hogwarts to get expelled from! ... Do you think he'll leave you or your families alone if Gryffyndor wins the house cup? If I get caught before I get to the Stone, well, I'll have to go back to the Dursleys and wait for Voldemort to find me there, it's only dying a bit later than I would have, because I'm never going over to the Dark Side! I'm going through that trapdoor tonight and nothing you two say is going to stop me! Voldemort killed my parents, remember?" **(p. 270)**

What could be worse than death? A selfish life without truth, love, and beauty, a life, that is to say, on the Dark Side, chosen in fear of physical death — a life which is not really life at all. A physical life without a soul is what happens to a dementor's victim. As Professor Lupin explains to Harry in **Prisoner**:

> "Get too near a dementor and every good feeling, every happy memory will be sucked out of you. If it can, the dementor will feed on you long enough to reduce you to something like itself...soul-less and evil. You'll be left with nothing but the worst experiences of your life." **(p. 187)**

> "What — they kill — ?" [Harry asked.]

> "Oh no," said Lupin. "Much worse than that. You can exist without your soul, you know, as long as your brain and heart are still working. But you'll have no sense of self anymore, no memory, no... anything. There's no chance at all of recovery. You'll just — exist. As an empty shell. And your soul is gone forever... lost." **(p. 247)**

Voldemort says of the dementors, "[They] will join us... they are our natural allies" **(Goblet, p. 651)**. Dumbledore, too sees the affinity. He tells Fudge to remove control of Azkaban from the dementors:

> "The rest of us sleep less soundly in our beds, Cornelius, knowing that you have put Lord Voldemort's most dangerous supporters in the care of creatures who will join him the instant he asks them!" said Dumbledore. "They will not remain loyal to you, Fudge! Voldemort can offer them much more scope for their powers and pleasures than you can!" **(Goblet, p. 707)**

The war taking shape between the forces of good and evil in the coming books is largely between those who think physical life (existence) is the greatest good and those that think what gives life meaning (the soul's ability to love and laugh) is more real and important than just what is visible (namely, continued physical existence). The fact that the Ministry of Magic depends on dementors naturally allied with the Death Eaters, who create a soul-less existence worse than death but not physical death, tells us the war will not be between the Ministry and Voldemort. Harry (and presumably his author) knows that death is not the greatest evil; living a soul-less existence in fear of death is much worse.

— *Death is not to be faced alone*
Rowling never has Harry enter the fray by himself. He often winds up by himself but he is always accompanied into the contest by friends who love him.

- In Book One, Ron and Hermione go through the trap door with Harry.
- In Book Two, Ron travels with him until a rockslide just before the Chamber blocks him.
- In Book Three, Hermione rescues Sirius Black on Buckbeak with Harry.
- In Book Four, Cedric joins Harry in mutual triumph — and a trip to Voldemort.

If Rowling is telling us that the answer to the riddle of death is not a personal, physical immortality but the love of family and friends, then it follows that there is no smarter way to confront death than with those you love.

How To Grieve — and How Not To

Rowling's "Bereavement Manual", written between the lines of her books, so far has five chapters:

- Talk It Out — and the Sooner the Better

- Honor the Dead in a Public Ritual

- Remember the Dead Will Always Be with You

- Get on with Your Life

- Grieving Well *is* a Civic Responsibility

Dumbledore has tutored Harry in these lessons book to book, and in **Goblet of Fire** he demonstrates how grieving is properly done. He is a model grief counselor to Harry after Cedric's murder and mourns Cedric ritually and with no little majesty at the Leaving Feast. This serves to unblock all present so they can get on with their lives.

Rowling hints at how not to grieve in two characters' responses to personal setbacks. In **Goblet**, Hagrid is exposed by Rita Skeeter as a half-giant, then in shame retreats to his cabin, offers his resignation, and drinks heavily. Only the love of his friends makes him realize "I bin stupid... I've bin an idiot" **(pp. 455-456)**. He resolves to get on with his life, unashamed, and at novel's end it has become clear that it is just the fact that he *is* a half-giant that qualifies him for a not-so-secret and critical mission for the Good Guys.

Winky, the Crouches' house elf, likewise takes the edge off her dismissal with a butterbeer binge and a good helping of paralyzing self-pity **(see Goblet, pp. 376-383 and 536-538)**. She is inconsolable to the end; she will not talk about her grief and experiences, and she cannot get on her life. Is it any accident that her hysterical and selfish way of mourning her loss results in the death of her masters, separation from whom she claims to be grieving? One word to Harry or Dobby and the secret mission of Master Barty would have been derailed. Grieving well is clearly a responsibility one undertakes for others as much as for one's self.

Death and the Popularity of *Harry Potter*

Rowling tells us the books are largely about death and bereavement and, sure enough, a closer look reveals the series is laden with implicit and explicit teachings about death and grief. A remarkable achievement in books most think of as cute and many think of as only a "rollicking good time"! Does this theme explain why the **Harry Potter** books are so popular? Are people worldwide so hungry to understand what death (and, in that, life) is about?

It makes more sense than, say, her teachings on prejudice, about which mankind seems determined to learn as little as possible. But as with prejudice, it seems a stretch to think the books are so popular because folks of all types are enamored of her lively sermons in engaging stories about difficult subjects. Other authors have written about 'love and death', and none of them have sold copies like **Harry Potter.**

Perhaps, as with prejudice, Rowling is able to make us aware of our own mortality in the books and how we should (and can) face death. That would be more powerful a presentation than a storybook homily and might explain her stratospheric sales. And indeed, that is what she does.

How? Turn back to the Formula map you were supposed to have dog-eared a few pages back. You may have thought that map was a vanity exercise by this author, but no, it actually serves some purpose. Follow Harry's journey from Privet Drive around clockwise through his adventure. In every book, he begins at home with the Dursleys, escapes to Hogwarts, and discovers a mystery. He, Ron, and Hermione do the Nancy Drew and Hardy Boys thing for a long while, as life goes on at Hogwarts (as with Tom Brown's Rugby) until the mystery comes to a crisis. Harry faces the crisis. He and one or more friends head underground to confront the evil "beneath and behind" the mystery.

Please remember your condition as a reader at this point in any one of the four stories. In my family, any event or person attempting to separate reader and story as Harry is about to face Voldemort or a Death Eater, is likely to be met with unflattering language and every bit of resistance short of physical violence. Disbelief has been suspended and, in our imaginations, we are right with Harry, we are even Harry himself, as the story rushes to a conclusion in battle.

Look at the chart again. What's the next thing to happen to Harry every time? In each battle, Harry goes through death.

- In *Philosopher's Stone*, Harry expires "[knowing] all was lost, and fell into blackness, down...down... down..." **(p. 295)**

- In *Chamber of Secrets*, Harry is poisoned by the basilisk. "Harry slid down the wall. He gripped the fang that was spreading poison through his body and wrenched it out of his arm. But he knew it was too late. ... 'You're dead, Harry Potter,' said Riddle's voice above him." **(p. 320)**

- In *Prisoner of Azkaban*, a dementor lowers his hood to kiss Harry. "A pair of strong, clammy hands suddenly attached themselves around Harry's neck. They were forcing his face upward... He could feel its putrid breath.... His mother was screaming in his ears.... She was going to be the last thing he ever heard.... [When released, Harry] felt the last of his strength leave him, and his head hit the ground as he fainted." **(pp. 384-385)**

• In *Goblet of Fire*, Rowling places Harry's seemingly hopeless battle with the risen Voldemort in a graveyard, so Harry is not only in an almost certain collision course with death, he is also already among the dead.

So what? Remember again your condition as a reader when Harry dies: in your imagination, you are with Harry, heart and soul, at his "death". *The reader dies with Harry — and, of course, rises from death with him, too.* This is Rowling's three-dimensional, one-two combination knock-out punch on death. She teaches explicitly through Dumbledore's sermonettes and deeds what we need to know about death; she follows this out-loud teaching with an imaginative experience of death and life after death to hammer it home. We see the truth she has to share with us about death as clearly after this cathartic experience as a child sees the dragon, knight, and castle rise up out of his pop-up book.

Have We Answered the Question?

This three-dimensional learning — by surprise ending and imaginative resurrection — is powerful stuff. It is only possible in a well-told tale that engages us so profoundly that we forget we are reading about and not experiencing the story ourselves. Rowling's success testifies to her ability to weave such enchanting fiction.

So is this the answer to the question of why the *Harry Potter* books are so popular? Yes and no.

Yes, we are a lot closer than critics who have dismissed Ms. Rowling's books as dangerous or "just slop". We know that her **Harry Potter** novels are about themes as profound as prejudice, love, death, and grief — and we know that she delivers her message explicitly in morals delivered at the end of the story, implicitly in the actions of characters, and most remarkably, in the experience of her readers identifying with Harry in death and being surprised at their own prejudicial errors.

That explains a lot about these books. They are great stories with meaningful lessons about questions we all must answer — and readers experience these answers three-dimensionally as they read. But that does not completely explain the popularity of Harry Potter in print and on screen.

Some questions remain. For example, Ms. Rowling has subversive opinions about government and the media that most people disagree with (or one assumes our government, newspapers, and teevee would not so resemble the picture she paints in her parallel world). How does a book critical of the regime of ideas in a liberal democracy enjoy such universal acclaim?

Did I say "universal"? There remains the unanswered question of why the *literati* and some Christians hate these books. These people aren't stupid (are they?). Ms. Rowling has said that, despite the criticism, she will not be deterred or distracted from her mission. Just what is this mission and why do objections from Christian groups get under her skin? These objections certainly have to be considered one cause of her popularity among the media and those others who feel drawn to love whatever churches damn.

Ms. Rowling has a secret mission. It is the task of the next chapter to peel away another layer of the onion and reveal this secret. Then, perhaps, we will have explained the phenomenal power and unparalleled popularity of the *Potter* novels.

Part Two

The Secret
of
Harry Potter

Part Two

The Secret
of
Harry Potter

T*he Hidden Key to Harry Potter* hopes to uncover the reason why Joanne Rowling's **Harry Potter** books are so popular. In Part One, we learned that Rowling does not discuss the "why" of her popularity, though she says this is the question most frequently asked her. A cursory survey of the critical response revealed that there are two "roads" of criticism so far: a Low Road of caution and disdain and a Middle Road of delight and gratitude. Neither of these approaches answers the question.

Critics on the Low Road hint or say right out loud that the reason the books are so successful is because they are so bad and people are so stupid they'll buy anything they're told to buy. Critics on the Middle Road say it is because they are so good that people like them. They write about themes and literary allusions and rave on about the great stories and clever characters Ms. Rowling has invented.

The Hidden Key is the first entry in a third approach to understanding Harry Potter, namely, the High Road. This perspective, in a nutshell, is that Ms. Rowling's novels sell so well, which is to say over 100 million copies in less than five years, because they are so *very* good and so *very* different. This may seem the obvious answer, but so far it has not been offered.

Part One plotted the relationships of the story connecting all the novels so far, drew a map of the Hero's Journey Harry takes in every book, and charted the various books that Rowling drew themes and narrative events from, consciously or unconsciously. After this groundwork was done, Harry was put under the microscope.

We looked at the themes of prejudice and death Ms. Rowling has admitted are central themes of the series and learned she has written the books in such a way that the reader gets her message three-dimensionally:

- baldly, by a character saying out loud what she is trying to say,

- in a picture, by character actions and plot events, and

- with a WOW!, by getting the reader to experience the message.

This WOW! third dimension of experience and catharsis, delivered via shocking endings and reader identification with Harry's death, separates Ms. Rowling from other writers and is certainly part of the reason she tops every chart of book sales other than the "Non-Fiction Best Sellers List". But it's only a part.

Middle Road critics explain Pottermania as a result of the fact that the books are well written. The High Road explanation in Part One doesn't say much more than this beyond saying they are "*really* well written". Not much height in that High Road. The **Harry Potter** books are so much more successful than other books that surely the difference is greater than just writing styles.

There is something in Ms. Rowling's reticence to discuss why her books are so popular, something about her annoyance with the critical response to Harry, that suggests there is a secret she is not sharing which explains Harry's profound effect on his readers. *The High Road explanation is that she attempts to satisfy a human need other writers neglect, even a human capacity — and that her attempt is on target, even a bull's-eye.* This Part, "The Secret of Harry Potter", is our search for the not-yet-revealed way in which the books are so *very* different and so *very* much better than other books — the way that might just explain their popularity.

Let's see if we cannot tease out this secret, to risk mixing metaphors, by peeling away another layer of the Harry onion. In this chapter we will look at two more themes of the books and track repeated images and symbols in search of the Secret. Whatever answer shows itself will be checked for plausibility against what little information is publicly available about Ms. Rowling's education, her religious beliefs, and her favorite books.

Chapter 5

Choice
in
Harry Potter

One of the delights of writing the High Road interpretation of Harry Potter is anticipating the Low Road response. Because only someone very well-educated can assert convincingly that readers love certain books because they are stupid and the books are bad, I more than half expect to be accused of a lack of sophistication and scholarship for asserting the obvious opposite. I am a small guy, but I learned in the Marine Corps that the small guy can win a fight if he throws the first punch. So here's a poke in the Low Road eye.

My favorite Low Road writer is Richard Abanes, author of ***Harry Potter and the Bible: The Menace behind the Magick***. Though he is undoubtedly a devout Christian and kind man, he says not one charitable word about Ms. Rowling or any of her ***Harry Potter*** books (not to mention Harry fans) in his 275 page philippic. She is chastened for her unbiblical spirituality, occult symbolism, moral ambiguity, bad language, poor writing, and causing a recession in Japan (well, he doesn't blame her for that). His concerns about careless spirituality and the dangers of the occult are real ones; sadly, they blind him to all and anything good in Harry Potter.

Take, for example, his charge of moral ambiguity. At first blush this seems a stretch. Harry Potter is a good guy and Voldemort the bad guy and there seems little common ground for confusion or ambiguity. To Mr. Abanes, however, because the "white hats" are a little gray, not lily white, and the "black hats" are not inhumanly evil without any redeeming virtues, the picture of right and wrong has been clouded. Let's hear him explain it.

> Rowling downplays Harry's other moral issues by elevating two virtuous characteristics above all others: bravery and courage. As she herself has stated, "If the characters are brave and courageous, that is rewarded." What Rowling seemingly fails to realize, however, is that even in her own books "evil" characters are brave and courageous, too. In the Potter series, we see some evil characters save each other's lives, magically heal other's wounds, remain loyal to their side in the face of enemy persecution and sacrifice

themselves for each other.... Of course, Voldemort's method of operation may be drastically unlike Harry's, but the two characters share the same motivation: self interest. Voldemort wants what he wants, as does Harry. The only difference between them rests in the rules they choose to break, the lies they choose to tell and the goals they choose to pursue. *(Abanes, Magick, p. 136)*

Really, the whole book is like that. That Harry's "self interest" is selfless and sacrificial (and, yes, sometimes means being out after curfew and protecting friends with a lie) is meaningless to Mr. Abanes. He acts from self-interest, Voldemort acts from murderous, pitiless self-interest; the two are morally indistinguishable. But there is another, better reason to reject Mr. Abanes' critical assertion as unfounded.

One of the last chapters in his book is a defense of C. S. Lewis and J. R. R. Tolkien in the face of frequently made assertions (usually in response to accusations from Christian critics) that the **Potter** books are "just like" Lewis' Narnia and Tolkien's Middle Earth. (If this book of mine has a single origin, it may be as a response to Abanes' "defense"; see Appendix A.) If Mr. Abanes had remembered some of the better defenses of Tolkien against Tolkien's critics when writing up the charge of moral ambiguity against Ms. Rowling, he would have recalled how Auden responded to the same charge against Tolkien. Tom Shippey, author of *J. R. R. Tolkien: Author of the Century*, explains:

Tolkien was, to put it mildly, not fortunate in his critics.... They accused him of making his good and bad characters morally indistinguishable: this was answered by fierce logic by W. H. Auden, who pointed out first in 1955, then in 1961, that a major difference was that the good characters, the Gandalfs and the Galadriels, could imagine becoming bad, whereas Sauron's great weakness, even tactically, is that he cannot imagine the self-destructive strategy of destroying the Ring forever. **(Shippey, *Author*, p. 147)**

As with Tolkien's good and bad lead players, the difference between Harry and Tom Riddle/Voldemort, over and beyond their purposefully-included similarities, is that Harry wrestles with his choices: he may not be tempted to the Dark Side but he knows that he is not pure of heart. Unlike Draco Malfoy and the Slytherins, Harry ponders the right and wrong of situations (and his darker impulses) in his desire to do the right thing beyond personal advantage and self interest.

Voldemort and his ilk lack this depth in not being troubled by their choices, a lack of depth that can be called "immorality". Because Ms. Rowling does not write fiction with a cartoon-like morality akin to the "Focus on the Family" radio serial "Adventures in Odyssey", choice and its central place in the examined heroic life are three-dimensional themes in her *Harry Potter* books.

Choice: The Three Dimensions

I use the word "choice" in its Aristotelian meaning: choice is the human faculty of mental discrimination between options (see Aristotle's *Nicomachean Ethics*, Book 2, for the real thing). If this faculty is well trained, that is, the person has a virtuous upbringing, she is able to discriminate or "choose well" between options of good and evil, right and wrong, advantage and disadvantage. Rowling lets us know — again, three-dimensionally — what constitutes "good choosing".

The first dimension of her treatment of choice is the "implicit" level. What choices does Harry make in the books and what do these choices tell us about "how to choose"? Harry makes two types of choices in every book — about what sort of person he is and what to do in a crisis — and he chooses "what is right" over "what is easy" every time.

Let's list the choices Harry makes in the four books that will define who he is. In each choice, Harry has options of loyalty to a high and difficult standard versus personal advantage. He chooses without exception loyalty to the good.

- In **Philosopher's Stone**, Harry asks not to be put in Slytherin House though Draco Malfoy and the Sorting Hat point to Slytherin as his path to power.

- At the same time, he chooses to be friends with Ron and Hermione, one poor, the other unpopular and of questionable lineage, despite being advised (again by Draco) to avoid hanging out with "riffraff".

- In **Chamber of Secrets**, Harry professes his loyalty to Dumbledore in the face of being murdered by Riddle/Voldemort, Dumbledore's enemy.

- In **Prisoner of Azkaban**, Harry chooses to spare Pettigrew, who betrayed his parents to their murderer, in loyalty to his understanding of what his father would have wanted.

- In **Goblet of Fire**, Harry refuses to reconcile with Ron, despite loneliness and love for Ron, in loyalty to the truth.

- Later in the same book, he withstands persecution by the media unabashed again because of his commitment to standing with what is true before what others think.

These internal choices are significant, but they are paired in each book with a life-or-death decision in a crisis in which Harry must choose between what is safe and easy for him versus resisting evil at risk of his life. He chooses each time to do the right, dangerous thing.

- In **Philosopher's Stone**, in a passage already cited, Harry chooses to pass Fluffy and enter the trap door in order to keep the Stone from Snape and Voldemort.

- In **Chamber of Secrets**, he opts to search for the Chamber to find Ron's sister Ginny, and in the Chamber he elects to fight Riddle against all odds.

- In **Prisoner**, Harry dives in front of Peter Pettigrew as Lupin and Black have wands drawn to kill him for betraying Lily and James Potter to Voldemort.

- In **Goblet of Fire**, Harry chooses both to warn Cedric of a giant spider about to attack him (though that would have cleared his way to victory — and the spider turns on Harry!) and chooses to resist and attack Voldemort in the graveyard — again against all odds.

Rowling delivers the implicit message "do the hard, right thing; don't take the easy, advantageous route" repeatedly through Harry's choices. What does Dumbledore teach us about choice in his discussions with Harry and others? You guessed it: "Your choices are what matters" and "choose what is right over what is easy".

In **Chamber of Secrets**, Harry is confronted repeatedly with suggestions that he is somehow akin to the Dark Lord. He learns at the end, from Voldemort and Dumbledore, that there is some truth in that. Harry then asks Dumbledore if he shouldn't have been put in Slytherin House where (Harry believes) the Sorting Hat thought he belonged. Dumbledore responds:

> "Voldemort put a bit of himself in *me*?" Harry said, thunderstruck.
>
> "It certainly seems so."
>
> "So I *should* be in Slytherin," Harry said, looking desperately into Dumbledore's face. "The Sorting Hat could see Slytherin's power in me, and it —"
>
> "Put you in Gryffyndor," said Dumbledore calmly. "Listen to me, Harry. You happen to have many qualities Salazar Slytherin prized in his hand-picked students. His own rare gift, Parseltongue — resourcefulness — determination — a certain disregard for rules," he added, his mustache quivering again. "Yet the Sorting Hat placed you in Gryffyndor. You know why that was. Think."
>
> "It only put me in Gryffyndor," said Harry in a defeated voice, "because I asked not to go in Slytherin...."

"*Exactly*," said Dumbledore, beaming once more. "Which makes you *very different* from Tom Riddle. It is our choices, Harry, that show who we truly are, far more than our abilities." (*Chamber*, p. 333)

Dumbledore makes this same point about the relative importance of our choices compared with our birthright in **Goblet of Fire**. Confronting the stuffed-shirt Minister of Magic, he bares Fudge's prejudice:

"You are blinded," said Dumbledore, his voice rising now, the aura of power around him palpable, his eyes blazing once more, "by the love of the office you hold, Cornelius! You place too much importance, and you have always done, on the so-called purity of blood! You fail to recognize that it matters not what someone is born, but what they grow to be! Your dementor has just destroyed the last remaining member of a pure-blood family as old as any — and see what that man chose to make of his life!" (*Goblet*, p. 708)

Your life is of value only if you choose the good before what is easy and evil. Dumbledore drives this point home in Churchill-like cadences to the assembled Hogwarts student body in the conclusion of his tribute to Cedric Diggory:

"Remember Cedric. Remember, if the time should come when you have to make a choice between what is right and what is easy, remember what happened to a boy who was good and kind and brave, because he strayed across the path of Lord Voldemort. Remember Cedric Diggory." (*Goblet*, p. 724)

So we have the *implicit* treatment of choice in what choices Harry makes, and we have the *explicit* dimension in Dumbledore's talks on choice per se. What is the WOW! experiential third dimension? Just as with her treatment of Death, Rowling projects her thoughts on Choice by placing Harry's choices in the scenes of greatest drama, when we are most engaged by the story. We identify with Harry and make the choice with him, usually amazed at our own virtue.

This is what literary theorist I. A. Richards called training in the Stock Responses: "a deliberately organized attitude which is substituted for the direct free play of experience" (for example, believing "that love is sweet, death bitter, virtue lovely, and children or gardens delightful"). One has to assume from reading C. S. Lewis' treatment in *A Preface to Paradise Lost* (pp. 54-61) that Richards didn't think much of deliberately organized attitudes or stock responses, or at least thought such conventions restricted the "free play of experience".

Lewis begs to differ:

> In my opinion such deliberate organization is one of the first necessities of human life, and one of the main functions of art is to assist it. All that we describe as constancy in love or friendship, as loyalty in political life, or, in general, as perseverance — all solid virtue and stable pleasure — depends on organizing chosen attitudes and maintaining them against the eternal flux (or "direct free play") of mere immediate experience.....[It] seems that most people's responses are not stock enough, and that the play of experience

is too free and too direct in most of us for safety or happiness or human dignity. ...

The older poetry by continually insisting on certain Stock themes — that love is sweet, death bitter, virtue lovely, and children or gardens delightful — was performing a service not only of moral and civic, but even of biological importance. Once again, the old critics were quite right when they said that poetry "instructed by delighting" for poetry was formerly one of the chief means whereby each new generation learned, not to copy, but by copying to make the good Stock responses. Since poetry has abandoned that office the world has not been bettered. **(Lewis,** *Preface,* **pp. 55, 57).**

Of course, Lewis is most famous today not for his scholarship in Medieval Literature, but for his own writing. As you might guess from the above passages, his fiction was largely about training in the Stock Responses. Anyone who has read his **Chronicles of Narnia** or **Space Trilogy** knows about "instruction by delighting" first hand. In engaging stories with believable and magical characters, Lewis enchants and teaches his Narnia audience "the right attitudes", namely, bravery, sympathy, perseverance, obedience, loyalty, sacrifice, love of nature and play, dislike of the wicked, self-important, and selfish — it's all there.

Rowling is a great fan of Lewis. When compared with him, she has volunteered her opinion that Lewis "is a genius and I am not" and that she is "physically incapable" even as an adult "to be in the same room with a Narnia book and not pick it up and read it."

I include this touch of the hat to Lewis to conclude my discussion of choice in Rowling's **Harry Potter** books because the WOW! of Rowling's treatment of choice — our experiencing and choosing alongside Harry the right, hard thing — points to Narnia and Lewis' Stock Responses. Her WOW! in this theme is not the choosing per se (as it was when dying with Harry) but *the goodness we experience as we choose the harder, virtuous, self-sacrificing option with Harry.* Rowling stands with Lewis in using her art to assist our growth in virtue. And her readers like that. A lot.

An aside before we move on: the fact that Dumbledore (and Rowling through him) points to our choices as shaping and showing what we truly are, does not mean that "we are what we choose to become" to the exclusion of having a destiny. Harry almost certainly has a King Arthur-like destiny to which he was born and of which he is not yet aware. **(Alas, see Part Four for details!)** His choices remain critically important, however, because this destiny is not a fate; he must choose to play the Harry Potter role **(Part Four!)** which is by no means automatic or pre-determined.

One more thought: Rowling's answers about choice are largely in response to the question of prejudice. If we aren't supposed to judge people by the standards of how much money they have, or how good looking they are, or what their parents are or do, how do we rightly judge people as "good" or "bad"? Ms. Rowling is not a relativist who might have us believe all judgments are prejudice and thus to be avoided (there are so many bad characters that readers are clearly meant to despise who have not — yet! — turned out to be good guys). We rightly judge others by what sort of people they choose to become, their decisions shaping whom they will change into. Which thought brings us to the theme of "change" in the **Harry Potter** books.

Chapter 6

Transfiguration, Transformation,
and
Alchemical Transmutations
in
Harry Potter

Dumbledore isn't the only philosopher at Hogwarts. Draco Malfoy knows a thing or two as well. Here is what sage Draco has to say about the importance and power of choices:

> [Malfoy] turned back to Harry. "You'll soon find out some wizarding families are much better than others, Potter. You don't want to go making friends with the wrong sort.... You hang around with riffraff like the Weasleys and that Hagrid, and it'll rub off on you." *(Stone,* pp. 108-9)

> "You've picked the losing side, Potter! I warned you! I told you you ought to choose your company more

carefully, remember? When we met on the train, first day at Hogwarts? I told you not to hang around with riffraff like this!" He jerked his head at Ron and Hermione. "Too late now, Potter! They'll be the first to go, now the Dark Lord's back! Mudbloods and Muggle-lovers first!" (*Goblet*, p. 729)

Draco understands that your choices shape who you become. We have discussed Choice in Harry Potter; let's move on to a look at the consequences of our choices, that is, what we become: our changes and transformations. It turns out that Joanne Rowling's **Harry Potter** novels are largely about transfigurations, transformations, and alchemical transmutations.

Transfiguration

"Transfigurations" comes from the Latin *trans* meaning "across" (hence "motion, change") and *figura* meaning "form, appearance, shape". *Transfiguration*, then, means "Shape Changing", and it is a major study at Hogwarts.

Most obviously, Transfigurations is a required classroom course in the curriculum. Young Wizards and Witches from the first year on are taught the basics of turning beetles into buttons, up to the advanced magic (not with teacher approval, it seems) of "turning [your] friend into a badger" (*Chamber*, p. 198). We meet the strict and proper Professor McGonagall, Master of Gryffyndor House, as a stiff backed tabby cat waiting on Privet Drive for Dumbledore in the first pages of the series. Professor McGonagall teaches Transfigurations and is a registered Animagus, one of the more difficult and advanced

accomplishments of the transfigurations art; animagi are able
to transfigure themselves into the shape of animals.

Dumbledore, too, was a Transfigurations professor (met
in Riddle's Diary and revealed later in *Chamber*, pp. 245, 312). It should
be noted that all the teaching masters of change are allied
with Gryffyndor and the good — even if not all shape
changers are good!

There is, for example, a rather nasty creature called a
"boggart" we meet in *Prisoner of Azkaban* that is a shape
changer who takes on the appearance of whatever any person
it meets fears most. It is dispersed by a "riddikulus" charm
and laughter. We know from the boggart and the Weasley
joke shop that Rowling values humor in fighting fear and
evil. (See Part Four to learn the importance Rowling may give to a joke
wand at series' end.)

More difficult even than taking the shape of animals is
changing into the appearance of another human being. This
requires a very involved potion of many ingredients and careful
brewing only the best wizards can pull off — and it only lasts
an hour at a time. Ron and Harry use the potion to good effect
in *Chamber* (Hermione has less impressive results) to turn into
Crabbe and Goyle for an hour. Barty Crouch, Jr., "becomes"
Mad Eye Moody for all of *Goblet* by drinking polyjuice potion
every hour on the hour.

One of the more poetic aspects of transfiguration is that
those who can take the shape of animals or who are forced into
the shape of animals become animals who are metaphors for
their human characters. When Moody punishes Malfoy for
attacking Harry when his back is turned, the sneaky and

rodentine Draco becomes a ferret that Moody bounces up and down with his wand. Hagrid tries to turn Dudley into a pig but only succeeds in giving him a curly pig's tail because, as he explains, Dudley is "so much like a pig there wasn't much left ter do" (*Stone*, p. 59). The obnoxious and nosy reporter Rita Skeeter (discussed in Chapter 1) of course becomes a "bug" for eavesdropping's sake as an (illegal and unregistered) animagus.

Of the animagi in Harry's father's class at Hogwarts, all take the animal shapes suggested by their names and characters. The always faithful Sirius Black becomes a big, black dog (*Sirius* is the "Dog Star"). Remus Lupin, the tragic werewolf and Defense Against the Dark Arts teacher, has a first name recalling one of the founders of Rome (suckled by wolves) and a surname that means "wolf-like". Peter Pettigrew, a.k.a. "Wormtail", the coward and turncoat who betrays his friends to Voldemort, becomes, of course, a rat as an animagus. Both his names suggest, alas, that he has a small penis. (*Pettigrew* parses to "petite growth"; *Peter* is U.K. schoolyard slang for the male sexual appendage; *Wormtail* also means, well, "worm tail".) Harry's father, James, transfigures into a majestic stag and is called "Prongs" — more on this in a little while.

The tragedy of Remus Lupin suggests one meaning about the importance of change in the **Harry Potter** series. The most accomplished wizards (usually good guys) are very skilled in transfigurations — they can control to a degree what shape they take and are in control of their changes. Lupin as a werewolf, however, is not in control of what he turns into and when it will happen. He is consequently a danger to everyone around him; if bitten by a werewolf, the person bit will also be unable to control their transfiguration into a monster.

Rowling has said that Lupin is one of her favorite characters and that he will return: no doubt as a member of The Order of the Phoenix. Rowling points through his tragic condition to our own human ability for meaningful and deliberate change as the hallmark of a well-educated, sophisticated, and socially responsible human being. Those who are unable to control their changes (what they become and when) are less-than-human monsters we are to fear (yes, to a degree), but also to pity for their compromised humanity.

Transformation

How Harry changes in each book makes the same implicit teaching about change as the human ability to choose and control "what sort of animal" every individual person wants to become. Harry changes via his choices and experiences from a child to a more mature, in-control, self-monitoring "human animal" (if you will) over the course of each year at Hogwarts. Let's review these changes book by book:

When we meet Harry in **Philosopher's Stone** he is a victim of his step-family's abuses and a seeming orphan. He has become, by book's end, a victor in battle against the Dark Lord and the heir of his family's legacy. How? It is through the heroic choices discussed above, where he chooses the good over his personal gain. **Chamber of Secrets**, too, opens with Harry literally and figuratively a prisoner; the Dursleys have locked him up in his room and Harry is mired in his own self-doubts and self-pity. He saves Ginny from her enchantment by the Dark Lord and escapes the Chamber at the end of the book on the wings of a phoenix, in every sense a free man. This transformation from prisoner to liberator is again, as explained above, a function of his choices of "what is right" rather than "what is easy".

Prisoner of Azkaban is Rowling's psychological *magnum opus* (as we'll see in **Part Three**). Harry's transformation in this book is, if anything, more profound than in any other book in the series. **Prisoner** opens with Harry not at all in control of his passions. Vernon Dursley's sister, Aunt Marge, patronizes Harry as an unwelcome burden on his brother and at last insults him and his parents as an example of bad blood and poor breeding. Marge is a bulldog fancier and, given her name and the bulldog's being to Britain what an eagle is to America, I have to suspect she is Rowling's rather transparent caricature of Margaret Thatcher and her uncharitable opinions about dole recipients.

Harry's response? He tries some self-control techniques to ignore her but of course fails. He has too many unresolved feelings and unanswered questions about his parents' death and especially about his Dad to suffer Aunt Marge gladly. In a rage (and without a wand), Harry makes this woman, so full of herself, into a three-dimensional picture of her character by "blowing her up" — not as a bomb blows up but as a balloon — Maggie Thatcher as self-important, self-inflating dirigible.

Harry experiences the death of his parents again and again in **Prisoner**, courtesy of the dementors and a boggart. He learns from his analyst, "Dr." Lupin (one of the turning points in the history of psychology is Freud's treatment of a patient he called "The Wolf Man"; again, see Part Three), how to fight off the depression and despair brought on by these nasties. When he learns the truth in the Shrieking Shack of Pettigrew's Judas-like betrayal, he has been changed so much by his choices in therapy and his consequent enlightenment that he not only does not attack Pettigrew but risks his own life to save Wormtail.

He has transformed from a passionate child rushing to judgment and punishment on Privet Drive to an adult capable of no little discernment and a semi-divine mercy. Both Dumbledore and Black comment that Harry at last is "truly [his] father's son" **(Prisoner, p. 415)**. He has become at book's end not really an orphan but a living image of his Father.

Harry begins **Goblet of Fire** as a boy understandably concerned about what others think and say about him. His experiences and choices consequent to a fight with Ron and an article in the *Daily Prophet* discussed above transform him into a mature young man more interested in "being" than "seeming", whose personal integrity and emotional maturity allow him to rise above popularity concerns or fear of slander.

When Rita Skeeter's second article about Harry in the *Daily Prophet* appears on the morning of the last TriWizard task (titled "Harry Potter: Disturbed and Dangerous"), Harry shrugs off her portrayal of him as a troubled mental defective. "'Gone off me a bit, hasn't she?', said Harry lightly, folding up the paper" **(Goblet, p. 613)**. This accomplishment is in a way more remarkable than his successes in the TriWizard tournament tasks and is the foundation of his ability to fight Voldemort to a draw at the Dark Lord's rebirthing party. The child leads in **Harry Potter** are never especially childish; by the end of **Goblet of Fire**, Harry has transformed into a real mensch and nearly a superhero.

Alchemical Transmutations

"Change" seems, then, to be shaping up as a major theme in Rowling's **Harry Potter** books. The persistent and large place given the subject of "Transfigurations" (and the witches and wizards who are accomplished in it) and the transformations Harry experiences in each book — from out-of-control victim to self-controlled, selfless victor — reveal Rowling's implicit teaching of the importance and preferred direction of change in human life.

But does Rowling give us a clear picture of what sort of person is ideal? Does she point to a human perfection as the goal of our transformations? Not yet explicitly, but in Dumbledore as alchemist and in the alchemical transmutations of the books she does give an implicit answer.

Professor Albus Dumbledore (*Albus*: Latin for "white", "pure", and "brilliant"; *Dumbledore*: archaic English for "bumblebee"), Headmaster of Hogwarts, Harry's guardian angel, and consensus pick as "greatest wizard of modern times" (**Stone**, p. 102, and elsewhere in each of the four books), has been explained by critics thus far as a poor man's cartoon image of Merlin, Gandalf, or Obi Wan Kenobi.

Certainly he looks and plays the part of wizened wizard and steward of the hidden king with more of a sense of humor than these other literary wizards. A more important difference between Dumbledore and these figures is that, to my knowledge, none of the others is an accomplished alchemist. (Merlin scholars, forgive me!) Albus Dumbledore is an alchemist, however, and in Dumbledore as alchemist Rowling gives us a picture of man in his perfection, the end or goal of human transformation.

Alchemy, to say the least, has a very bad reputation, so forgive me this lengthy aside to explain what alchemy is and is not. Unless you are a very rare bird indeed, your preconceptions about alchemy may keep you from understanding the Secret behind the popularity of Harry Potter. First, then, what alchemy was not.

Alchemy was not a crackpot pseudo-science with the sole purpose of changing lead into gold and gaining immortality via the synthesis of substances into a "philosopher's stone". It was not "infantile chemistry" from the Middle Ages from whose cradle "real chemistry" grew up, albeit after centuries of experiment and the scientific method. Traditional Alchemy is not "black magic" for selfish advantage and enrichment — any more than it is merely "bad science".

There is a historical reason why alchemy has this bad rap. In its degenerate form in the ironically called "Enlightenment" after the Middle Ages, not a few men tried to learn enough alchemy to get rich quick and put off death. These "charcoal burners" as they were called were just the sort of chemist hacks (believing alchemy to be a materialist *scientia* or "knowledge") all alchemists are believed to have been today.

However, these hacks weren't idiots, by any means. Isaac Newton, for example, was a full time alchemist and stock speculator whose scientific and mathematical treatises on optics, physics of motion, and calculus were only plague year diversions he kept in a drawer. Sadly, he wasn't much at playing the stocks or at alchemy; he lost a fortune in the South Sea speculative bubble and was the model "dark arts" alchemist with an unfortunate taste for "Black Masses". Biographies of Robert Boyle also reveal a closet alchemist.

If these latter-day "wannabe"'s were not real alchemists, what were the real sort about? The authentic alchemists, if the better History of Science books can be believed, lived in countries around the globe — China to Egypt to Western Europe — and practiced their esoteric spiritual art only within their revealed tradition. Christianity, Islam, Judaism, Buddhism, Confucianism, and the Taoist tradition share a history of alchemy *as a profoundly spiritual work rather than a materialist science*. As Titus Burckhardt, Swiss authority of comparative religions and sacred art, explains in his **Alchemy: Science of the Cosmos, Science of the Soul**:

> [A]rtistic creation, as it appears within a sacred tradition, ... [is] an inward process whose goal is the ripening, "transmutation", or rebirth of the soul of the artist himself. Alchemy too was called an art — even the royal art (*ars regia*) — by its masters, and with its image of the transmutation of base metals into the noble metals of gold and silver, serves as a highly evocative symbol of the inward process referred to. In fact alchemy may be called the art of the transmutations of the soul. In saying this I am not seeking to deny that alchemists also knew and practised metallurgical procedures such as the purification and alloying of metals; their real work, however, for which all

these procedures were merely the outward supports or "operational" symbols, was the transmutation of the soul. The testimony of the alchemists on this point is unanimous. **(Burckhardt, *Alchemy*, p. 23)**

Alchemy, then, before its degeneration in Enlightenment Europe into crank scientism outside the Church, "was essentially a symbolic process involving the endeavor to make gold, regarded as the symbol of illumination and salvation" **(J. E. Cirlot, *A Dictionary of Symbols*, p. 6)**. "Spiritually understood, the transmutation of lead into gold is nothing other than the regaining of the original nobility of human nature" **(*Alchemy*, p. 26)**.

The alchemical process itself is the universally understood path to spiritual perfection: purification, illumination, and divinization *within a revealed tradition*. Burckhardt is emphatic on this last, perhaps thinking of New Age alchemist pretenders as well as Newtonesque black magicians:

[A]lchemy, which is not a religion by itself, requires to be confirmed by the revelation — with its means of grace — which is addressed to all men…. It is thus a major error to believe that alchemy or Hermeticism by itself could possibly be a self-sufficient religion or even a secret paganism. **(Burckhardt, *Alchemy*, p. 21)**

Cirlot describes the steps in the alchemical work from purification to perfection:

The four stages of the process were signified by different colors, as follows: black (guilt, origin, latent forces) for "prime matter" (a symbol of the soul in its original condition); white (minor work, first transmutation, quicksilver); red (sulphur, passion); and finally gold ….

Alchemical evolution is epitomized, then, in the formula *Solve et Coagula* (that is to say: analyse all the elements in yourself, dissolve all that is inferior in you, even though you may break in doing so; then, with the strength acquired from the preceding operation, congeal). **(Cirlot, Symbolism, pp. 6-8)**

Burckhardt explains at greater length:

In order to free the soul from its coagulation and paralysis, its essential form and its *materia* must be dissolved out of their crude and one sided combination. It is as if spirit and soul had to be separated from one another, in order, after their "divorce", to become "married" again. The amorphous *materia* is burnt, dissolved, and purified, in order finally to be "coagulated" anew in the form of a perfect crystal. ...

Alchemical transmutation brings the centre of human consciousness into direct contact with that divine ray which irresistibly attracts the soul upwards and lets it savour by anticipation the Kingdom of Heaven. ...

The soul must first be extracted from base metal, the alchemists say. The remaining body is to be purified and burnt until it is no more than ashes. Then the soul is to be reunited with it. When the body is thus "dissolved" in the soul, so that both constitute a pure *materia*, the Spirit acts on the soul and confers on it an incorruptible form. That is to say, it transmutes individual bodily consciousness back into its own purely spiritual possibility, where, in all its fullness and according to its own essence, it remains motionless and indivisible. Basilius Valentinus compares this state with the "glorious body" of the resurrected. **(Burckhardt, Alchemy, pp. 72-73, 87).**

An authentic alchemist, then, is something of a holy man or saint. Rowling lets us know that Albus Dumbledore is an authentic alchemist rather than a voodoo pretender by both telling and showing us just that. Harry reads on the back of Dumbledore's trading card found inside Harry's first pack of chocolate frogs that the Headmaster is "particularly famous for… his work on alchemy with his partner, Nicholas Flamel" (*Stone*, **pp. 102-103**). That he and Flamel are not alchemists focused on free gold and endless physical life is revealed at the end of **Philosopher's Stone** when Dumbledore and Flamel destroy the Stone though it means Flamel's death. Dumbledore comments then to Harry, who is astonished by this:

> "To one as young as you, I'm sure it seems incredible, but to Nicolas and Perenelle, it really is like going to bed after a very, *very* long day. After all, to the well organized mind, death is but the next great adventure. You know, the Stone was really not such a wonderful thing. As much money and life as you could want! The two things most human beings would choose above all — the trouble is, human beings do have a knack of choosing precisely those things that are worst for them." (*Stone*, **p. 297**)

Dumbledore and Flamel are alchemists sufficiently accomplished to conjure the Philosopher's Stone. However, they are not interested in its mundane uses for private gain as much as its capability for spiritual work: the purification, illumination, and salvation or perfection of their souls. That spiritual work being done, the Stone is a happy by-product and symbol of the illumined soul's victory over the material world and profane, physical life — not to mention something of a nuisance! Think of all the precautions taken in **Philosopher's Stone** to keep it from the unworthy and dangerous.

In classical Greek tradition, the bee is a symbol of the soul; Cirlot explains that this is so "not only because of the association with honey but also because they migrate from the hive in swarms, since it was held that souls "swarm" from the divine unity in a similar manner" **(Symbolism, p. 24)**. Albus Dumbledore, then, literally "the white or pure soul", is Rowling's head man at Hogwarts and greatest of wizards because of his spiritual perfection. In a work pre-occupied with choice and change — and, please remember, death — Dumbledore, the master of transfiguration and alchemy, is the model or goal towards which good choices and change should lead.

Rowling is "big" on alchemy and spiritual transmutation as a book-by-book second look reveals.

The title of Book One was originally (and remains in the U.K.) **Harry Potter and the Philosopher's Stone**. Scholastic, Rowling's American publishers, changed it to **Sorcerer's Stone** because they did not believe Americans sufficiently sophisticated to know what a "Philosopher's Stone" is and, even if so, to buy a book with the word "philosophy" in it. In addition to the title giveaway, we know the book is about alchemy when we meet Hermione Granger.

Hermione is the female version of "Hermes"; alchemy is often called the "hermetic art"; Hermes Trismegistos was a legendary alchemist in whose name most alchemical works were written; and Hermes (or "Mercury") was patron god to ancient alchemists. The Gold and "Red Lion" of Gryffyndor House, beyond a tip of the hat to Lewis' Aslan, is the name given to the Elixir of Life drawn from the Stone for immortality (*Alchemy*, **p. 91**). For the drama of **Philosopher's Stone** as alchemical process, see the discussion of **Stone**'s meaning in Part Three.

The next three **Potter** books don't have alchemy in their titles, but in their dramatic endings they all feature a crucible-like environment in which something corrupt or hidden is revealed or returned to its innocence. This alchemical work of purification and revelation is done in the heated resolution of contraries (in alchemical language, "the marriage of quicksilver and sulphur"). In **Chamber of Secrets**, Fawkes and Harry do battle with the Basilisk and Riddle. Riddle is revealed to be the young Voldemort (and destroyed) while Ginny — that name should be read "Virginia" or "virgin innocence" — near death, is restored. In **Prisoner of Azkaban**, the crucible is the Shrieking Shack. The battling contraries are Harry and Sirius Black and, in their battle, Peter Pettigrew is revealed and Sirius reclaims his "innocence".

Voldemort rises from the dead via something like a Black Mass at the end of **Goblet of Fire**. He admits to Harry after his rebirth that he is not capable of the spiritual work necessary to conjure a Philosopher's Stone (*Goblet*, **p. 656**) so he must "set [his] sights lower" than immortality and invent a spell to get his body back. Voldemort is no alchemist. Check his desk drawer for a paper on the reflection of light in crystals.

The alchemical crucible in **Goblet** is the Golden Cage of Phoenix Song in which Harry and Voldemort, the contrary heirs of Gryffyndor and Slytherin, face off. Voldemort's victims are restored to a shadowy, temporary form in which form they judge and attack him. Harry is revealed, *mirabile dictu*, as Voldemort's equal in battle by the Golden Cage and escapes with Cedric's body.

Purification, dissolution, perfection: this is the work of alchemy, the sacred art of meaningful change. Rowling's **Harry Potter** books are in general about changing for the good by making "good" choices, and they are specifically the story of Harry's transformation, really his book-by-book purification and perfection by fire. Within each book and from book to book, with every choice he makes for the good instead of for what is easy, Harry becomes the man he was born to be, an image of his Father. We get our WOW! cathartic identification with Harry and his changes as we survive the transformation he goes through in each book's crucible.

If you can remember that far back, we began exploring the meaning of Harry Potter (by way of themes that run through the books) in hope of figuring out why Joanne Rowling's **Harry Potter** books are so popular. In the first three themes we looked at — prejudice, death and grief, and choice — we found that Rowling not only offers an implicit and explicit moral through the actions and speeches of characters, but also zaps the reader with a WOW! third dimension. This third dimension (vicarious experience of her meaning) forces the reader to take her meaning to heart. Take a peek at the chart which includes our fourth theme, Change:

Theme	Implicit	Explicit	WOW!
Prejudice	Prejudice everywhere	Dumbledore	Surprise endings
Death	Harry's parents, Cedric	Dumbledore	Cathartic identification: Death
Choice	Harry's choices	Dumbledore	Cathartic identification: Choice
Change	Changes everywhere	Not yet	Cathartic identification: Alchemy

So far, so good. I'm not too concerned that Dumbledore has not yet explicitly spoken about change because I think that may be part of Rowling's secret and big finish for one of the remaining books or for the whole series (**see Part Four…**). What bothers me is that all we seem to have demonstrated is that Ms. Rowling is a great writer with meaningful lessons powerfully delivered.

Though they haven't teased out her themes very well or touched on the WOW! extra dimension of her presentation, this isn't very different from what Ms. Rowling's delighted Middle Road critics have offered as explanation of her success. Where is the High Road secret of her being so popular because the books are so *very* different and so much better? Let's take another look at each theme's WOW! that drives Ms. Rowling's lessons home.

What is most important about the WOW! for each theme, the experience that reaches out and grabs you, is our engagement with the story. If we believe that what is going on is really happening, if we feel that we are there and forget we are only reading a story (and, c'mon, a pretty wild story at that), then and only then does what I call "cathartic identification" kick in.

"Cathartic Identification"? Long words, simple meaning. If I'm right in there with Harry and what he's doing, then, by my believing "I" am "he", through my imagination I experience what he experiences. I am as shocked by the surprise ending (and my errors in having judged the good as bad and vice versa), purified by his death and resurrection, edified by his sacrificial and courageous choices, and as transformed from fallen victim to perfected victor as Harry is. Even though these things only "happen" in my imagination!

The word *catharsis* is the Greek word for purification. Aristotle uses it in the **Poetics** to describe what happens to the audience at a well done play (specifically, at a tragedy) when it is overcome by terror and pity for the players. As the drama reaches its climax and the plot lines are resolved, the audience, again, because of its identification with what is happening, is "purified" (experiences *catharsis*) through its imagination as if it had been the players in "real life". This is the value of edifying drama: concentrated experience of the virtues and the resolution of universal conflicts. Our souls are remade after a fashion by the power of vicarious images and experiences.

As we've explored the four main themes, so far the best answer we've come up with to the question "why are the books so popular?" is the cathartic second-hand experience of death, courageous choices, and soul perfecting changes. This catharsis — our purification and transformation via shared imaginative experience — is the alchemy of good stories and theater. Let's look at what the alchemy of symbolism tells us for another explanation of Harry's popularity.

Chapter 7

The Symbolist
Outlook

Symbolism. Did you groan when you read the word "symbolism"? If you did, I bet I know why. You had a "Survey of American Literature" teacher like mine in High School that made sure you "got" the symbolism in everything you read — from the Great White Whale in **Moby Dick** to the all-seeing billboard eye-glasses in **The Great Gatsby**. Problem was, she never explained how symbolism worked or why these supposedly great writers were spending so much time hiding what they meant behind silly images and metaphors. I figured it was just another adult game for writers and English teachers to enjoy.

So let me take a moment here (before doing the English teacher thing and pointing out the symbols in **Harry Potter** and what they mean) to try and say what symbols are and aren't — and why there may be as powerful an alchemy in imagining these symbols as in any good play or story. It's also possible that the cathartic experiences we enjoy in stories and plays may be due to the symbols they contain.

First, what symbols aren't:

- Symbols aren't just one thing. Peek at the chart **(on p. 109)** and you'll see that there are at least eight types of symbols. The types of symbols differ in the sort of thing or idea they represent.

- Next, most of these symbols are not mechanical equations of a picture with a natural thing or idea which the picture represents. That is true only of signs, ciphers, and some allegory.

- Lastly, what symbolism is will be lost on you (even while it can still work profoundly on you) without your grasping the possibility of both the existence of *multiple states of being and points of correspondence between these states.*

This last point will require a little explanation. In a nutshell, what symbolism requires is a different way of thinking about the world, one that doesn't deny the possibility that anything exists beyond nature, which is to say the world of chemistry and physics. Symbolism requires the perspective of metaphysics, which transcends nature.

No need to shudder! Metaphysics just means "more than nature" (from the Greek *meta*: "with, before, besides"; *physics*:

"nature"). We have a cultural aversion to "metaphysics" because of anti-metaphysics-immunization- shots we get from school and the daily teevee. To understand how a symbol works, though, you have to put off this aversion for a minute.

We live in a materialist culture. You've heard that before, so and you may think when I say we're materialistic, that I am trying to criticize your priorities at Christmas-time or our collective effort to live as comfortably as possible. Not true! What I wish to stress is that living in a materialist culture fosters a world view, a way of looking at things, which is restricted to what is visible and tangible. In essence, we are taught from an early age to look at the world as a chemist would; everything is a thing made up of measurable and manipulable energy and matter that can be rearranged to create other phenomena. This includes not only stuff like chairs and camels but thoughts and feelings and the stuff of dreams as well.

The materialist perspective is flat or one-dimensional. Again, most of us can only peek through the holes in our head through these materialist-colored glasses, unless we have labored hard at putting it off. It is the lowest-common- denominator perspective created by democracy and a desire-driven culture. Any alternative to the materialist perspective, allowing the possibility of a reality greater than or prior to "natural" reality, is not allowed in the schools because naturalism (another word for materialism meaning "visible, natural world only") is our state religion.

Symbolism — beyond the mechanical equations of street signs ("picture of deer means deer crossing"), pictures, word descriptions, and tit-for-tat allegory — requires a perspective on the world that allows for the possibility of other, greater, more real worlds than the measurable universe. In this perspective, our existence is actually only a shadow or symbol of higher realities or states of being. Maybe an example or word picture will help.

Imagine the natural world of energy and matter, the world of the sciences, as a circle we live on (diagram A). We cannot see a circle larger than ours or a center to our circle. We imagine, consequently, there is nothing but our circle and believe our circle is self-creating and sustaining. We spend a lot of time poking at it to figure it and us out.

Then someone with especially sharp sight spies the center and sees the innumerable radii radiating from the center that create our circle (diagram B). Or the sky peels away one day to reveal a greater world, like our own but much more beautiful and clear (diagram C). We are compelled, consequent to either of these revelations, to concede that our circle and we ourselves are dependent on this center or greater circle, that our existence is somehow a projection of their greater being.

This multiple-world perspective, heresy though it may be to the naturalists, is the perspective of symbolism. In fact, this "symbolist outlook" — rather than "spiritualism" or sentimentality — is the true opposite of materialism (more on that in Part Three). A symbol, going back to our example, is a *point of correspondence* between a greater and lesser circles or a *radius* between circle and center *through which the greater reality or being of one world pours into the other.*

From the symbolist outlook, the human being is designed to understand and pursue these points of correspondence for a life of greater truth, beauty, and virtue. Please be careful here. As one of C. S. Lewis' Oxford students reminds us, "attaching to the symbol for its own sake apart from its higher meaning", the mistake of the materialists, separates man from the greater, transcendent life for which he is designed, and condemns him to what Lewis called a life in the "Shadowlands" (Martin Lings, *Symbol and Archetype*, p. 4).

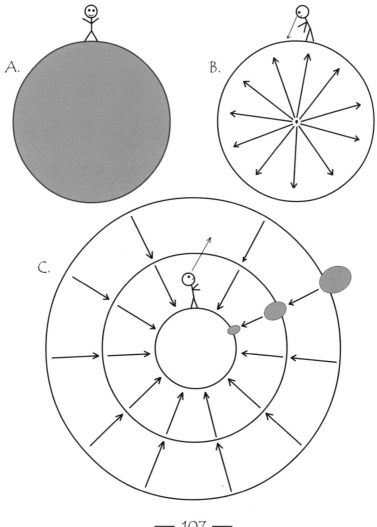

Please note that symbolists are not writing "allegories". Allegories are story-puzzles that are often just ironic or satirical retellings of other stories, sometimes historical, sometimes "spiritual", but all are about *our world and its realities* as we experience it. Tolkien, a symbolist extraordinaire, resisted every attempt to categorize **The Lord of the Rings** as an allegory with tremendous verbal violence; he felt there could be no greater misunderstanding of what he was doing than to explain it as an allegory of the second world war or some other event. If anything, the second world war was a symbol of the eternal conflicts and verities **The Lord of the Rings** illumined. The same can be said of Lewis' fiction and Rowling's; this is writing of a different kind than the allegorical **Gulliver's Travels**, or even **Pilgrim's Progress**. (For Lewis' careful distinction between "Allegory, Supposal, and Symbolism", especially as it applies to his **Chronicles of Narnia**, see Walter Hooper's *C. S. Lewis: Companion & Guide*, pp. 423-429.)

Back to **Harry Potter**. There is a lot of symbolism in **Harry Potter** and, outside of a few cartoon-like caricatures (remember Aunt Marge and Margaret Thatcher?), almost all of it is not mechanical or allegorical but symbolic in the sense described above. That's the fourth symbolism on the accompanying chart, called simply, "symbolism".

All the types of symbolism below the fifth (from "icon" down) are not points of passage looking out but intrusions of greater realities into our world. They are consequently not the subject of "Literature" but "Theology". (If you want to know something about that, an excellent introduction is "The Iconic and Symbolic in

Orthodox Iconography" by Bishop Auxentios. It can be found on the web at *www.orthodoxinfo.com.*) For us Harry Potter fans, the symbolic will be hard enough to "get" even without the theology.

Symbol Type	Example	Object Represented	Faculty Affected
Sign	Deer Crossing	Natural, material	Sight, reason
Cipher	Words, Painting	Natural, material or idea	Sight, reason
Allegory	Pilgrim's Progress	Natural, Supernatural	Imagination, reason
Symbol	*Water, Unicorn*	*Supernatural*	*Imagination, heart*
Icon	Icon, Scripture	Supernatural, Contranatural	Sight, heart, person
Signal	Lightning, Eagle	Supernatural	Sight, heart, person
Eruption	Communion	Contranatural	Sense, heart, person
Incarnation	Christ	Contranatural	Sense, heart, person

The alchemy of symbols (that is, "how we are changed by them for the better") is this: It is a principle of traditional literature and sacred art, East and West, that ***by looking at or imagining authentic symbols (those corresponding to greater realities than themselves by virtue of some quality or virtue they possess) with a non-critical attitude, we absorb some form or quality of the thing represented.*** Risking over-simplification, this is the power of religious painting and architecture, as well as of meditation on natural beauty and figures.

Praying before an icon or "raising one's eyes up to the hills" gives our spirit or soul's noetic faculty an experience of the formal majesty or perfection in the symbol as point of correspondence. Ever been awestruck by the nobility and grace of a swan? Your awe is a measure of the impression and change this symbol has made on you through its correspondence with the qualities of nobility and grace further up the "great chain of being".

What does this have to do with Harry? Ms. Rowling has filled her **Harry Potter** books with symbolic stories, characters and images. If the symbolist outlook of multiple states of being and correspondences between these states via natural and artistic symbols is indeed not just a possibility but true, then we may have an explanation of the **Potter** books' popularity better than "they are well written". We may even have uncovered her secret. So let's look at the symbols in **Harry Potter** and see what they have to tell us about the greater realities each reflects.

Chapter 8

Story and Character Symbolism in Harry Potter

I've divided the symbols in the *Harry Potter* books into three categories:

- story symbols;
- character symbols; and
- flat-out symbols.

We've looked at the stories already for themes; let's look at those themes again, this time from the symbolist outlook, and see what we see.

Story Symbols

Put on your symbolist eyeglasses. (If your book didn't come with a set, you'll just have to look diagon-ally.) Symbolist eyeglasses have a prescription that corrects our carnival-house, materialist vision so we can easily see the symbols connecting our world with greater realities. We can also see through these glasses and sense in our hearts that this way of looking at and experiencing the world gives us a real rush, as if we are more alive than we have been. Talk about a WOW!

Without our glasses, we looked at the stories and, working from Dumbledore's explicit morals at the end of each book and the implicit messages of what happens in each book, we deduced what Rowling was trying to tell us about prejudice, death, choice, and change. We shall see the same things with our symbolist glasses on — but with them on, we ourselves shall have changed.

Before putting on the glasses, we thought of ourselves as genetically shaped packages of energy and matter: basically, a body bag of organic chemistry motivated only for advantage and reproduction of our individual genetic blueprints. With our glasses on, we see ourselves still as bodies, yes, but not bags of ephemeral protoplasm as much as we are bags of eternal qualities. Truth, beauty, courage, love, life, nobility, loyalty — you name something good, you can find it in the bag.

The more of these good things we have in our bag, the more alive we become and feel. We can see (with our glasses) these qualities all around us: in other people and what they do, in animals and nature, and in things people have built, written or created. Even more bizarre, we see that these qualities are just "exports" from other more meaningful and alive worlds or dimensions around ours.

The things around us that are full of the qualities we want in our bags — my dog with "loyalty", my Mother with "love" and "sacrifice", the ocean with "beauty" and "majesty" — seem to be projections or extensions into our world from this better place. We connect with them because we can fill our bags with their good stuff just by being in their company (imitating them works too). Part of us realizes that we belong in this other dimension, glimpsing it perhaps out of the corner of our eyes, when our bags take on a new quality or a big scoop of an old one.

What does the bespectacled Harry Potter have to say to us symbolists?

The **Harry Potter** books are still "about" prejudice, death, choice, and change. Now they also seem to be about my efforts to fill my person bag with the shining qualities. Harry is always choosing the people and deeds that fill his bag. Sometimes he judges others as "good" or "bad" based on what he's been told or wants to believe and misses out on a good quality he might have put in the bag. More often, though, he is right on target and his bag is much more full at the end of his journey through each book than it was at the beginning. His bag is loaded with bravery and courage, loyalty, love, sacrifice, determination, humility and laughter.

What I like about Harry is that *my* bag is filled too by reading the books. By making the choices, going through the changes, and dying the deaths Harry does, even though only vicariously, I get some of the qualities he has (not a few of which are new to my bag). I feel a real surge in my body bag, in fact, when Harry and I die because we always rise from the dead.

I remember in experiencing this second-hand, imaginative resurrection that the qualities in my bag are eternal and, so much as I embody them, even when my bag gives way, my form of these qualities will live forever. I can't wait for the next book to remind me again of what I'm ultimately about. I need all the inspiration I can get to make the right choices and change into a brilliantly full bag, a bag without unfilled spaces or dull qualities. If only I could glue these glasses on — without them, it's like I'm living in a cave. I can't see anything but shadows on the walls.

Symbols and Characters

Enough of the glasses; go ahead and take them off. My point in asking you to try them on is that Rowling is almost certainly a symbolist writer. The popularity of her stories spring from the fact that human beings want to believe, indeed, seem to be designed to believe in sacred dimensions or heavens and to see themselves as reservoirs or living symbols of eternal virtues and qualities. As Mircea Eliade and others have written, man is historically (and currently) more obviously removed from the animals by his capacity for belief and faith (*homo religiosos*) than by his ability to think (*homo sapiens*). The **Harry Potter** books nourish this capacity with symbolic stories of heroic virtues and cathartic resurrection from death.

Assuming she is a symbolist, then, let's have a look at her major human characters and mythological creatures and symbols to see if her symbols have a particular bent or flavor. Is she drawing from a particular stream of symbols, say, out of classical Greek or Norse mythology? Is she a closet Buddhist? A great fan of themes and images from American Indian folklore? Or are the symbols in **Harry Potter** just a rich collection of "volunteer flowers" from the compost pile of Ms. Rowling's reading? Let's see.

The heroes of the **Harry Potter** books are Harry and his two close friends Ron and Hermione. Each is the embodiment of certain abilities and qualities.

- *Hermione*: Of all Harry friends, indeed of all students in Hogwarts, Hermione is the smartest. Harry comments once, when Hermione answers a teacher's question about the properties of the mandrake plant with unbelievable detail, that it seemed "she had swallowed the textbook" (*Chamber*, **p. 92**). She is remarkably studious, true, but her brilliance is not limited to what she picks up in her hours at the Library. She is a whiz as well in logic, as she demonstrates by figuring out the potions obstacle in *Stone*, the Basilisk mystery in *Chamber*, Lupin's handicap in *Prisoner*, and the Skeeter secret in *Goblet*. She takes herself and her ideas a little too seriously, in fact (remember S.P.E.W.?) Hermione's a thinker and, if she seems a little cold blooded at times, she embodies the capacities and virtues of the mind.

- *Ron*: Hermione's refrain with Ron is "Don't be stupid." This is not cruelty; Ron's guesses are way off the mark almost without exception. Outside of a talent for wizard chess, Ron has little promise as a thinker. He is, however, always interested in an adventure (well, except for those with spiders) and willing to follow Harry anywhere (to include into spiders dens). He also loves to eat, tell a story, and enjoy a party. He is a great one for jokes. He complains about anything and everything uncomfortable or not to his immediate liking. He is self-conscious, self-pitying, and sensitive about being from a poor family. In defense of his honor, then, or that of his friends, this redhead is ready to fight anytime. Ron's a lovable, walking bag of desire and passions, who, apart from his friend's influence, is something of "a loose cannon".

- *Harry*: Not a great thinker or joker and not one to complain or be preoccupied with his own ideas, Harry lacks the virtues and failings of his two close friends. He says when asked his strengths, "I haven't got any" **(Goblet, p. 344)** and only his skills and accomplishments as a Quidditch seeker boost his self-esteem. Such humility, even after saving the world from Voldemort time and time again! He is remarkable, then, at least in his modesty and lack of self-importance. Dumbledore remarks on his resourcefulness, determination, "pure nerve and outstanding courage". He is the decision-maker in a crisis; Ron and Hermione always yield to his judgment when the chips are down because he has an internal compass for the right thing to do. He is loyal to his friends and even more to his sense of right and wrong. Harry is a man of heart.

Are these characters symbols? I think so. Another symbolist thinker, Plato, in his "Myth of the Charioteer" tells a story when trying to illustrate the human soul's three faculties or powers with three figures not unlike Harry, Ron, and Hermione. Plato tells us the human soul is like "the union of powers in a team of winged steeds and their winged charioteer". These two steeds which the charioteer struggles to control are white and black:

> [The white horse] that is on the more honourable side is upright and clean limbed, carrying his neck high, with something of a hooked nose; in color he is white, with black eyes; a lover of glory, but with temperance and modesty, one that consorts with genuine renown, and needs no whip, being driven by the word of command alone. The other is crooked of frame, a massive jumble of a creature, with thick, short neck, snub nose, black skin and grey eyes; hot-blooded, consorting with wantonness and vainglory; shaggy of ear, deaf and hard to control with whip and goad. **(Plato, *Phaedrus*, 246b, 254 c-e).**

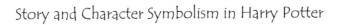

Plato explains that one of the chariot's horses is obedient and good, the other passionate and difficult. The charioteer's job is to control the one and guide them both so they pull the chariot upward. (These are flying horses, remember?) What faculties of soul do these symbolic figures represent?

Plato in the Republic explains that it is the intellect that guides will and appetites in the rightly ordered soul **(Republic, 441e-442b)**. Constantine Cavarnos, trusty guide to all things Greek and philosophical, explains the relationship of the intellective, appetitive, and "high-spirited" powers of the soul as delineated in the Myth and *Republic*:

> In the myth of the Phaedrus, the human soul is compared to a chariot drawn by two winged horses, one noble, the other ignoble, and guided by a pilot. The noble horse represents the "spirited" or honor and power seeking part of the psyche, while the ignoble represents the "appetitive" part, the animal desires. The pilot represents noesis, the purely cognitive aspect of reason…. The horses can pull the chariot forward, but it is the pilot that has to guide them upward. Each horse has an independent power of his own, but the noble steed obeys the charioteer, while the ignoble steed disobeys him. In the healthy soul, the pilot — the cognitive aspect of reason — is master, and the ignoble steed — the desiring part of the soul — has been transformed and is fully obedient. **(Cavarnos, *Plato's View of Man*, pp. 31-32)**

You may think it's a stretch to claim that Ms. Rowling is making a reference to Plato — or symbolizing the three powers of the soul in her Harry, Ron, and Hermione — but hear me out. C. S. Lewis in his famous essay about the aims of education, "Men

Without Chests", talks about the human person as having just these three faculties, which he labels "head, chest, and belly":

> We were told it all long ago by Plato. As the king governs by his executive, so Reason in man must rule the mere appetites by means of the "spirited element". The head rules the belly through the chest.... It may even be said that it is by this middle element that man is man: for by his intellect he is a mere spirit and by his appetite mere animal. (Lewis, *Abolition of Man*, p. 34)

We have already cited Lewis (a great favorite of Rowling, remember) as an advocate of using literature to train the soul in the stock responses, "instructing while delighting". He asks writers to teach the virtues to each of the soul's powers so they think, will, and desire the right things. Beyond this, in the passage above he also advocates training the soul so that its capacities are in right alignment: head over chest over belly. But I'm getting ahead of myself.

I can hear you thinking, "So what if Plato and Lewis believe the soul has three powers or that the head tells the belly what to do through the chest? What makes you think Harry, Ron, and Hermione are symbols of the soul's three powers?" Well, two reasons. There's a match there and it's been done before. Just so you can see this has been done before in books, teevee shows, and in movies you may be familiar with, I provide a chart. Everyone from Dostoevsky to George Lucas uses it; it's something of a cliché or *topos*.

I will go so far as saying that if you don't "get" this, a large part of what these authors are saying will be lost on your conscious mind. Take **The Lord of the Rings**, for example.

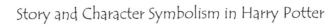

Tolkien has these three hobbits on Mount Doom at the climax of the Ring part of their adventures and, unless I am very much mistaken, that Smeagol's destruction means their salvation (and they did not kill him) reflects the author's Roman Catholic conviction about the baser, desiring qualities of the soul. If the selfish desires cannot be subdued or redeemed (and every effort you remember is made to bring Gollum into service or obedience to Sam and Frodo), then their elimination is one's salvation. **(See Matthew 5:29-30.)**

Work	Body (Desire)	Mind (Will)	Spirit (Heart)
Fyodor Dostoevsky's **Brothers Karamazov**	Dmitri Karamazov	Ivan Karamazov	Alyosha Karamazov
C. S. Lewis' **Narnia Chronicles**	Edmund Pevensie	Susan Pevensie	Peter Pevensie
J. R. R. Tolkien's **Lord of the Rings**	Smeagol (Gollum)	Sam Gamgee	Frodo Baggins
Gene Rodenberry's **Star Trek**	Bones	Spock	Kirk
George Lucas' **Star Wars**	Han Solo	Princess Leia	Luke Skywalker
Joanne Rowling's **Harry Potter**	Ron Weasley	Hermione Granger	Harry Potter

The American producers think a lot more of the desires (surprise!), so Bones is never especially joyous in obedience to Kirk, and Hans Solo answers to no one. Ron Weasley is much more reminiscent of Lewis' Edmund than to more recent (or Catholic) symbols of the "dark horse" or desiring faculty of soul — but that's an inconsequential opinion. What I hope to have demonstrated is that, if Rowling is a symbolist and writing Harry, Ron, and Hermione as symbols of our tripartite souls, she isn't doing anything especially novel or innovative. She's right in line with the best writers and successful movie/teevee producers.

Given the credibility of this usage, let's check to see if we have a match.

I don't think we do on the strict Platonic model. (Hermione can be willful — remember her assault on Draco in **Prisoner**, her fight with Rita Skeeter, and the lecture she gave Hagrid in **Goblet**? — but that's hardly her defining characteristic, yet.) Change the division into "carnal/rational/spiritual" or body-mind-spirit as do Dostoevsky, Lewis, and company, however, and all three line up: Ron, the comfort-focused complainer, Hermione, the thinker, and Harry, the heroic heart that leads the company.

So what? To understand the purpose and power of this literary *topos*, take a moment to think of Harry, Ron, and Hermione's relationships — when they work and when they don't. Harry is clearly in charge. Hermione is the best thinker. Ron is the cheer leader and flag waver (in his best moments). When they follow Harry's lead in line, Harry, Hermione, Ron, one, two, three, all goes well. Think of their assault on the obstacles leading to the Stone or their teamwork to get to the Chamber of Secrets: amazing work for pre-teens.

But when the team breaks down and the players don't play their roles or won't play them in obedience to Harry, things go wrong in the worst way. In the four books already out, this has happened twice, both times because Ron, low man in the hierarchy of faculties, takes the wrong role.

In **Prisoner of Azkaban**, he takes the lead position. Ron gets into a bitter fight with Hermione about her decision to tell Professor McGonagall about Harry's broom and then about her pet cat's seeming to have made a meal of his pet rat. As Hagrid points out to them, a broom and a rat are hardly reason to throw off a friend and especially a friend in need, but no matter, Harry follows Ron's passionate cues and stops speaking to her. Harry also decides to go to Hogsmead on Ron's advice and against Hermione's pleas — and narrowly misses being expelled. Lupin shames Harry; Ron comes to his senses, apologizes to Harry, and they reconcile with Hermione — with Ron again in a place of service to his friends.

In *Goblet of Fire*, Ron breaks entirely with Harry out of jealousy and meanness of spirit when Harry is chosen by the Goblet to be a school champion. Ron is pathetic on his own and Harry misses his friend terribly but he learned his lesson in *Prisoner*; the heart following selfish, spiteful passions gets you nowhere good fast. Ron returns to the fold after the first TriWizard task, the draconian danger of which seems to have jerked him back into remembrance of his rightful place in Harry's service.

It should be remembered that it is Hermione that almost has nervous breakdowns during her time apart from Harry and Ron and during Ron's break with Harry. This is not feminine weakness but Rowling's conviction about the fragility of an intellect that is disembodied and heartless. Part of Hermione's brilliance is her determined dependence on her friends; she understands that her jewel intelligence is glorious in its right setting and almost inhuman on its own (remember Hermione at the beginning of *Philosopher's Stone*?).

The power of this usage, from Dostoevsky to Rowling, is that we identify with the symbolism. If the reader doesn't understand the match-ups consciously, the reader is still powerfully affected *because the match-ups exist independently of understanding*. When writers like Rowling follow Lewis's instructions about the Stock Responses, training the three faculties and their right alignment for the reader's edification, as Rowling has done, the reader experiences in cathartic sympathy something like a chiropractic "adjustment" to the soul. Spirit, mind, body: one, two, three. Did you hear the crack?

I do not want to seem to be saying this adjustment happens because Plato and his admirers' right-alignment is gospel truth, for someone might object that it only works because we all are taught it is so. True or believed true, the effect of the symbol is as captivating and rich a WOW! as any of the themes in the series. The trio's love for one another and our identification with them makes their hard times with each other the most painful parts of the stories — and their reconciliation and realignment the most joyous. We become aligned in this identification — spirit to mind to body — and feel strangely upright and all right for the change.

This experience is an answer, or at least more of an answer to why the **Harry Potter** books are so popular. Let's go on to look at the more obvious symbols Rowling uses to see if they have anything in common with each other and with the symbols in the stories and the characters.

Chapter 9

Symbols of Christ
in
Harry Potter

I think our experience of animals makes believable the symbolist contention that there are multiple states of being and multiple points of correspondence between them. I can see the possibility that our response to certain animals is a trained response, but the power of the connection between an animal and its symbolized quality — even as felt by my small children — makes me doubt it. A dog embodies and radiates the virtue of loyalty, a cat feminine beauty and grace, a lion power and majesty, an eagle freedom, a horse nobility.

The animals in **Harry Potter** are not your conventional domestic pets or zoo beasties. Rowling has a rich imagination and a special fascination for fantastic beasts; she has even written a Hogwarts "school book", **Fantastic Beasts and Where to Find Them**, cataloguing her favorites A-Z. Are these products of her imagination symbols in the way eagles and lions are symbols?

Yes and no. No, I don't think a fictional lion (say, the one that occurs throughout the **Potter** books on the banners of Gryffyndor house or the lion Aslan in Lewis' **Chronicles of Narnia** books) has the same power to suggest "majesty" as a real lion on the savanna. One works through the sense of vision and the other through the imagination. But, yes, if the fictional beast is capably depicted, both contain the quality which makes the lion regal and stirs the heart.

If my unfamiliarity with the source of their names is any indication, many of Rowling's animals are her own invention (although her Acromantula reminds the Tolkien fan of the giant spider Shelob and the den of spiders in **The Hobbit**). I will not talk about these creatures and their symbolic value — although in Part Four, I may have to try to explain what role Nifflers and Skrewts will have in upcoming installments. Let's focus on the creatures Rowling uses throughout her books that have a history as symbols in European literature.

I choose to focus on these traditional symbols because, though their meanings are not especially obscure or arcane, I am delighted to be able to point to reference books to "back up" my interpretation of what supernatural quality they reflect. If there is a single "giveaway" of the secret behind the popularity of **Harry Potter**, it is in the uniform meaning of the symbols she uses — and it is such a surprise to many of her fans that not a few have insisted I cite a source or two for my contentions.

The magical creatures and figures we will consider as symbols are:

- the Griffin;
- the Unicorn;
- the Phoenix;
- the Stag;
- the Centaur;
- the Hippogriff;
- the Red Lion; and
- the Philosopher's Stone.

The references I will cite are J. E. Cirlot's **Dictionary of Symbols**, T. H. White's **Bestiary**, Paul Ford's **Companion to Narnia**, Titus Burckhardt's **Alchemy**, and two guides to the **Harry Potter** books, David Colbert's **The Magical Worlds of Harry Potter** and Allan and Elizabeth Kronzek's **The Sorcerer's Companion**. When appropriate, Rowling's descriptions of the beasts from the **Harry Potter** books and **Fantastic Beasts** will be included as well.

The Griffin

There is only one mention of a griffin per se that I have found in the **Harry Potter** books, and it is a detail mentioned in connection to Dumbledore's office. Professor McGonagall is bringing Harry there in **Chamber** after he has been discovered next to the petrified forms of Justin Finch-Fletchley and Nearly Headless Nick. "Harry saw a gleaming oak door ahead, with a brass knocker in the shape of a griffin" (**Chamber**, p. 204).

Rowling describes a griffin in **Fantastic Beasts** as having "the front legs and head of a giant eagle, but the body and hind legs of a lion" (**Beasts**, p. 20). It is an important symbol in the **Potter** series because:

> Harry's House, Gryffindor, literally means "golden griffin" in French (*Or* is French for "gold"). (**Colbert,** *Magical Worlds*, **p. 107)**

So spell it "Griffin d'or" — though the House is not named for a golden griffin per se, but for Godric Gryffyndor, one of the four founders of Hogwarts. The Gryffyndor house emblem does not include a griffin, favoring an image of the lion instead (about which symbol, see below). As Harry is considered a "true Gryffyndor" in Dumbledore's estimation (**Chamber**, p. 334) and Harry's parents lived in Godric Hollow, put a bet on there being great significance on the meaning of golden griffin (skip to Part Four if you can't wait) for the identity of Harry Potter.

Burckhardt explains the alchemical meaning of the leogriffin and griffin in **Alchemy**:

> Sometimes one of the two reptiles [entwined or biting each other's end] representing Sulphur and Quicksilver is winged, whereas the other is without wings. Or instead of two reptiles, there are a lion and a dragon in combat. The absence of wings always refers to the "firm" nature of Sulphur, whereas the winged animal, be it a dragon, a

griffin, or an eagle, represents "volatile" Quicksilver. The lion, which conquers the dragon, corresponds to Sulphur, which "fixes" Quicksilver. A winged lion, or leogriffin, can represent the union of the two natures, and has the same meaning as the image of the male-female androgyne. **(Burckhardt, *Alchemy*, p. 137)**

That's a little obscure and arcane for the average reader if you don't recall who is the resolution and completion of combatting contraries, so Colbert in his ***Magical Worlds*** allows scholar Hans Biedermann to spell out the supernatural referent of the griffin symbol:

A fabulous animal, symbolically significant for its domination of both the earth and the sky because of its lions body and eagle's head and wings.... [T]he creature later became a symbol of the dual nature (divine and human) of Jesus Christ, precisely because of its mastery of earth and sky. The solar associations both of the lion and eagle favored this positive reading. **(Colbert, *Worlds*, p. 109)**

That the griffin in "Griffin d'or" is golden only highlights "these solar associations" and its reflection of the Christ. Some door knocker!

The Unicorn

Harry first meets a unicorn in the Forbidden Forest under the worst of conditions. The unicorn is dying or dead; Voldemort as something like a snake is drinking its blood, which "tonic" curses the drinker but keeps him alive **(*Stone*, p. 256)**. Unicorns pop up again in Ms. Grubberly Plank's and Hagrid's Care of Magical Creatures Classes **(*Goblet*, p. 436)**.

I remember as a young boy being taken to the Cloisters, a New York museum of stolen, plundered, and purchased Medieval art and artifacts in an authentic castle brought stone by stone from Europe. Best field trip ever. The highlight of the trip, beyond just walking around the castle, was the tapestries — specifically the Unicorn tapestries. The guide told us that the unicorn was the symbol of Christ preferred by the weavers of these giant pieces. Though I was a child of no special faith (or sensitivity, believe me), I was moved by the woven images of the unicorn being chased, captured, and resting its head in a virgin's lap.

J.E. Cirlot notes that Carl Jung made mention of this symbolism with a reference to an author contemporaneous with the tapestries:

> The very fierce animal with one horn is called unicorn. In order to catch it, a virgin is put in a field; the animal then comes to her and is caught, because it lies down in her lap. Christ is represented by this animal, and his invincible strength by its horn. He who lay down in the womb of the virgin has been caught by the hunters; that is to say, he was found in human shape by those who loved him.
> **(Honoris of Autun, *Speculum de Mysteriis Ecclesiae* [Eyeglass of the Mysteries of the Church], quoted in *Symbolism*, pp. 357-358)**

Paul Ford in his encyclopedic **Companion to Narnia** confirmed my memory and this interpretation. The unicorn, he reports, is "a mythological beast with a single horn in the center of its head. It variously symbolizes purity, chastity, and even the Word of God as brought by Jesus Christ" (*Companion to Narnia*, p. 430). A check in **Strong's Concordance to the Bible** reveals mentions of unicorns in the Old Testament books of Deuteronomy, Numbers, Job, Psalms, and Isaiah **(p. 1133)**. Colbert comments on these biblical usages:

> The Old Testament refers to unicorns several times: "God brought them out of Egypt; he hath as it were the strength of the unicorn" (Numbers 23:22); "His horns are like the horns of the unicorns: with them he shall push the people together to the ends of the earth: (Deuteronomy 33:17; "My horn shall thou exalt like the horn of a unicorn" (Psalms 92:10); "Will the unicorn be willing to serve thee, or abode in thy crib?" (Job39:9). These references, to some scholars, indicate that the unicorn is actually a symbol of Christ. **(Colbert, Worlds, p. 182)**

The Phoenix

My flat-out favorite beastie in Rowling's menagerie is Fawkes the phoenix, Dumbledore's pet. Harry meets him in **Chamber** on a "dying day" when he bursts into flame and rises as a chick from his own ashes. Cirlot confirms this process as characteristic of the phoenix rather than a Rowling invention:

> [The phoenix is] a mythical bird about the size of an eagle, graced with certain features of the pheasant. Legend has it that when it saw death draw near, it would make a nest of sweet smelling wood and resins, which it would expose to the full force of the sun's rays, until it burnt itself to ashes in the flames. Another phoenix would then arise form the marrow of its bones....In the Christian world, it signifies the triumph of eternal life over death. In alchemy, it corresponds to the color red (Sulphur), the regeneration of eternal life and to the successful completion of a process. **(Cirlot, Symbolism, p. 254)**

Harry Potter experts echo the Christian symbolism. Colbert: "In Egyptian hieroglyphics, the phoenix image conveys the passage of time, and it remains a symbol of immortality today" (*Worlds*, **p. 82**). Kronzek: "During the Middle Ages the phoenix became part of Christian symbolism, representing death, resurrection and eternal life" (*Sorcerer's Companion*, **p. 188**).

If this weren't enough, T. H. White, author of *The Sword in the Stone* and translator of a medieval compendium called *The Bestiary*, details the obvious symbolism of the phoenix as "resurrection bird":

> Now our Lord Jesus Christ exhibits the character of this bird, who says, "I have the power to lay down my life and take it up again". If the phoenix has the power to die and rise again, why, silly man, are you scandalized at the word of God — who is the true Son of God — when he says that he came down from heaven for men and for our salvation, and who filled his wings with the odours of sweetness from the New and the Old Testaments, and who offered himself on the altar of the cross to suffer for us and in the third day rise again?...The symbolism of this bird therefore teaches us to believe in the resurrection. (White, *Bestiary*, **p. 126**)

Given the phoenix Fawkes' role in the defeat of the Basilisk in *Chamber*, Harry's draw with Voldemort in *Goblet* in the cage of phoenix song and light, and Book Five's tentative title being *Order of the Phoenix*, this symbol is central to any interpretation of the books or understanding of their power and popularity. But let's finish our list before we get back to that point.

The Stag

Lupin and Black explain to Harry in the crucible of the Shrieking Shack that his father James was an animagus. Harry discovers later that night what form his father took after transforming into an animal: a majestic stag with a full rack of antlers. His nickname at school, Prongs, came from these antlers, which are the stag's weapon and defining characteristic (*Prisoner*, p. 424). That Harry's "patronus" likewise takes the shape of a stag gives this already powerful symbol even more importance. With what supernatural qualities or figure does it correspond?

Ford defines the stag as "a beast, the quest of great hunting parties, who was said to grant wishes to his captors. Lewis, as a student of the Middle Ages, would know of the symbolism of the stag for Christ" (*Companion to Narnia*, p. 440). Narnia fans recall that the Pevensie children in ***The Lion, the Witch, and the Wardrobe*** only return to Earth from their Narnia kingdom because they pursue the White Stag into a thick wood. Lewis points to their search for Christ as the cause of their return, because Christ is to our world what Aslan is to Narnia.

Maybe you don't see how a big deer can become a correspondence point linking our world and the Christian creative principle. Cirlot explains that the power of the symbolism comes from the antlers:

> Its symbolic meaning is linked with that of the tree of life ... inexhaustible life, and is therefore equivalent to a symbol of immortality ... because of the resemblance of its antlers to branches. It is also a symbol of the cycles of regeneration and growth.... The stag...came to be thought of as a symbol of regeneration because of the way its antlers are renewed. Like the eagle and the lion, it is the secular enemy of the

serpent....[and acts] as [one of the] mediators of heaven and earth... In the West, during the Middle Ages, the way of solitude and purity was often symbolized by the stag, which actually appears in some emblems with a crucifix between its horns. (**Cirlot,** *Symbolism*, **pp. 347, 308-309**)

Given what has been said above, it is no accident that when Harry first sees the stag patronus who saves him from the dementor's kiss — the living, soulless death worse than death — he sees it "as a unicorn" (*Prisoner*, **p. 385**). The stag in *Harry Potter*, as elsewhere, is a symbol for Christ.

The Centaur

In medieval literature and classical mythology, the centaur is anything but a Christ symbol. This beastie with the head and chest of a man and the body of a horse is not perfect man, but a man controlled by animal passion instead of the spirit. "From a symbolic point of view the centaur is the antithesis of the knight, that is, it represents the complete domination of a being by the baser forces: in other words, it denotes cosmic force, the instincts or the unconscious, uncontrolled by the spirit" (**Cirlot,** *Symbolism*, **p. 40**).

There were notable exceptions. Our guides to myths and legends relevant to *Harry Potter* mention these. "Some centaurs were recognized to be noble. Chiron, having been taught arts such as medicine and hunting by the gods Apollo and Artemis, founded a school where he taught some of the great heroes of the time, including Achilles and Odysseus" (**Colbert,** *Worlds*, **p. 52**). "Chiron also practiced astrology and divination. Based on the ability of Ronan, Bane, and Firenze to read the future in the sky, we suspect these centaurs may have descended from Chiron's side of the (centaur) family" (**Kronzek,** *Sorcerer's Companion*, **p. 36**).

C. S. Lewis, renowned classicist and medieval scholar of Oxford and Cambridge, was certainly familiar with these interpretations and uses of the Centaur as symbol. His centaurs in the *Chronicles of Narnia* are astrologers like Chiron and, beyond their insight, they can be heroic and sacrificial in their service to the King.

In *The Last Battle*, the centaur named Roonwit — literally "he who knows the ancient languages" (Ford, *Companion to Narnia*, p. 358) — reveals to King Tirian the portents of calamity in the stars. Roonwit sends this edifying, otherworldly message after he has been shot by the invading Calormenes while on a mission for the King: "Remember that all worlds draw to an end and that noble death is a treasure which no one is too poor to buy" (*The Last Battle*, p. 193).

Lewis didn't see the horse, the Centaur's driving part, as a passionate creature, but as the desires (or "belly") in alignment and in service to will and spirit ("chest and head"), especially when hosting a human rider. Ford explains the symbolism of horse and rider and, consequently, of the centaur:

> The horse for Lewis is a complex symbol, the personification of all that is best in our natural desires. Thus good horsemanship, the harmonic interaction of horse and rider, is symbolic of the ultimate reconciliation of our spiritual and physical nature. (Ford, *Companion to Narnia*, p. 235)

The centaur, "a semi-divine being with the head and chest of a man and the body of a horse" the embodiment of horse and rider, represents this reconciliation. "For Lewis, the Centaur represents the harmony of nature and spirit" (Ford, *Companion to Narnia*, p. 102).

Ford does not share the origin of Lewis' interpretation of the Centaur, which Rowling follows certainly in the case of her heroic character, Firenze. This centaur is anything but frenetic despite his name (pronounced "frenzy"). He saves Harry Potter from Voldemort in the forest in violation of the centaurs' otherworldly doctrine of non-interference. Lewis and Rowling, I think, are both familiar with a tradition that links a man on a passionate beast with omniscience coupled with heroic, sacrificial, and saving actions.

The traditional Christian explanation of why Christ rides in triumph into Jerusalem on a jackass rather than a noble steed is that he wanted to show the hosanna-shouting assembly on the sides of the road a three-dimensional icon or symbol of the perfect man. Thus the jackass (certainly a cipher for willful, stubborn desire) serves his Master, spirit and God incarnate, on Palm Sunday in cheerful obedience. Lewis, the great Christian apologist, blends the classical Centaur and this scriptural image of the God-man and the rightly-ordered soul. The centaur in **Harry Potter** becomes (following Lewis' usage) another symbol of Christ.

The Hippogriff

I confess to thinking that Buckbeak the Hippogriff was another one of Rowling's mythological innovations — and a hoot. I had certainly never heard of one. Turns out, he is the creation of a 16th century Italian Court poet named Ludovico Ariosto in his **Orlando Furioso**, after a saying from Virgil (for the full story, see Colbert, *Magical Worlds*, pp. 113-116). Compare this description to Buckbeak the Firebolt:

> Like a griffin, Ariosto's hippogriff has an eagle's head and beak, a lion's front legs, with talons, and richly feathered

wings, while the rest of its body is that of a horse. Originally tamed and trained by the magician Atalante, the hippogriff can fly higher and faster than any bird, hurtling back to earth when its rider is ready to land. **(Kronzek, *Sorcerer's Companion*, p. 109)**

Cirlot makes an observation that is helpful in seeing the symbolism of the lion/bird/horse:

[The hippogriff] is a kind of supercharged Pegasus, a blend of the favourable aspects of the griffin and the winged horse in its character as the "spiritual mount". **(Cirlot, *Symbolism*, p. 149)**

To help decipher Rowling's hippogriff, let's see how Ford explains Lewis' symbolic usage of the flying horse in his ***The Magician's Nephew***:

Strawberry, the cart horse whose transformation into Fledge is the very image of risen nature in its glory…carries Digory and Polly to the garden, and is the vehicle of their ultimate salvation, illustrating Lewis' feeling that humanity and nature must be in harmony in order to enter Aslan's country. **(Ford, *Companion to Narnia*, p. 236)**

Rowling, the Lewis fan and accomplished student of Medieval lore (had you ever heard of ***Orlando Furioso***?), understands this symbolism of "spiritual mount" and "risen nature in its glory" implicitly. The noble — even supernatural — Buckbeak in ***Prisoner*** pecks the disrespectful and shameless Malfoy, is persecuted by the Ministry, and is almost executed by the Death Eater McNair. He escapes death at the hands of a world that cannot understand him (and which chooses to hate and fear him) to serve as Sirius' salvation. As in the griffin and centaur double-natured symbols explained above, Rowling uses the hippogriff as a symbol of Christ, the God-man.

The Philosopher's Stone

As discussed above, the production of the philosopher's stone was the "net result" of spiritual purification, dissolution, and recongealed perfection. Cirlot backs me up:

> As for the philosophers' stone in alchemy, it represents the "conjunction" of opposites, or the integration of the conscious self with the feminine or unconscious side (or in other words, the fixing of volatile elements); it is, then a symbol of the All. As Jung rightly says, the alchemists approached their task obliquely — they did not seek the divine in matter but tried to "produce" it by means of a lengthy process of purification and transmutation. According to Evola, the touchstone is symbolic of the body, since it is "fixed", as opposed to the "wandering" characteristic of thought, the spirits and desires. But only the resuscitated body — in which "two will be one" — can correspond to the philosophers' stone. Evola points out that, for the alchemist, "between eternal birth, reintegration, and the discovery of the philosophers' stone, there is no difference whatsoever. (Cirlot, *Symbolism*, pp. 314-315)

A little heady? Burckhardt makes it simple:

> From the Christian point of view, alchemy was like a natural mirror for the revealed truths: the philosophers' stone, which turned base metals into silver and gold, is a symbol of Christ, and its production from the "non-burning fire" of sulphur and the "steadfast water" of quicksilver resembles the birth of Christ-Emmanuel". (Burckhardt, *Alchemy*, page 18)

How could a stone promising eternal life and golden (that is, solar or spiritual) riches be anything else?

The Red Lion

Narnia fans have told me they do see Aslan, Lewis' Christ figure from the *Chronicles of Narnia*, in the Gryffyndor House Lion symbol. I think that is a reasonable link, especially in light of the symbolic meaning of Gryffyndor and its opposition to the Slytherin serpent. Rowling, however, needn't be seen as "lifting" this from Lewis — the lion and specifically the red lion has been a symbol of Christ from the first century.

St. John the Evangelist has no need to explain this usage in the book of Revelations: "Weep not; lo, the Lion of the Tribe of Judah, the Root of David, has conquered..." **(Revelation 5:5)**. It is a topos of Christian literature and heraldic signs, consequently, throughout the Middle Ages. Lewis draws from this tradition both for Aslan (Persian for "Lion") and Aslan's devotees in Narnia. Remember Peter's Shield? "The Shield was the colour of silver and across it there romped a red lion, as bright as a ripe strawberry at the moment when you pick it" **(Lewis, *The Lion, the Witch, and the Wardrobe*, p. 104)**.

Rowling uses alchemical imagery throughout the four *Harry Potter* books and, even if Lewis was unaware of it (the silver and red in Peter's shield makes me doubt his ignorance), we can assume Rowling knows what the "Red Lion" means to an alchemist. Burckhardt tells us:

[T]he divine spark in man corresponds to the sun (gold). It seems to die when the soul enters the house of Saturn (becomes lead). In truth, however, it arises anew and

ascending through the seven levels of consciousness, becomes the "red lion" — the all transmuting elixir.
(Burckhardt, *Alchemy*, p. 91)

The "red lion" is the Elixir of Life coming from the Philosopher's Stone, a symbol of the blood of Christ received in Communion. The Red Lion is another point of correspondence between Christ and the world.

Eight symbols examined, eight symbols of Christ revealed. Here is a chart of this work for your easy reflection. Not a particularly obscure pattern!

Symbol	Meaning	Therefore
Philosopher's Stone	Transforming Lead to Gold = Immortality Fount of "Elixir of Life" = Communion	Christ
Red Lion	Life-giving alchemical elixir; Aslan Revelations 5:5	Christ
Gryffyndor = Golden Griffin	Eagle/Lion = Kings of Heaven/Earth = God/Man = Two natures of Christ	Christ
Unicorn	Biblical references: Numbers, Psalms, Job Christian tapestry & literary tradition	Christ
Phoenix	Resurrection bird; immortal life Medieval Literature topos	Christ
Stag	Tradition: "Tree of Life" in antlers Regeneration of Antlers = Resurrection	Christ
Centaur	Perfect man in control of passions Christ riding donkey into Jerusalem	Christ
Hippogriff	Eagle/Lion/Horse, Heaven/Earth, God/Man Two natures of Christ	Christ

Chapter 10

The Ironic Secret
of
Harry Potter

Remember Mrs. Smith, my English and Latin teacher? She taught her ignorant and unwilling students (all of whom she loved) not only how to find traces of Homer in Beatles' lyrics, but how to write an expository composition as well. Thesis paragraph, major supporting reasons, conclusion: I can see her red marks on my one-sheet essay papers just thinking about it.

I have foregone the usual sequence in this second part of **Hidden Key** and given you my major supporting reasons before my thesis statement. Mrs. Smith wouldn't have liked it, but what's the fun of a secret if you give it away before laying out all the clues? Here at last is the secret of Joanne Rowling's *Harry Potter* and the answer to the question "why are these books so popular":

Joanne Rowling is a Christian novelist of the Inkling School writing to "baptize the imagination" and prepare our hearts and minds for the conscious pursuit of the greater life in Jesus Christ. Harry Potter is a Christian Hero.

This is not only a secret, it is also a real surprise to most. If a non-reader knows anything about the Potter phenomenon from news reports, it is that many Christian groups do not like the books. What is the evidence that she is a Christian writer, of all things?

The clues we have reviewed above are her themes, her symbolist perspective, and the referents of the symbols she uses. If these have Christian meaning, it's not much of a leap to the conclusion that she is a Christian writer ("walks like a duck, looks like a duck, sounds like a duck — must be a ....").

The Themes

The three-dimensional themes resounding through the *Potter* books are Prejudice, Death, Choice, and Change. A look at each one (and its lessons) from the traditional Christian perspective shows a match with Christian teaching.

Prejudice or "the rush to judgment" is a failure in love. Love is the defining mark of Christians: "By this shall all men know that ye are my disciples" **(John 13:35)**. One of the few commandments given by Christ to his followers is the love of

God and neighbor **(Mark 12:30-31)**. Another commandment, really an application of the commandment to love, is the prohibition of judging one's brother's sins **(Matthew 7:1-5)**. This is not a prohibition of discernment and virtuous discrimination, but the proscription against identifying the neighbor with his sins and the pretense (inevitable to this posture) of being without sin oneself.

Can you think of a single character in Rowling's books that suffers from others' prejudices — and there are a host — that you didn't sympathize with? As we saw in the last chapter, Rowling teaches us the evil of prejudice implicitly, explicitly, and via her WOW! surprise endings. Love is her answer and she is clearly in the Christian camp on this issue.

But being against prejudice and for love is a little bit like being against drunk driving. Christians are against drunk driving, but so are sentimental nihilists and Christian-baiting communists. We have seen that the **Potter** books are about death; what is the traditional Christian teaching on death, and does Rowling agree with the Church?

St. Paul teaches that "the wages of sin is death" **(Romans 6:23)** and that "carnal mindedness is death" **(Romans 8:6)**. Death is the life spent in selfish pursuit of advantage rather than with the God Who is Life and Love Himself. This pseudo-life apart from God is a death worse than a physical death, because it promises an eternity in darkness outside the Glory of God. Only by a life of love in resistance to selfishness and evil, by the life spent in pursuit of communion with God, by a victory over death made possible by the life and by the death-destroying Resurrection of Christ, do we have eternal life.

Harry Potter doesn't lay out Christian doctrine explicitly, but Dumbledore comes close. Death, he tells us, to the well-organized mind is just the next great adventure. Life is not a value to be pursued in itself, but what value it has we create by our choices — for the good over what is easy. Those who love us live on in us after their death because of this love, a love which is their immortality and which protects us. Dumbledore teaches Harry not to fear death as much as a life without love, which is the real death.

Moreover, the WOW! of Rowling's presentation of this theme is our vicarious experience of dying heroically in resistance to evil with Harry in every book, then rising from the dead with him to talk with Dumbledore and those we love. This shared Resurrection in *Stone*, in case you resist the Easter parallel, comes after three days (*Stone*, p. 296). Ms. Rowling has us share in the spoils of a life spent in love and resistance to darkness by this cathartic death and resurrection — and it is the great joy, relief, and lesson of each book. Death is not final. Death has been overcome by Love Himself.

Choice and Change parallel these themes of "love and death". In Christian language, Rowling's exploration of a choice is instruction in our free will to pursue or deny God. She teaches that our choices are a life and death matter of what we will become. Change, as Rowling presents it, is an echo of the Christian doctrine of transformation from the "old man" into the life of "Christ in me". We are called spiritually to the alchemical purification, dissolution, and perfection of our persons that we see Harry undergoing in each book, and which is already accomplished in Albus Dumbledore, the "brilliant, radiant soul".

Symbolism

We've seen that Rowling's themes check out as at least nominally Christian. Let's talk next about her symbolism.

The "symbolist outlook", which is the opposite of cultural materialism and exclusive naturalism, holds that there are multiple states of being in a hierarchy of lesser and greater states. According to this view, we have access to the worlds of more being, the greater realities via points of correspondence or symbols through which we can see and receive as graces the qualities and figures we can know only in shadow on this plane of being.

We looked at Ms. Rowling's books through the symbolist glasses and found it not only consistent with this perspective, but also much more understandable. Her stories, characters, and animal figures unfold their meaning and highlight her themes when considered as referents to greater realities. But is the symbolist perspective a Christian way of looking at things?

I'll go so far as saying if a Christian isn't a symbolist, he or she cannot be Christian. A God in heaven whose Son becomes man and returns to heaven, and whose Spirit creates the world and perfects mankind in Christ, is inconceivable without worlds or dimensions of being greater than our own. Without correspondence or revelation or avenues of grace between these worlds, there could be no knowledge of God, or salvation by participation in the barrier-destroying resurrection of his Son, or experience of the Holy Spirit.

Iconography, sacred architecture, liturgy, and the mysteries (sacraments) of the Church only make sense to the symbolist; to a materialist who thinks of symbolism as only mind games and conventional signs, these things are barren of meaning and opiates for the self-deluded (think of the dwarves in the shack at the end of Lewis' *Last Battle*). The naturalists are hard of heart and blind to a God beyond nature, despite the fact that — because nature is inadequate to explain itself — nature cannot be a god.

Not only are Rowling's symbols beyond cardboard imagery, not only do they reflect traditional belief in multivalent worlds, they are symbols of Christian doctrines and of Christ. We saw that Harry, Ron, and Hermione are types of the powers of the soul. I cited Plato as the source of this doctrine, but C. S. Lewis gets his formula "the head rules the belly through the chest" from Plato through St. Alanus. Dostoevsky's use of it in *The Brothers Karamazov* comes from St. Isaac the Syrian, the Optina Elders, and the Fathers of *The Philokalia*. This idea of the soul is trinitarian and is used by countless theologians to explain what is meant by man having been created "in God's image".

And the eight mythical animals and figures we looked at? All were symbols of Jesus Christ, traditional and recent. Either Joanne Rowling is a Christian author or she has a remarkable fetish for Christian imagery and teaching. I think the former possibility easier to believe.

That she is a Christian author does not explain the popularity of her books, however. At first blush, it seems pretty unlikely in our times that a fantasy novel series with Christian hero and themes would conquer and maintain a lasting grip on the bestseller lists. More than unlikely: it's flipping unbelievable!

The Inklings

What makes her a successful Christian author is her fellowship with a group of Christian writers who called themselves "The Inklings", all of whom were long dead before she took up pen to write. The formal group comprised such notables as Charles Williams, C. S. Lewis, and J. R. R. Tolkien. But other popular authors have worked within this Inklings stream of Christian fiction, including George MacDonald, G. K. Chesterton, Dorothy L. Sayers, and currently (I contend) J. K. Rowling.

As I have mentioned before, the first defense of Middle Road critics against Christian critics of Rowling is, "Hey, c'mon, take a valium; these *Potter* books are just like Narnia and Middle Earth: good, clean fun." This comparison causes Christians to go over the edge, in my experience; with the same zeal (too often, with greater zeal) as they might share the Gospel, they propound the differences between the *Chronicles of Narnia*, *The Lord of the Rings*, and *Harry Potter*. They are, sadly, usually mistaken about all of the authors of these three works.

The working assumptions of the Christian critics are that Lewis and Tolkien are conventional Christians, that Rowling is not a Christian of any sort (and not very smart to boot), and that they understand what these authors' books are all about. My reading and research tell me that each of these assumptions is unfounded.

I do not wish to single out the Christian side of this argument. These "take a valium" critics offer what I think is the right answer, but for none of the right reasons. They charge the Christian critics with hypocrisy for dissing Rowling and adoring Lewis and Tolkien as if they were the fifth and sixth evangelists. (Wheaton College, an esteemed Evangelical college outside Chicago, has something of a shrine — only larger — to Lewis and Tolkien in its library.) Some Rowling defenders think the Inklings were writing Christian allegory of the battle between good and evil — and the triumph of the good — so they see common ground by viewing Rowling as writing fantasy literature about the same battle. That sells short all three writers.

Lewis and Tolkien were not composing paper cut-out allegories of Christian doctrine. This is especially clear in the case of Tolkien; he described his work as Catholic fiction, but few of his readers see this Catholicism as easily as anyone can see the Christian elements and figures in *The Lion, the Witch, and the Wardrobe*. But neither of these men were conventional Christians; instead, they were traditional Christians at war with the Christian conventions and compromises of their time.

Tolkien was an unreformed Vatican I Roman Catholic who practiced his faith without compromise. Lewis was not Catholic, but a more Catholic Protestant (or Catholic Catholic) you could not find in our day. He received Communion as sacrament (believing in the Real Presence), confessed to a Cowling Father monastic, and had no truck with liturgy that was "spontaneous" or not the traditional ritual.

Both Lewis and Tolkien were WWI combat veterans with "firsts" in Classics and English Literature, and both became chaired professors at Oxford and Cambridge as the acknowledged authorities in their fields (Medieval and Renaissance Literature and Anglo-Saxon, respectively). Their familiarity with and fluency in Classical languages, literature and philosophy, the mythological traditions of the

Mediterranean and Nordic countries, and the history, philosophy, and literatures of Christian medieval Europe (all reflected in their fiction) are mind-boggling.

Besides being stuffy churchgoers and eggheads, though, they were remarkably unconventional in their way of looking at the world — they were radical Christian symbolists. Lewis' conversion to Christianity, in fact, came about after Tolkien convinced him that the "myths" he delighted in were not lies but truths from God for human reflection, and that Christianity as myth was not only such a truth but an historical and personal truth as well. (See *The Inklings* by Humphrey Carpenter, pp. 42-45, or any good biography of Tolkien or Lewis for this conversion experience; read James Cutsinger's lecture "C. S. Lewis as Apologist and Mystic" at *www.cutsinger.net* for insight about the Inklings' unconventional "diagonal" view of reality.)

They may have been traditional Christians, but they also included among their better friends and intellectual peers Owen Barfield, an Anthroposophist, as well as the novelist Charles Williams, whose spiritual formation took place largely in "The Order of the Golden Dawn", a self-styled esoteric stream of Christianity. Don't expect to meet many Anthroposophists or Christian magicians and alchemists at Wheaton College! While these men did not share Lewis or Tolkien's traditional religious faith or observances, they did look at the world in much the same way, that is, not as materialists but as symbolists.

Lewis and Tolkien resolved in 1937 to write the sort of fiction they liked and was not being written: mythopoetic epic of detailed worlds composed in imitation of God's creation.

These "sub-creations" (as Tolkien called them) and the adventures they told would train their readers in the stock responses, to excite and foster the spiritual (or noetic) faculty of soul, and (in Lewis' words) to "baptize the imagination" with Christian symbols and doctrines.

Readers of Inkling fiction are being readied for real-world spiritual combat, interior and exterior spiritual warfare in the Christian trenches: this is *Literature to prepare one for Life and Liturgy*. That's what the best literature and fairy stories did, in their opinion, and this conviction shaped **The Lord of the Rings** and the **Narnia** books.

Hogwarts and the magical world of **Harry Potter** are just such a detailed, mythopoetic sub-creation. It prepares the young for their later conscious life in the Church and steels those already Christian in their faith. It is not by chance that Rowling is writing a seven book series; both the Narnia and Middle Earth series are seven books long (using Tolkien's original division of **The Lord of the Rings** into six "books" plus **The Hobbit**), and she points to the parallel and her debt to them.

I wonder, too, if Rowling's publishers are being entirely on the level when they say the reason they put Ms. Rowling's name on the dust jacket as "J. K. Rowling" was because they didn't think boys would buy a book by a woman. The suggestion of "C. S." and "J. R. R." is fairly obvious in the "J. K.", which would have been lost in "Joanne".

Enumerating all of Rowling's specific allusions to Narnia and Middle Earth would require another chapter. We have already mentioned the Lion of Gryffyndor House, the giant spiders, and Dumbledore as Gandalf. Here is a less obvious one.

Symbolists believe that icons, pictures, and word pictures have the power to cross worlds and bring the observer in formal contact with what is represented. Lewis demonstrates this belief by having the children "fall into" Narnia through a picture of a ship on the high seas. The picture comes to life and, lickety split, they're in the other side, soaking wet, being brought aboard the ship (*The Voyage of the Dawn Treader*, pp. 5-7). If you don't think Lewis is employing icons here, remember that the Latin for sea is "mare" and the better western churches are styled as ships for the body of Christ. Every Orthodox Christian home has an icon of the Virgin Mary holding the Christ child in its prayer corner to foster the same effect of the painting in **Voyage**: our transportation through the picture to the forms depicted.

The paintings are all alive at Hogwarts castle, too, as are all the photographs taken. What tips us off that these photos are living symbols is that they are not movies of what happened, but reflections of what the portrayed are really about. Think of Colin Creevy's snapshots of Harry and Gilderoy Lockhart. In "real" life, Harry is unhappy but lets Colin take the picture. In the *more-real* life of the pictures, Harry resists and pulls away from Lockhart (**Chamber, p. 106**). No Madonna with Christ Child here, but the theology of icons and the symbolist perspective are present. Icons do not "look like" natural pictures, because they represent the supernatural existence of the portrayed Saint or event in eternity, the *more-real* image of that greater life with which we have contact in viewing the icon. Rowling and Lewis are reading from the same page.

These specific crossovers in the **Harry Potter** books are not as important as the signature elements in Inkling fantasy: *training* *in stock responses, the right alignment of the soul, and initiation into Christian images and doctrines.* This is the secret of Rowling's success. I said in the beginning of this chapter that we would check the secret if we found one against what we know of Rowling's favorite writers, religious beliefs, and education. Time to check it out.

Her favorite authors are Jane Austen and Charles Dickens and their shadow is visible in the books. As Joan Acocella wrote in *The New Yorker*:

> Rowling's favorite writer, she has told interviewers, is Jane Austen. She also loves Dickens. And it is in their bailiwick — English morals-and-manners realism, the world of Pip and Miss Bates, of money and position and trying to keep your head up if you have neither — that she scores her greatest victories. **(Acocella, "Under the Spell",** *New Yorker*, **July 31, 2000)**

Rowling, as mentioned previously, thinks Lewis a genius and confesses a great love of his ***Narnia*** books. She has combined brilliantly, as no other author, the "morals and manners realism" of nineteenth century English fiction that engages readers with the struggles of characters and the edifying Christian fantasy of the Inklings.

Though she does not discuss her religious beliefs in interviews, she does admit to believing in God. One ***Potter*** guidebook reports: "Some more paranoid book banners have incorrectly alleged that Rowling is a witch, attempting to convert children to black magic. An attendant of the Church of Scotland, Rowling resents such accusations" **(Schafer,** *Exploring Harry Potter*, **p. 33)**. Rowling, it turns out, is a Christian. Surprise!

And her education? She is famous for being unemployed, on the dole, and a hapless single mother as she prepared *Philosopher's Stone*. I don't doubt that she was in a bad way, but anyone who concludes from this rags-to-riches tale that Rowling was a street person without an education is making a grand mistake. She has an educational pedigree that might not be the equal of Lewis and Tolkien, whose species of intellectual is nigh on extinct, but is extraordinary for our times nonetheless.

She was head girl of her secondary school, passed A-level exams in French, German, and English, and, at the University of Exeter, she took a double first in French and Classical Languages. As were the Inklings, she is familiar and fluent with the languages, philosophy, and literature of the classical and medieval worlds. I suspect, too, that she has read the twentieth century traditionalists and writers on symbolism in French. Surprise! Her books reflect an understanding of the truths of Plato, Aristotle, Augustine, and Aquinas because she has read these greats.

Why are her books so popular? Three reasons.

- They teach us traditional doctrines we long to hear;

- They give us some experience of the truth of these doctrines; and

- Rowling delivers it all inside a wonderfully engaging, entertaining story.

The Hidden Key claims to be the High Road approach to *Harry Potter*, but perhaps I am stretching your ability to take me seriously when I say *Harry Potter* has taken the world by storm because the world wants desperately to experience Christian truths. Really, though, that is the reason. You just have to see the fiction novel as Lewis, Tolkien, and a few others have, to understand why Inkling books outsell all others (and are doing pretty well at the box office, too).

Huston Smith, famous authority on the world's religions, tells this story in his *Why Religion Matters*:

> At the Press Conference that the university mounted on [Saul Bellow's] arrival, one of the reporters asked him, "Mr. Bellow, you are a writer and we are writers. What's the difference between us?" Bellow answered, "As journalists, you are concerned with news of the day. As a novelist, I am concerned with news of eternity." **(Smith, *Why Religion Matters*, p. 120)**

People who read novels are looking for this eternal news. They look for it, as said above, because, even in a profane, desacralized, and materialist culture — with, as one symbolist put it, "a low ceiling and a deep basement" — the human heart longs for some experience of the sacred. We find it, according to Mircea Eliade, in our entertainments and especially in the books we read:

> Nonreligious man *in the pure state* is a comparatively rare phenomenon, even in the most desacralized of modern societies. The majority of the "irreligious" still behave religiously even though they are not aware of the fact. We refer not only to modern man's many "superstitions" and "tabus", all of them magico-religious in structure. But the modern man who feels and claims that he is nonreligious still retains a large stock of camouflaged myths and degenerated rituals....

A whole volume could be written on the myths of modern man, on the mythologies camouflaged in the plays that he enjoys, in the books that he reads. The cinema, that "dream factory", takes over and employs countless motifs — the fight between hero and monster, initiatory combats and ordeals, paradigmatic figures and images ... Even reading includes a mythological function, not only because it replaces the recitation of myths in archaic societies and the oral literature that still lives in the rural communities of Europe, but particularly because, through reading, the modern man succeeds in obtaining an "escape from time" comparable to the "emergence from time" effected by myths. Whether modern man "kills" time with a detective story or enters such a foreign temporal universe as is represented by any novel, reading projects him out of his personal duration and incorporates him into other rhythms, makes him live in another "history". **(Eliade, *The Sacred and the Profane*, pp. 204-205)**

The Inkling writers, to include Rowling, understand and embrace the fact that their sub-creation novels act as detailed little worlds *which serve a mythological function in a profane culture.* This contrasts to theocentric cultures with a living revealed religious tradition (and the ancillary mysteries, sciences, arts, and vocations), which do not feel the same need for novels or movies as ours does. But in our culture, Inkling books touch us where we live, feeding our hunger for some experience of a greater existence than our flat, mundane concerns.

It is a patristic formula after Terrtullian that "all souls are Christian souls". Obviously, this does not mean that everyone is a professing Christian; instead, it points to the doctrines that all men are made by God's creative Word to receive the same

Word — because there is a correspondence (amounting to "identity") between human intellect or "logic" and the Logos of God creating man and the world. Even in our post-Christian culture, it is possible to see two things in the great success of the Christian symbolist stories from Narnia, Middle Earth, and Hogwarts:

- First, the great mass of people, despite materialist immunizations and naturalist booster shots, still long for explicitly Christian spiritual experiences; and

- Second, the prevalent culture is so profane and bereft of what is good, true, and beautiful, that the unsated desire for these things is overwhelming when presented with what it craves.

Hence, Pottermania.

I wish to emphasize that, whatever our spiritual condition, except for Ms. Rowling's remarkable artistry with these themes and symbols, and except for her great care in creating an at times hilariously detailed world, none of us would have ever heard of Harry Potter. She claims that Lewis is a genius and she is not, but I beg to differ.

Lewis may have been the better writer and Christian apologist, but he was what he was in the company of other writers and thinkers who loved and supported him. It is not to belittle Lewis to say that Rowling's achievement is the more remarkable, less because of her book sales than because of the height she has achieved in an environment which Lewis dreaded, foretold, but never lived in.

Certainly Lewis had his Christian critics (more on that in a moment), but his books were written in what was only then becoming a spiritual desert; post-war Britain was not already, visibly Eliot's wasteland. His audience may have known what a teevee was; they didn't know 300 station cable, DVD, and MTV as a way of life. Harry Potter springs from and has conquered this world, perhaps his greatest and least-noted victory over Voldemort.

Do you find this secret and reason for Harry's popularity unbelievable? I confess I don't blame you. I read the books three times (once to myself, once to the children, and then again via cassette on a long trip) before it hit me what **Harry Potter** was about. But I think even the profoundly skeptical should be drawn in and won over after reviewing each book and title from this High Road perspective, as we shall do in Part Three.

I close with this response C. S. Lewis made to Christian critics who objected to the magic in his **Narnia** series:

> Do you think I am trying to weave a spell? Perhaps I am; but remember your fairy tales. Spells are used for breaking enchantments as well as inducing them. And you and I have need of the strongest spell that can be found to wake us from the evil enchantment of worldliness which has been laid upon us for nearly a hundred years. (**Lewis, *The Weight of Glory and Other Addresses*, p. 7**)

We still have need of counter-spells, enchantments to do battle with our profane world view, stronger and perhaps more dangerous spells and magic than warranted in Lewis' day. But that's all the more reason to celebrate Ms. Rowling's genius and success. Let's take a closer look at the individual books to see if the Inkling hypothesis holds water and whether the greatest surprise ending of all may be the revelation, despite the media and the fundamentalists, of Harry's identity as a Christian hero.

Part
Three

The Meaning
of
Harry Potter:
A Book-by-Book Look

Part Three

The Meaning
of
Harry Potter:
A Book-by-Book Look

 T *he Hidden Key to Harry Potter* really only aims to answer one question: Why are Joanne Rowling's *Harry Potter* books so popular? Their critics and admirers have not explained Harry's success worldwide. Those that dislike them tell us only that they are bad (poorly written, uninspired, or, at best, of questionable spiritual value) and are read only by the stupid or foolish. Those that like the series say the opposite, that the books are brilliantly conceived and written, and only the narrow-minded and ridiculous avoid them.

The Hidden Key takes the high-road approach. It offers the common sense response to the question posed; if the books are more popular than any other children's books — or any books, frankly — of recent memory, then the reason must be because they are that much better than the other books. Our work in the last two chapters was the attempt to isolate this qualitative difference in Ms. Rowling's oeuvre that puts her in a different, higher class than other authors.

The high-road answers to the question "Why are the *Harry Potter* books so popular?" are:

- Their meaningful themes;

- The three-dimensional presentation of these themes; and

- Their Christian meaning.

Their Christian meaning (evident in Rowling's symbols, teaching, and characters) uncovered Ms. Rowling's secret. She is a closeted Inkling, which is to say, she is a Christian author like Tolkien and Lewis, teaching the "Stock Responses" and right alignment of the soul's powers, in an effort to "baptize the imagination" of her readers in the edifying symbols and teaching of the Christian faith.

The keys, then, to unlocking Harry Potter and understanding his popularity are her Christian symbolism, the Resurrection plot formula used in each book, and her implicit and explicit teachings that model the virtues and doctrines we need for spiritual warfare. The books "strike a nerve" or satisfy a human need; they both teach us and give us an imaginative experience of the answer we crave to our struggles with hatred and death: love and life in Christ.

Our materialist "post-Christian" culture, having abandoned religion as delusion, still looks to popular fiction and movies for its fix of transcendent, religious experience. *Harry Potter*, as have only *Narnia* and *The Lord of the*

Rings before them, satisfies this need in the only forms even our desacralized world is able to recognize, namely, the Christian ones.

Rowling's books, despite — or should I say "especially because of"? — much publicized Christian objections to them, enjoy unprecedented sales and marketing spin-offs. Some folks like the series because they don't seem to be Christian. Really.

This book was originally written as four lectures given at the Carnegie Library in Port Townsend, Washington. After the second lecture, Beth deJarnette, the Children's Librarian, invited me to talk to two classes at the local elementary school. She hoped that I could share with a fifth and a sixth grade reading class the secret behind the *Harry Potter* books they loved. Sure, I thought — why not? Should be fun.

She warned me in the school parking lot that there was a big difference between the fifth and sixth graders — that something happens in the summer between those years. I had no idea what she was talking about, but sagely agreed as if I were familiar with this disease. She introduced me to the first class, which was the sixth grade bunch.

Piranhas display more kindness with strangers. As I expected, they knew the books fairly well so, after answering a few questions, I dropped the bombs: Harry Potter is a Christian hero and Rowling writes to prepare her readers for spiritual combat and a life in Christ's Church (like her predecessors Lewis and Tolkien).

The class went for my throat.

I assume a few of the children were from Christian families (some, at least, volunteered that they had not been allowed to read the **Potter** books), but these never said a word. But the Politically Correct Ideology Enforcement Hit Squad lost no time taking aim: "Who are you kidding? We know these books are anti-Christian, not pro-Christian. You're here to try and convert us, aren't you?"

Despite my protests that evangelizing them was not my agenda or ambition, and no matter the barrage of evidence I offered them, these skeptical consumers weren't buying anything I had to sell. We went at it for an hour: I talking about the books, they questioning my motives and religious beliefs in *ad hominem* attacks.

I made the mistake (!) of admitting my Christian faith in answer to one javelin hurled at me; consequently the game was over. The P.C. Hit squad threw up their hands in victory. Nothing I had to say about the books could be trusted because of my outrageous prejudice. Did I want to talk to them about creation science to boot?

I thought "what a peculiar reaction" and resolved never to let my children experience sixth grade! Beth was right: by contrast, the fifth graders asked great questions, were polite, and (if not entirely convinced of my thesis) they remained receptive to the possibility that they had something to learn about Harry.

The local television station had broadcast my lectures at the library, so I began to hear responses to my thesis from thoughtful readers of various beliefs (and non-beliefs). Most agreed with me that a "higher criticism" was necessary to explore the phenomenon of Pottermania; most, however, also rolled their eyeballs at the idea of Rowling as an Inkling "wanna be".

Few attempted to explain their reticence, and no one decided to make it openly an issue of my faith ("You're a Christian, and this jaundiced perspective makes you think everything is Christian"). A little reflection on this resistance both to my idea and to the evidence that Rowling is a Christian author — an author of no little sophistication, a peer of Lewis and Tolkien and an echo of Austen and Dickens — has led me to the following possibility.

Rowling herself points to the answer in **Goblet of Fire**. No matter how outrageous a *Daily Prophet* story may be — even about people they know, and even when they are well aware that Rita Skeeter is mercilessly disdainful of the truth — everyone in the magical world believes what they read in that rag. I suspect that Rowling makes this subversive theme such a prominent one in her most recent book because it parallels the common inability of her critics and fans to see through the story they read in papers or see on teevee, and perceive what she's really doing.

Almost every media story touches at least tangentially on the same two "base truths": that the author is a single mother on welfare and that Christians don't like her books. No matter that Rowling's time on the dole was short, or that many Christian groups embrace the **Potter** series — she has been branded a welfare mom and enemy of the Christian right.

This story has no doubt helped her sales. I imagine even members of the Christian right must want to deny this effect (except in their church basements or cable programs) for fear of being lambasted by the mainstream media. Despite attacks on the press in her books, Rowling remains a media darling.

Her rags-to-riches story, after all, is charming. Some friends have told me they first bought a **Potter** book in order to "help the lady out".

But when I say the lady is brilliant and lay out the evidence — not only of her intellectual breadth and of her skill with themes and plotting, but also of her Christian intentions — many people look at me as if I were joking or selling drugs. You'd think I was trying to convince them that Abraham Lincoln was a gay skinhead and died of AIDS. I can hear them thinking behind their blank looks: "Welfare moms aren't brilliant, and enemies of fundamentalists don't write Christian propaganda pieces. What is this guy trying to pull?"

What I am trying to put over is this: if you have Ms. Rowling pigeonholed as some kind of "lottery winner", as a woman who got lucky with some Christian-bashing stories about witchcraft and English kids, then you've been sold a bag of trash by the popular media. She is a writer of the first order and her books are the most edifying fiction to be published in fifty years. The book-by-book look in the following chapters should drive these points home.

Chapter 11

The Meaning
of
Philosopher's Stone

I have briefly discussed in Parts One and Two the themes of prejudice, death, choice, and change that run through all four of the **Harry Potter** books to date. Let's try to focus here on each individual book, and examine its themes and meanings with an eye out for specific Christian doctrines and symbols.

The first book's title lets us in on a good starting place to look for its meaning: the philosopher's stone is the byproduct of spiritual alchemy, so we need to review that esoteric art.

We learned in Part Two that alchemical work was essentially spiritual, and only had symbolic supports from metallurgy. This work or process followed the universal path common to the great revealed traditions of purification, illumination, and perfection. The alchemical language for this salvation journey is purification, dissolution, and recongealing — the "solve et coagula" of hermetic lore. The end of this process is a soul which has turned or "transmuted" from lead to gold, from base desires and concerns for individual advantage to a Christ-like love and freedom.

We learned, too, that the process is distinguished by four colors:

> The four stages of the process were signified by different colours, as follows: black (guilt, origin, latent forces) for "prime matter" (a symbol of the soul in its original condition); white (minor work, first transmutation, quicksilver); red (sulphur, passion); and finally gold. **(Cirlot, Symbolism, p. 6)**

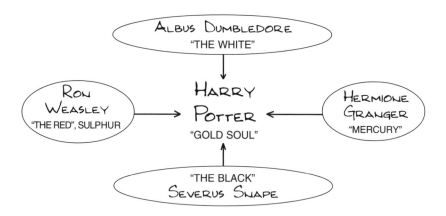

The first book, our introduction alongside Harry to the brave new world of magic, is largely an exposition of the alchemical method writ in human character chemical reagents. It is centered on Harry's spiritual purification into gold (if you will), so that he might be able to grasp or be worthy of the philosopher's stone at the book's end; this requires his purification, dissolution by contraries, and *philosophic congealation*. Taking a peek at the major characters in **Stone**, we see the colors alluded to and the relevant contraries for his dissolution.

Working from above, we have Albus Dumbledore, whose name (meaning "white") points to his being the "first transmutation or minor work". In **Stone**, Dumbledore allows Harry to see his parents in the Mirror of Erised, then coaches him through the major obstacle to his being able to look in the Mirror and see himself: Harry's tremendous longing for family.

Working from below, we have the dark Potion's professor, Severus Snape, always described as dressed in black with black unclean hair. Snape's name is a description of the dissolving effect his mysterious hatred has on Harry, in polar opposition to the love he gets from the "White" Dumbledore ("Severus" means to sever or cut asunder; "Snape" is the past tense of snip or cut).

Working from side to side on Harry, also towards his purification and dissolution, are the incarnations of the alchemical reactants sulphur and quicksilver, namely, Ron and Hermione. Ron Weasley, as we have already discussed, is the passionate aspect of the soul. That and his flaming red Weasley hair point to him as representative of sulphur. Hermione may not seem "mercurial" or flighty, but she is a match with the alchemical reagent quicksilver, which is another name for mercury: Hermione is the feminine of Hermes, who is the Greek version of Mercury.

That Ron is the boy and Hermione the girl reflects that "sulphur — the opposite of quicksilver — is the active power of the solar or masculine cause" and that "the alchemists represent the...feminine cause... by quicksilver" **(Burckhardt, *Alchemy*, p. 81)**. Rowling is spelling out her alchemical meaning by the names and characters of Ron and Hermione, the two alchemical catalysts.

In Part Two's discussion of "Change in Harry Potter", we noted that Harry changes in *Stone* from an orphan in a muggle home into a wizard hero capable of saving the world from Voldemort's return. This happens in stages as the various character reactants distill the muggle out of him. His final trials "to get the stone" are symbols of his soul's journey to perfection.

Let's look at these trials. They begin with Fluffy, the giant three-headed dog that guards the trap door. Hagrid purchased Fluffy from a "Greek chappie" in a bar — which makes sense, because the dog is clearly Cerberus, who played a role in several Greek myths as the monster guarding the gates of hell. Orpheus got past Cerberus by lulling him to sleep with a lyre, and that is Fluffy's weak point as well. Quirrell uses a harp (much like a lyre), and Harry uses Hagrid's gift flute.

Cerberus, the otherworldly doberman, is at the gates guarding the gauntlet of trials to the Stone (or spiritual perfection), because the first step in spiritual life and alchemical work is renunciation of the world. This is the first rung on "the ladder of divine ascent" **(see St. John Climacos, *The Ladder*, chapter 1)** and the most difficult. As a sign of this, Quirrell struggles with the Fluffy obstacle above all others, which is why it takes him so long to enter through the trap door.

Renunciation is the better part of purification, and it is not until Harry throws off earthly concerns (the House Cup, detentions, being expelled, life itself) that he is able at last to enter the trap door:

> "I'm going out of here tonight and I'm going to try and get to the Stone first."
>
> "You're mad!" said Ron.
>
> "You can't!" said Hermione. "After what McGonagall and Snape have said? You'll be expelled!"
>
> "SO WHAT?" Harry shouted. "Don't you understand? If Snape gets hold of the Stone, Voldemort's coming back! Haven't you heard what it was like when he was trying to take over? There won't be any Hogwarts to get expelled from! ... Do you think he'll leave you or your families alone if Gryffyndor wins the house cup? If I get caught before I get to the Stone, well, I'll have to go back to the Dursleys and wait for Voldemort to find me there, it's only dying a bit later than I would have, because I'm never going over to the Dark Side! I'm going through that trapdoor tonight and nothing you two say is going to stop me! Voldemort killed my parents, remember?" (*Stone*, p. 270)

In Part Two, we discussed Harry, Ron, and Hermione as living symbols of the powers of the soul. This platonic doctrine (after its baptism and correction) became the teaching of the Church, and especially of the Eastern Church fathers.

The Western Church and the East parted company after the West was invaded by Arian Goths, Huns, and Franks. Following several hundred years of isolation from classical philosophy and Eastern Christian tradition, the West was reintroduced to Aristotle by the Spanish Muslims. Throughout the subsequent Middle Ages and Reformation, Roman Catholics and Protestants thought of the soul in Aristotelian language instead of in Plato's terms.

This is relevant to our story, believe me. Each trial Harry faces in his race to get the Philosopher's Stone reflects a faculty or kind of soul in the Aristotelian scholastic model. Rowling is careful to create an obstacle course symbolizing the soul's qualities and powers; to reach perfection (the Philosopher's Stone), Harry must necessarily show himself to have surpassed each obstacle within himself.

The scholastic model, following Aristotle and Aquinas, is that there are three kinds of soul: vegetative, sensitive, and intellective. The powers or faculties closely tied to each kind are: (1) nourishment and reproduction with the vegetative; (2) discrimination and will with sensitivity to data; and (3) the rational and spiritual with the intellective kind (see Aristotle, *On the Soul*; William Wallace, *The Elements of Philosophy*, p. 62; and the relevant articles on soul in *The New Catholic Encyclopedia*).

What do Harry, Ron, and Hermione find when they jump through the trap door? They descend, of course, "miles under the school" into a netherworld crucible where their worthiness will be tested.

First is the test for the vegetative kind of soul, by means of the vicious plant "Devil's snare". It wraps itself around Ron and Harry without their knowledge, and only the application of fire (it prefers the dark and damp) saves them from being strangled by it. The powers associated with the vegetative kind of soul are nourishment and reproduction; let's call them food and sex.

Hermione, the Mr. Spock of Hogwarts, is unaffected by these most carnal of temptations, so scrambles free easily. Ron and Harry, representing desire and the heart respectively, clearly have unresolved issues with this vegetative part of the soul, which is tied to the body and its needs. Hermione saves them after Harry (always cool under pressure) guides her to the answer: light and heat to treat the dark and damp within us. The upwardly-moving or spiritual elements in fire move us beyond our downward, earth-tied concerns for the physical body. Think Four Elements!

On to the next test, which is one of "discrimination" or choice (see **Aristotle's** *Nicomachean Ethics*, **Book III, chapter 4**). The team has to find the single winged key that fits the locked door on the opposite end of the chamber, out of hundreds of flying keys. After discerning that the key must be an old, big, and silver one, they mount broomsticks and fly into the cloud of keys. Harry spots the right one and coordinates their attack; Desire (Ron) attacks, Reason prevents escape, and Spirit makes the grab.

What's the poetry of this passage? The only way to right choosing is alignment of the soul's powers in obedience to the spirit, which discriminates correctly among all choices and "grabs the ring". Desire or Mind cannot find or catch the right key except in obedience to the Heart. Next test, please.

To pass the magical chessboard test, they must become players and win the game. Ron is in charge here, because this is the ultimate test of the willing or desiring faculty he embodies. Of course, Ron chooses the passionate, erratic knight, and assigns the linear, analytical-thinking Hermione the rook (which only moves in straight lines). Harry, the heart or spiritual center, becomes — what else? — a Bishop. No doubt the diagonal motion of this piece reflects the thinking of a symbolist.

Why is the chess game, what Americans think of as an egghead sport, the test for will — and the last or highest test for Ron, our desiring part? Because to win this game, Ron must sacrifice himself. There is no greater challenge for the appetitive faculty than to forego its selfish interests and focus on the greater good. Ron transcends himself in selfless sacrifice and the test is passed. On to the next test.

It's a freebie! Harry and Hermione get a pass on tackling the troll for Quirrell has already knocked it out. At this level of the soul's perfection — we're up to the intellective kind and spiritual faculty — the troll fight wouldn't have made any sense. If you were disappointed to miss out on this fight, remember that the Terrible Trio already dispatched of a troll in their friendship-forging adventure on Halloween (*Stone*, p. 176). Next test!

"Pure logic" — Snape has left a word puzzle beside seven bottles of potions that will kill or liberate. This is Hermione's exam, of course, and Mind solves the puzzle without trouble. But there's only enough left in the bottle for one of them to go forward and one to return. Harry takes charge and sends Mind back for help. Hermione hugs him and tells him he's a great wizard before retiring.

Harry, because virtue at its purest is unaware of its goodness, thinks she is the better of the two. However, he knows that he must be the one to go on, because the next test is the final exam: spiritual perfection or death. This is the end of the alchemical process, Harry's Final Judgment.

And this test? It's our old friend the Mirror of Erised! Quirrell and Voldemort are standing in front of it, trying to find the Stone, and all Quirrell can see is himself giving it to Voldemort. Dumbeldore tells Harry why after the test:

> "How did I get the Stone out of the mirror?" [Harry asked.]
>
> "Ah, now, I'm glad you asked me that. It was one of my more brilliant ideas, and, between you and me, that's saying

something. You see, only one who wanted to *find* the Stone — find it, but not use it — would be able to get it, otherwise they'd just see themselves making gold or drinking Elixir of Life. My brain surprises even me sometimes…" **(Stone, p. 300)**

Quirrell is clueless in front of the mirror, but not Harry. Because of Dumbledore's coaching about the Mirror months before, explaining that the happiest man in the world would see only his reflection, Harry knows what he will see — it won't be his family. After the trials of purification he has just passed through, Harry knows he will see himself only wanting the Stone for itself.

What I want more than anything else in the world at the moment, he thought, is to find the Stone before Quirrell does. So if I look in the mirror, I should see myself finding it — which means I'll see where it's hidden! But how can I look without Quirrell realizing what I'm up to? (Stone, p. 297)

This passage is key; it's one of very few italicized paragraphs in the **Harry Potter** books that is not either a letter or book passage, and the only one in **Stone**. In Part Two's treatment of alchemy, we learned that the authentic and accomplished alchemist is able to produce the Stone in consequence of his spiritual achievement. It is a *byproduct* of that perfection, as are immortality and the riches of transcending the world, rather than the *end* or goal of it. We know Dumbledore and Flamel are of this perfected type because they destroy the Stone at book's end.

Dumbledore has set up the final hurdle to getting the Stone in poetic fashion; the mirror reflects the spiritual quality of whoever stands before it. To produce the Stone from the mirror, the seeker must be passionless, "spiritually apathetic" as the

Greek Fathers say, not desiring any private gain or advantage. One's worthiness to hold or find the Stone *is a reflection* of the quality of one's desires. Quirrell, consumed by Voldemort and his own lust for power, cannot get the Stone — but Harry, of course, sees himself put the Stone in his own pocket.

This is all very interesting, I hear you saying, but what do alchemy, Aristotle, and this Mirror/Stone puzzle have to do with Christianity? Good question. The answer is "quite a bit".

You probably remember that alchemy was not its own religion or spiritual path — it only existed as a discipline within revealed traditions. To Christians, the alchemical process was symbolic of the way to spiritual perfection or *theosis* (divinization), and the Philosopher's Stone, as the end result of this process, was a symbol for Christ.

Having completed a trial by fire and spiritual purification, Harry is able to see and receive this symbol of Christ, because he has no desire to use it for his own advantage but seeks it in loving service to others. Only the pure of heart will see God (see Matthew 5: 8); the Mirror reflects the heart's desire.

The purified Harry sees and receives the Christ, then flees from the two-faced evil of Quirrell/Voldemort — and something fascinating happens. The two-headed monster is unable to touch or have any contact with Harry without burning, quite literally. Dumbledore saves Harry in the end and (after Harry's three-day resurrection) explains what happened:

"But why couldn't Quirrell touch me?"

"Your mother died to save you. If there is one thing Voldemort cannot understand, it is love. He didn't realize that love as powerful as your mother's for you leaves its own mark. Not a scar, no visible sign... to have been loved so deeply, even though the person who loved us is gone, will give us some protection forever. It is in your very skin. Quirrell, full of hatred, greed, and ambition, sharing his soul with Voldemort, could not touch you for this reason. It was agony to touch a person marked by something so good." **(Stone, p. 299)**

If there is a single meaning to the **Potter** books, it is that love conquers all. And of all loves, sacrificial love is the most important, because it has conquered death. Harry's protection against the assault of the evil one is the love shown years ago by someone who made the greatest sacrifice for him. His bond with that sacrifice and the love it demonstrated permeates his person and repels all evil. Voldemort cannot touch him because of Harry's worthiness to receive the Christ, and because of the Christ-like love and sacrifice that shield him.

If that's not plain enough a Christian message for you, there are two more Christian doctrines taught in **Philosopher's Stone**.

Traditional Christians are struck especially by the Unicorn scene in the Forbidden Forest. Harry and Draco Malfoy have been given a detention, requiring them to help Hagrid find what is killing the unicorns in the forest. What they find is a dead unicorn — and its murderer.

It was the unicorn all right, and it was dead. Harry had never seen anything so beautiful and sad. Its long, slender legs were stuck out at odd angles where it had fallen and its mane was spread pearly white on the dark leaves.

Harry had taken one step toward it when a slithering sound made him freeze where he stood. A bush on the edge of the clearing quivered.... Then, out of the shadows, a hooded figure came crawling across the ground like some stalking beast. Harry, Malfoy, and Fang stood transfixed. The cloaked figure reached the unicorn, lowered its head over the wound in the animal's side, and began to drink its blood. (*Stone,* **p. 256)**

Harry is saved by Firenze the Centaur, who explains to Harry why someone would drink unicorn's blood:

"Harry Potter, do you know what unicorn blood is used for?"

"No," said Harry, startled by the odd question. "We've only used the horn and tail hair in Potions."

"That is because it is a monstrous thing, to slay a unicorn," said Firenze. "Only one who has nothing to lose, and everything to gain, would commit such a crime. The blood of a unicorn will keep you alive, even if you are an inch from death, but at a terrible price. You have slain something pure and defenseless to save yourself, and you will have but a half-life, a cursed life, from the moment the blood touches your lips." (*Stone,* **p. 258)**

The centaur is a symbol of a perfect man and an imaginative icon of Christ riding into Jerusalem. Here, this Centaur is talking about another symbol of Christ, the unicorn (see **Part Two for an explanation of this symbolism)**. That the blood of the unicorn will curse those who drink it unworthily, and that it has life-giving power, echoes St. Paul's discourse on the unworthy reception of Communion, which is the blood of Christ:

For I have received of the Lord that which I also delivered unto you, That the Lord Jesus the same night in which he was betrayed took bread: And when he had given thanks, he brake it and said, Take, eat: this is my body which is broken for you: this do in remembrance of me.

After the same manner also he took the cup, when he had supped, saying, This cup is the new testament in my blood; this do ye, as oft as ye drink it, in remembrance of me. For as often as ye eat this bread and drink this cup, ye do shew the Lord's death till he come.

Wherefore whosoever shall eat this bread, and drink this cup of the Lord, unworthily, shall be guilty of the body and blood of the Lord. But let a man examine himself, and so let him eat of that bread, and drink of that cup. For he that eateth and drinketh unworthily, eateth and drinketh damnation to himself, not discerning the Lord's body. **(1 Corinthians 11: 23-29)**

Another Christian echo is in the burning of Quirrell's hands and skin when they make contact with Harry; Quirrell burns and dies in agony. Rowling wheels out here traditional Christian doctrine concerning God's judgment and the nature of heaven and hell. Dr. Alexandre Kalomiros cites St. Peter Damascene, St. Symeon the New Theologian, and St. Makarios the Great in support of this explanation:

God is Truth and Light. God's judgment is nothing else than our coming into contact with truth and light. In the day of the Great Judgment all men will appear naked before this penetrating light of truth. The 'books' will be opened. What are these 'books'? They are our hearts. Our hearts will be opened by the penetrating light of God, and what is in these hearts will be revealed. If in those hearts there is love for God, those hearts will rejoice seeing God's light. If, on the contrary, there is hatred for God in those hearts, these men will suffer by receiving on their opened hearts this penetrating light of truth which they detested all their life. **(Kalomiros, *River of Fire*, p. 18)**

The late Reverend Dr. John Romanides, Professor of Patristic Theology at the University of Thessalonica, concludes:

> God himself is both heaven and hell, reward and punishment. All men have been created to see God unceasingly in His uncreated glory. Whether God will be for each man heaven or hell, reward or punishment, depends on man's response to God's love and on man's transformation from the state of selfish and self-centered love, to God-like love which does not seek its own ends.... The primary purpose of Orthodox Christianity, then, is to prepare its members for an experience which every human being will sooner or later have. **(Romanides, *Franks, Romans, and Feudalism*, p. 46)**

Back to Harry and Quirrell. Professor Quirrell is possessed by the Evil One. He stands before the judging mirror looking at the quality of the desires reflected from his heart. It sees what possesses him: a selfish and self-centered love apart from God. He is unworthy of the Stone/Christ and the ensuing Elixir of Life, so these are kept from him. When he touches someone blanketed by the sacrificial love of the savior (here, of course, Harry's mother) and worthy of having Christ in him, the love of God therein burns Quirrell. He is "judged" and "goes to hell" aflame.

So what is ***Harry Potter and the Philosopher's Stone*** about? Written in the symbolism of alchemy and traditional Christian doctrine, it is an ode to the purification and perfection of the soul in Christ and His saving, sacrificial love. The perfected soul at death will experience the glory and love of God as joy; the soul that has not transcended, that has consumed itself with pursuit of power and love of self apart from God, will experience the same glory as agony and fire.

Chapter 12

The Meaning
of
Chamber of Secrets

And what was the response to the publication of ***Philosopher's Stone***? It sold very well. Scholastic Press bid six figures for the American publishing rights. Some Christian groups, not just peripheral fundamentalist sects but several mainline churches in England and America, objected to the magical milieu of Harry's world. Other reviewers rushed to its defense (usually reducing objections to straw men while defending all fantasy and fiction); a few noted its literary references. There was no interpretation of the book per se, and no defense from the position that ***Stone*** is a remarkably Christian book.

I think that this last must have startled Ms. Rowling. She has admitted in several interviews that she never expected anything like the sales her books have enjoyed — and she bristles at Christian objections, especially those that suggest she is a Satan worshipper. She remarked at the release of *Goblet of Fire*, that it and *Chamber of Secrets* were the hardest to write and her favorites among the books. She doesn't tell us why, but I have a good guess.

Chamber of Secrets operates on several levels. As in all the books, it tells a rollickin' good yarn while advancing the larger story of Harry and Voldemort. But *Chamber* also provides an answer to her Christian critics within its story, and is a "book about books" to boot. It couldn't have been easy to write, but I have to agree with her, *Chamber* is the best single volume of the series. It is, simultaneously:

- A wonderful mystery/adventure story, tightly plotted;
- A series of revelations about Riddle and other characters, which move along the larger storyline; and
- A response to critics via a textbook demonstration of the meaning and power of Inkling literature.

As a book about books, *Chamber* discusses the quality, value, and dangers of three separate books: Riddle's Diary, Lockhart's oeuvre, and the very *Harry Potter* book the reader is holding and experiencing. Let's see what Rowling has to tell us about each of these three books and speculate on her real-world referents.

Chamber turns on Tom Riddle's diary and what happens when it returns to Hogwarts. When Harry and Ron discover the diary in Moaning Myrtle's toilet, Ron warns Harry about the dangerous magic contained in books.

> Harry looked under the sink where Myrtle was pointing. A small, thin book lay there. It had a shabby black cover and was as wet as everything else in the bathroom. Harry stepped forward to pick it up, but Ron suddenly flung out an arm to hold him back.
>
> "What?" said Harry
>
> "Are you crazy?" said Ron. "It could be dangerous."
>
> "*Dangerous?*" said Harry, laughing. "Come off it, how could it be dangerous?"
>
> "You'd be surprised," said Ron, who was looking apprehensively at the book. "Some of the books the Ministry's confiscated — Dad's told me — there was one that burned your eyes out. And everyone who read *Sonnets of a Sorcerer* spoke in limericks for the rest of their lives. And some old witch in Bath had a book that you could *never stop reading!* You had to just wander around with your nose in it, trying to do everything one-handed. And —"
>
> "All right, I've got the point," said Harry.
>
> The little book lay on the floor, nondescript and soggy.
>
> "Well, we won't find out unless we look at it," he said, and he ducked around Ron and picked it up off the floor.
> (*Chamber*, pp. 230-231)

Rowling is having a little fun here. Notice that the only dangerous book title mentioned by Ron contains the word "Sorcerer" — a word rarely used in the **Harry Potter** series, except that it appears in the title of the American edition of **Philosopher's Stone**. Could she be accusing her American

Christian critics of making laughable accusations? Few if any of those who read **Stone**, after all, have been magically transformed into Wicca coven devotees.

Harry, after Ron's hysterical warnings and barely concealed prediction of a fate worse than death, decides he'll have to read it to find out. I don't doubt that Rowling is advocating this course for the sensible, sober reader: in the matter of a controversial or supposedly dangerous book, you should read it and decide for yourself what it is about.

However, we know for sure that Rowling is not dismissing the possibility that books can be dangerous — for Riddle's diary certainly is. Let's lay out what we know about this evil book:

- It is the diary of Tom Marvolo (a.k.a. Lord Voldemort)
- delivered by Lucius Malfoy
- in a Transfiguration Textbook
- to Ginny Weasley.

Lucius Malfoy's intentions in planting the book in Ginny Weasley's textbook are not, as one might think, to restore Lord Voldemort. Malfoy could have done that on his own, in Quirrell fashion, with any stooge. Dumbledore tells us that the book planting was a "clever plan" to undermine Arthur Weasley's standing among wizards and to destroy the sponsors of the Muggle Protection Act **(Chamber, pp. 335-336)**. Mr. Malfoy is understandably nervous about this Act and the consequent raids to round up "dangerous toys" from dark wizards. Draco Malfoy also suggests that his father was trying to remove the "muggle loving" Dumbledore from Hogwarts — which he succeeded in doing, at least for a while.

Rowling makes her point about the effects of authentically dangerous books through the example of Riddle's diary:

- The innocent (again, *Ginny* should be read as "Virginia" or "virgin")

- are transfigured (the diary is placed in the Transfiguration textbook)

- into the wicked (the possessed Ginny is the one that opens the Chamber and releases the Basilisk)

- by the author of a book of dark magic (Riddle/Voldemort is the bad guy)

- hidden inside their textbooks and pretending to be what they are not.

The effect of the book on Ginny is that she turns into a rooster-murdering, basilisk-releasing servant of Riddle. She thinks she is losing her mind — and she is right. Her mind is now Voldemort's; in this is the death of her innocence and purity. The effect of the book on Harry, too, is remarkable. After his time inside the memory of Tom Riddle, he more than half believes that Hagrid is the heir of Slytherin. It is a pretty powerful drug or confundus charm — or evil magic — that could make Harry suspect his friend, the Dumbledore-adoring gamekeeper.

Rowling isn't telling us to beware of the sneaky diaries of dark wizards. *She is pointing to the dangers hiding in children's textbooks.* In this, she follows C. S. Lewis who discusses just this problem in his book ***The Abolition of Man***. The lead essay,

"Men Without Chests", exposes the harm done by the insidious and sentiment-destroying "moral philosophy" of textbook writers. His powerful conclusion:

> The operation of *The Green Book* and [textbooks of] its kind is to produce what may be called Men without Chests. It is an outrage that they should be commonly spoken of as intellectuals. This gives them the chance to say that he who attacks them attacks Intelligence. It is not so. They are not distinguished from other men by any unusual skill in finding truth nor any virginal ardour to pursue her. Indeed it would be strange if they were: a persevering devotion to truth, a nice sense of intellectual honour, cannot be long maintained without the aid of a sentiment which [the textbook writers] could debunk as easily as any other. It is not excess of thought but defect of fertile and generous emotion that marks them out. Their heads are no bigger than the ordinary: it is the absence of the chest beneath that makes them seem so.
>
> And all the time — such is the tragi-comedy of our situation — we continue to clamour for those very qualities we are rendering impossible. You can hardly open a periodical without coming across the statement that what our civilization needs is more "drive", or dynamism, or self-sacrifice, or "creativity." In a sort of ghastly simplicity we remove the organ and demand the function. We make men without chests and expect of them virtue and enterprise. We laugh at honour and are shocked to find traitors in our midst. We castrate and bid the geldings be fruitful.
> (Lewis, *Abolition of Man*, pp. 34-35)

In other words, the hidden "dark wisdom" in our children's school books are transforming them from something human into people who are somehow less than human. Because of their having grown up "having read the wrong sort of books" (see Eustace Scrubb in Lewis' *The Voyage of the Dawn Treader* and Mark Studdock in *That Hideous Strength*), they are incapable of the sentiments and emotions that buttress and create moral excellences such as courage. Rowling communicates this real danger of the vacant naturalism and godlessness endemic in textbooks, through the mind of Tom Riddle hidden in Ginny's Transfiguration schoolbook. This danger is so much more real today, having won the day, that it is perhaps less apparent to us than it would have been in Lewis' time.

I think this is also part of Rowling's intended response to the objections to Magic in her books. We have already read Lewis' response to his own Christian critics: magic, he explained, can be a counter-spell, and magic in edifying fiction is just that — a counter-spell to the enchantment of modernity. One way to appreciate Rowling's genius (as well as the tragi-comic objections of some Christians) is in understanding this enchantment and Rowling's attack on it in her books. So let's take a closer look at it.

Phillip Johnson, Professor of Law at the University of California, Berkeley, and author of *Darwin on Trial* and *Reason in the Balance*, is America's most pointed critic of the materialist regime that monopolizes public discourse and education. He has argued persuasively that the religious belief that nothing exists outside the realm investigated by science (i.e., energy and matter or "nature") has become the *de facto* and often *de jure* state religion of the United States.

This irks him because naturalism is illogical and self-contradictory; nature is unable to explain itself (or even explain "explaining") without reference to something (say, "truth") outside of nature. Consequently, he urges a return to rationality through open consideration of the more credible alternatives to materialism. He hopes this will create a wedge or break in the stranglehold the materialists have on the academy, media, and government.

Johnson proposes *theistic realism* as one such alternative to our naturalist state religion. However, the belief in a God outside nature, even a God who creates nature, does not supplant the cultural core belief that matter and energy are the core reality. In my experience, theists usually imagine their Creator God as a white-bearded grandfather or ball of energy akin to a nebula galaxy in motion (that is, as materialists caricature the Christian God — some to dismiss, some prudentially to adore).

There is no necessary harm in this; such anthropomorphism is in part consequent to Christian language describing the three persons or hypostases of the Holy Trinity. There is a more credible alternative to materialism than this theism, though, in "the symbolist outlook". Symbolism is the opposite of materialism and the preferable alternative, because it posits that the greater reality is not in what is visible and ephemeral, but is in the eternal, supernatural verity that the natural object reflects (see Lewis' *The Discarded Image*, p. 85). A Sufi artist and sheikh described this outlook, the beyond-allegory perspective of Lewis and Tolkien's neo-platonism, as follows:

> It would be quite false to believe that the symbolist outlook consists in selecting from the exterior world images on which to superimpose more or less far-fetched meanings. This would be a waste of time incompatible with wisdom.

On the contrary, the symbolist vision of the cosmos is ... based on the essential nature — or the metaphysical transparency — of phenomena, which are not detached from their prototypes.

The symbolist outlook sees appearances in their connection with essences ... That is to say, it sees things, not "in surface" only, but above all "in depth". It sees things as much in their "participative" or "unitive" dimension as in their "separative" dimension. **(Frithjof Schuon, "The Symbolist Outlook",** *Tomorrow,* **Winter 1966, pp. 52-53)**

To break the "head lock" of materialism requires looking at objects differently — in effect, not as realities in themselves that we can only experience through our passive observation as abstractions, but as "realities which pass into us from God undivided" (Cutsinger, "C. S. Lewis as Apologist and Mystic", *www.cutsinger.net*). This symbolist perspective ties the material world to the greater Reality which creates it and also transcends and informs it.

In this understanding — that beauty, truth, and goodness are not abstractions but real, not ephemeral but eternal, and that their opposites and the material things in which these three qualities appear to us are "as grass in the fire" — is both the root of the symbolist outlook contra materialism and the genius of Rowling's use of magic. Rowling's magical world, existing alongside the pale, materialist Muggle world, is the same world experienced "diagonally" — revealing what is eternal in the ephemeral, the quality in the quantity.

"Diagon Alley", as not a few critics have noted, is word play for "diagonally". This street hidden in the heart of London is a magical avenue of commerce with a Wizard's bank (run by goblins), a wand shop, and the best book store. The numbers on this street are without exception prime numbers (see **Philip Nel, *J. K. Rowling's Harry Potter Novels*, pp. 31-32**). Is this just cleverness run amuck, or is Rowling telling us something?

Rowling asks us to look at the world magically, which is to say, to not accept what we see as all there is. Seen "diagonally", material things (including people!) are better understood in light of their qualities, beauty, truth, and virtue. Rowling's use of prime numbers points us to consider "the quality in quantity": each prime differs from other numbers by representing an essential quality that is irreducible to lesser constituents. She suggests that we look for what is irreducible and eternal in the world, rather than only its "straight on", ephemeral, quantitative value.

And the magic? "Magic" itself is activity that is not obedient to naturalist law and material quantities. Rowling is writing a broadside, Christian attack on the reign of quantity, error, evil, and ugliness in the modern world — what better place to cast the counter-spell to the enchantment of modernity, than in a technology-free world of magic hidden alongside our own? And yet, because of the poetry of magic she uses to defend and symbolize the greater view, she has drawn fire from the very community she defends.

The irony of these Christian objections is that they are uniformly directed against **Harry Potter**'s magic and "occult elements". I do think there is real danger in the occult, but I believe the far more prevalent and spiritually-damning danger is the materialist world view of our time — the very world view Rowling attacks in her fiction. Naturalism makes Christian belief, or any revealed faith, seem ridiculous; in its monopoly upon public discourse, materialist ideology reduces the path to communion with Truth down to a private and eccentric struggle, which sentimental individuals may attempt on the far periphery of the public square.

Those who object to her magic do so with good intentions, I am sure — but they are blind to the great service she does them in her attack on the mortal, invisible enemy inside our gates. It is the materialist heresy that undermines and belittles the traditional world view of Christianity; it is naturalism that immunizes hearts to graces available from the two-fold revelation of God in nature and in scripture. By comparison to this spiritual cancer, in reaction to which many souls are attracted to "spiritualism", the dangers of magic and the occult are mostly in that they distract us from the greater evil.

Now let us return to **Chamber of Secrets**, the **Harry Potter** "book about books".

We have looked at the portrait of evil Rowling paints in Riddle's diary, depicting the dark moral philosophy hiding in modernist textbooks — let's move on to the most comic figure in the **Potter** series, Gilderoy Lockhart.

First, the bad news. Rowling has said in interviews that Gilderoy Lockhart will not return. Any of you having bet on his being the next Defense Against the Dark Arts teacher will have to pay up; **Chamber** will be his only appearance.

But there is good news. In an interview with Amazon.com, Rowling mentioned that Gilderoy Lockhart "started as an exaggerated version of a person I've met." I will give you my best guess as to who is the real Gilderoy. You will have learned it in **The Hidden Key to Harry Potter**!

Break With a Banshee, Gadding with Ghouls, Holidays with Hags, Travels with Trolls, Voyages with Vampires, Wanderings with Werewolves, Year with the Yeti, Gilderoy Lockhart's Guide to Household Pets, Magical Me — Gilderoy Lockhart sure has written a bunch of books. Here is what we know about them:

- Their only purpose is to generate money and fame for Gilderoy;

- The adventure stories are all other magical persons' accomplishments; and

- Women (that is, witches) love them; wizards do not.

Beyond his being "Order of Merlin, Third Class, Honorary Member of the Dark Force Defense League, and five time winner of *Witch Weekly's* Most-Charming-Smile Award" (which he "won't talk about", but manages to mention four times in **Chamber**) — what we learn about Gilderoy himself is:

- He is despised by the teachers as an empty-headed braggart;

- He is adored by the girl students, but he sickens the boys;

- He lives for publicity, large photos of himself, and other people's admiration;

- He favors effeminate colors in robes (jade, lilac, midnight blue, etc.);

- He has one good trick (the memory charm); and

- He is a Coward, "Order of Scaredy Cat, First Class".

His cowardice is revealed in spades when Ginny Weasley is taken by Riddle into the Chamber of Secrets, and the teachers tell Lockhart he has a "free rein at last" to slay the monster.

When Harry and Ron go to him to explain where they think the Chamber is, he tells them this sort of work wasn't "in the job description". He reveals that he has done none of the heroic deeds recounted in his books — and tries to work a memory charm on the boys to protect his secret.

Harry and Ron disarm him, then force him to join in their pursuit of the Chamber. When he grabs Ron's broken wand while "miles under the school", he causes a cave-in by trying another Memory Charm (the wand explodes). The backfiring Charm obliviates his memory, which tragedy compels Dumbledore to say later, "Impaled upon your own sword, Gilderoy!" **(p. 331)**. Most everyone cheers, professors and students alike, when it is announced at the Leaving Feast that Professor Lockhart "would be unable to return next year, owing to the fact that he needed to go away and get his memory back" **(p. 340)**.

In books promoting the virtues of bravery, selflessness, and loyalty, you're not supposed to like Gilderoy. We can laugh at him, but Rowling clearly doesn't want us thinking of him as a role model. Gilderoy is a cartoon figure of everything self-important, self-promoting, superficial, effeminate, and emasculating: everything the **Harry Potter** books hope to overcome and replace with heroic, masculine virtues.

Even if we never met him, the name Rowling gave him would tell us we weren't supposed to like him. "Gilderoy Lockhart" breaks down to "gilded" (given a deceptively attractive appearance) "roi" (French for king) and "lock" (shut tight) "hart" (heart). His name tells us he is a false, "pretty boy" prince with a closed heart, which is to say a "hard heart" and spiritually dead. What more could she tell us? Not much.

The fact that his only magic (his "sword") is the Memory Charm, reveals Rowling's estimation of the value of the real Gilderoy's books. They are lies, only written for the promotion of their author, and, one has to guess, "not for guys". Their strength is they help you forget; they're an escape wherein you can forget what you are about — and what the author really is about, too.

Rowling hates Gilderoy's kind of fiction; it's everything her fiction is not. In this "second book within the book", she offers this character to her critics as a foil for her own work. Children's literature that does not come from true belief nor genuine love and concern for young readers, demeans them and distracts them from spiritual combat-readiness. There are no "stock responses" in Gilderoy's books, no right alignment of soul, and certainly no baptism of the imagination in Christian doctrines and symbols. Rather than Christ, the true king, all we find in Lockhart's books is himself: Gilderoy, the "false king".

So who is the real-life model for Gilderoy Lockhart? My guess is Philip Pullman, author of the **Dark Materials** trilogy and many other much-admired children's books. I have a few reasons for guessing Pullman — some good, some silly. Let's start with the "off the wall" stuff.

1) Every person I have met or read about that loves Pullman's books (to include my daughters) is female. Here are a couple of rave reviews written in the New York Times — by women:

> War, politics, magic, science, individual lives and cosmic destinies are all here. They are not flung together, they are shaped and assembled into a narrative of tremendous pace by a man with a generous, precise intelligence. If you are going to preface your books with passages from Milton,

Rilke and John Ashbery, then you had better write well. Pullman does. His prose has texture and flexibility, like excellent fabric. And he gives us so much. Suspense of course, but such degrees of pleasure, excitement (the excitement of meeting characters, not just adventurers) and grief. And such joy — the joy of thinking, of testing your senses and feelings, of knowing your imagination is entering worlds not dreamed of in the usual philosophies. **(Margo Jefferson, "Harry Potter for Grown-Ups",** *New York Times,* **January 20, 2002)**

One can only hope that where Pullman leads [the children] will follow, and discover the dissenting tradition from which these books spring. This is remarkable writing: courageous and dangerous, as the best art should be. Pullman envisions a world without God, but not without hope. **(Erica Wagner,** *London Times,* **quoted in Sarah Lyall, "The Man who Dared Make Religion the Villain",** *New York Times,* **November 6, 2000)**

2) When *Harry Potter* was still just a new title from a small publishing house, his *Dark Materials* trilogy was big news and Pullman a star at English book fairs — and it was at one of these events that Rowling said she met her "Lockhart" model; and

3) One of the lead characters in multiple Pullman books is named Sallie *Lockhart*.

Onto more serious reasons for Rowling to choose Pullman as her "Man Without Chest" Lockhart model:

4) Pullman feels nothing but disdain for C. S. Lewis and the *Narnia* school of children's fiction.

Mr. Pullman's book offers an explicit alternative to C. S. Lewis' "Chronicles of Narnia", with their pervasive Christian message. In the Narnia books, nestled inside the delightful stories of talking animals, heroic challenges and whimsical scenes, the meaning is clear: the heroes find true happiness only after death, when their spiritual superiority buys them passage to heaven.

It is a conclusion with which Mr. Pullman thoroughly disagrees. "When you look at what C. S. Lewis is saying, his message is so antilife, so cruel, so unjust," he said. "The view that the Narnia books have for the material world is one of almost undisguised contempt. At one point, the old professor says, 'It's all in Plato' — meaning that the physical world we see around us is the crude, shabby, imperfect, second-rate copy of something much better."

Instead, Mr. Pullman argues for a "republic of heaven" where people live as fully and richly as they can because there is no life beyond. "I wanted to emphasize the simple physical truth of things, the absolute primacy of the material life, rather than the spiritual or the afterlife," he said. **(Lyall, *New York Times*, November 6, 2000)**

He opposes the tradition of children's literature as Christian allegory, made famous by the Narnia Chronicles of C. S. Lewis. He is a disciple of that sensual visionary William Blake. And by revising (as Blake did) Milton's theology of Paradise lost and regained, he is paying tribute to Milton the poet and political dissident. He thinks it's dangerous to believe that innocence is at its best when untouched by experience. Or that morality is at its purest when untouched by joy. **(Jefferson, *New York Times*, January 20, 2002)**

5) He is a public atheist and despiser of organized religion.

Shockingly, Mr. Pullman, a 53-year-old former school teacher, has created a world in which organized religion — or, at least, what organized religion has become — is the enemy and its agents are the misguided villains....The author grew up in Wales listening to fantastical stories of his maternal grandfather, an Anglican priest bursting with imaginative energy. "I think he would be shocked by some of the things in [***Dark Materials***]," said Mr. Pullman, who was raised a Protestant but became an atheist as a teenager. (Lyall, *New York Times*, November 6, 2000)

Pullman has made clear in a lovely essay called "The Republic of Heaven" that he is passionately against any religion that puts its vision of the spirit and the afterlife above human life and the natural world, where our moral and spiritual tests as well as our pleasures are found..... And what does he mean by "the Republic of Heaven"? "No kings, no bishops, no priests," says one of the rebels. "The Kingdom of Heaven has been known by that name since the Authority first set himself above the rest of the angels. And we want no part of it. This world is different. We intend to be free citizens of the Republic of Heaven." (Jefferson, *New York Times*, January 20, 2002)

6) The feeling is mutual.

Already, the Catholic Herald in Britain has condemned [Pullman's ***Dark Materials***] trilogy as "truly the stuff of nightmares." (Lyall, *New York Times*, November 6, 2000)

I would not be surprised if Rowling has been condemned by the Catholic Herald, too, as a black magic promoter and Satanist — but I have to hope not. Pullman's fiction is not, as he imagines, of the "dissenting tradition" of Blake and Milton (!), but imaginative stock straight from the materialist warehouse. He doesn't believe in the fantastic realms he creates, only in the naturalist, "this-world-ly" atheism and anti-clericalism he promotes beneath its surface.

The brilliance and real dissent in Lewis' anthropology and cosmology is lost on him; one has to assume because Pullman forgot his grandfather's wisdom after having been enchanted by the demons in his school textbooks. To believe that the natural world and joy in this life are diminished by discerning between what is eternal and what is fleeting in the natural is to have never experienced the natural world in its depth, breadth, and height.

Enough about Pullman and Lockhart — onto the third "book" inside *Chamber of Secrets* — which is the storyline of *Chamber* itself. In contrast with the Pullman/Lockhart genre and Riddle's diary, Rowling does not demean or diminish her readers by indoctrinating them with worldly philosophies.

This book ends instead with an answer for her Christian critics, which one would think they would have a hard time rejecting: the best books for children are the ones that model for them a heroic life in battle with the Evil One, dependent on the graces only available in Christ. That "best book" model is evident in the battle scene at the end of *Chamber*, a Christian morality play for anyone with "eyes to see".

Christian morality plays were the first theater in Western Europe. They were almost without exception either portrayals of Bible stories or "Everyman" allegories of the soul's journey to salvation through thick and thin. Imagine medieval street dramas at public markets and fairs, with itinerant players putting on variations of *Pilgrim's Progress* and the Passion Play. The finish to *Chamber of Secrets*, as morality play, is the most transparent Christian allegory of salvation history since Lewis' *The Lion, the Witch, and the Wardrobe*. Let's look at in detail.

Harry, our "Every Man", enters the Chamber of Secrets to find and rescue Ginny Weasley. He finds her unconscious, and Harry cannot revive her. He meets Tom Riddle. Since he thought Riddle was a friend, Harry asks for his help in restoring Ginny. No deal.

He learns then that Tom Riddle is anything but his friend; Riddle is instead the young Lord Voldemort, Satan's "stand in" throughout the **Harry Potter** books, the Dark Lord or Evil One. Far from helping him revive Ginny, Riddle has been the cause of her near death. Harry boldly confesses to Riddle's face his loyalty to Albus Dumbledore and his belief that Dumbledore's power is greater than Lord Voldemort's.

The Chamber is filled with Phoenix song at this confession, heralding the arrival of Fawkes (Dumbledore's Phoenix), who brings Harry the Sorting Hat of Godric Gryffyndor. The Dark Lord laughs at "what Dumbledore sends his defender" (p. 316) and offers to teach Harry a little lesson: "Let's match the powers of Lord Voldemort, Heir of Salazar Slytherin, against famous Harry Potter, and the best weapons Dumbledore can give him" (p. 317). He releases the giant Basilisk from his reservoir, and the battle is joined.

The look of the Basilisk is death, so Harry runs from it with eyes closed. Fawkes the Phoenix attacks the charging Basilisk and punctures its deadly eyes. Harry cries for help to "someone — anyone" (p. 319) as the Phoenix and blind Basilisk continue to battle, and is given the Sorting Hat — by a sweep of the Basilisk's tail.

Harry throws himself to the ground, rams the hat over his head, and begs for help again. A "gleaming silver sword" comes through the hat (p. 320).

Evil Tom Riddle directs the blind Basilisk at this point to leave the Phoenix and attack the boy. When it lunges for him, Harry drives the sword "to the hilt into the roof of the serpent's mouth" — but one poisonous fang enters Harry's arm as the Basilisk falls to its death. Harry, mortally wounded, falls beside it. The Phoenix weeps into Harry's wound as Riddle laughs at Harry's death.

Too late Riddle remembers the healing powers of Phoenix tears and chases away the Phoenix. He then confronts the prostrate boy and raises Harry's wand to murder him. The Phoenix gives Harry the diary, and Harry drives the splintered Basilisk fang into it. Riddle dies and disappears; red ink pours from the diary. Ginny revives, and they escape by holding the tail feathers of the Phoenix, who flies from the cavern "miles beneath Hogwarts" to safety and freedom above. Harry celebrates with Dumbledore.

Now let's translate this Morality Play and allegory. First, we need to know the cast of characters (*dramatis personae*) and what reality each figure represents:

- Harry is "Every Man";
- Ginny is "Virgin Innocence, Purity";
- Riddle/Voldemort is "Satan, the Deceiver";
- The Basilisk is "Sin";
- Dumbledore is "God the Father";
- Fawkes the Phoenix is "Christ";
- Phoenix Song is "Holy Spirit";
- Gryffyndor's Sword is "the Sword of Faith/Spirit" **(Ephesians 6:17)**;

- The Chamber is "the World"; and

- Hogwarts is "Heaven".

The action of this salvation drama, then, goes like this:

> Man, alone and afraid in the World, loses his innocence. He tries to regain it but is prevented by Satan, who feeds on his fallen, lost innocence. Man confesses and calls on God the Father while facing Satan, and is graced immediately by the Holy Spirit and the protective presence of Christ.

> Satan confronts man with the greatness of his sins, but Christ battles on Man's side for Man's salvation from his sins. God sends Man the Sword of Faith which he "works" to slay his Christ-weakened enemy. His sins are absolved, but the weight of them still mean Man's death. Satan rejoices.

> But, behold, the voluntary suffering of Christ heals Man! Man rises from the dead, and, with Christ's help, Man destroys Satan. Man's innocence is restored, and he leaves the World for Heaven by means of the Ascension of Christ. Man, risen with Christ, lives with God the Father in joyful thanksgiving.

I can imagine where different types of Christians could disagree with this thumbnail sketch of Everyman's salvation drama, in terms of emphasis and specific doctrines. However, it would be a very odd Christian indeed that could not understand what this story is about, and would not admire the artistry of Rowling's allegory. Using only traditional symbols, from the "Ancient of Days" figure as God the Father to the satanic serpent versus the Christ-like phoenix ("the Resurrection Bird"), the drama takes us from the fall to eternal life without a hitch. There's nothing philosophical or esoteric here. (Can you say, "no alchemy"?)

Rowling spells out here, for anyone with eyes to see, that her books are Christian and in bold opposition to the spiritually dangerous books our children are often given. *Chamber of Secrets* is an unequaled example in the genre that provides an engaging, enlightening, and edifying reading experience for children — as well as a powerful rebuke and wake-up call to her Christian critics.

What is *Chamber of Secrets* about? Perhaps in response to the absence of intelligent discussion of *Stone's* meaning, Rowling reveals in her second book that she is writing Inkling fiction: stories that prepare children for Christian spiritual life and combat with evil. Talk about baptizing the imagination with Christian symbols and doctrine!

She also points out to her Christian critics that their real enemies are not her counter-materialist magic, but both the dark magic hidden in their children's textbooks and the "good children's books" written by atheists and the worldly minded.

Chamber of Secrets is a *tour de force* operating on at least three levels of meaning simultaneously. I can understand Rowling's struggle in writing it, and I agree with her that it is the best single volume of the series. As a nod to its movie adaption, I give *Chamber* Five Stars and Two Thumbs Up.

Chapter 13

The Meaning
of
Prisoner of Azkaban

Remarkably, the critical reaction to **Chamber of Secrets** was not the revelation of Rowling's meaning and purpose in writing. The books continued to sell well; in fact, Rowling became something of a celebrity as word spread about these wonderful children's books. Unfortunately, this popularity stirred a well-reported Christian backlash, especially insofar at it conformed to the media's prejudices about Christian believers' zeal to ban and burn witch books.

The spectrum of Christian opinion about the **Potter** books split between "they're OK" and "they're not OK" — without any notice that they are implicitly and explicitly Christian works. Despite this reaction (or because of it), sales of the first two books exploded. Their popularity with hard-to-reach boys and girls led not a few librarians and educators to laud the books as important tools in the fight against illiteracy.

However, the release of the third book in the series, *Prisoner of Azkaban*, earned a different response than the first books. Sales continued to grow, yes, along with the beginning of the idea that "Pottermania" was more than just a fad. But for the first time, not a few complaints were heard and printed that the latest *Potter* installment wasn't really a children's book. *Prisoner's* ending especially upset some fans, who viewed it as too complicated and confusing, too dark and scary, too unhappy and unsatisfying. Voldemort isn't even vanquished this time; he seems stronger in the end than at the beginning!

Rowling has said many times that her books have all been outlined in some detail for years — down to the last word in the seventh book! So perhaps it is just my own churlishness that I see — in the tone change between the second and third books — the possibility of a change in Ms. Rowling herself, born of frustration. Could it be that the third book was made so much more difficult because of the disappointingly "childish" and mechanical critical response to her first two books?

Let there be no confusion: there is a change from *Stone* and *Chamber* to *Prisoner*. As rich and tightly woven as the first books were, *Prisoner* represented a big jump in complexity and opaqueness. Of the four books published to date, **Prisoner** is the most remarkably dense, dark, and challenging work.

It is also obviously psychological in a way that the first two books were not. Among other things, Rowling makes implicit references throughout **Prisoner** to specific cases in the history of psychology. Lupin the werewolf, for example, is a nod of the head to Sigmund Freud's ground-breaking interpretations in his case published and known as "The Wolf-Man". Hermione's adventures and struggles with her "Time Turner" point to Carl Jung's doctrine of synchronicity.

Also reappearing are alchemy and purification through the conjunction of opposites, a favorite Jungian theme. The layers of meaning, specific archetypes, interpretation of dreams, and father figures in **Prisoner** all point to Jung (transcending Freud's mechanical Oedipal complex). I have come to think of **Prisoner** as "The Psychological Novel for Jungian Analysts".

Not many of us are Jungian analysts, though, so the psychological interpretation of the book may take us far afield. As with its predecessors, **Prisoner** is clearly an Inkling novel — albeit more akin to Lewis' **Space Trilogy** and Tolkien's **The Lord Of The Rings** than to the **Narnia** books (aside from the darkness and psychological profundity of certain scenes in **The Silver Chair** and **The Last Battle**). We will stick to the obvious, then, rather than the obscure. Let's take a look at **Prisoner** as being:

- really "The Return of Voldemort: Book One", leading to apocalyptical World War; and

- about "Escape" and "Revealed Secrets".

We can see in **Prisoner** the opening shots of the World War about to begin in the fifth book, with Harry learning much more about the death of his parents and Peter Pettigrew escaping to aid Voldemort's return to a physical body. The stage is set at the end of **Prisoner** for the drama that unfolds at the end of **Goblet of Fire** and the crisis that will be resolved in the last three books.

Prisoner is also largely about Escape and Revelation. Who Escapes? Who is Revealed?

- *Sirius Black* escapes from Azkaban and is revealed to be, not the murderer of Harry's parents and servant of Lord Voldemort (as everyone assumes), but Harry's long-suffering protector and authentic God-father;

- *Buckbeak the Hippogriff* escapes execution and is revealed to be, not the dangerous bird the Ministry thinks he is, but the means of Sirius' salvation;

- *Peter Pettigrew*, we learn, escaped Sirius and a death sentence years ago (by feigning his own murder at Black's hands), and he is revealed to be the real Judas "secret keeper", servant and spy of Voldemort — as well as the betrayer of James and Lily Potter;

- *Pettigrew* also escapes execution in the present (because of Harry's mercy) along with capture, and is revealed to be an animagus — a rat literally and figuratively;

- *Lupin*'s werewolf status is revealed at last, but he "escapes" from his own mistaken beliefs both about his friends Black and Pettigrew, and about the limits of Dumbledore's ability to understand and forgive.

The most important escapes, changes, and revelations in *Prisoner*, though, revolve around Harry Potter himself:

- He escapes from Privet Drive and the badgering of Aunt Marge at the beginning of the book, revealing himself to be an angry young man with a host of "unresolved issues" about his parents and his own identity;

- He escapes from these passions via dissolution of his confusion (and revelation of his past) in the alchemical crucible of the Shrieking Shack, revealing himself by his protection of Pettigrew, to be the merciful son of his father; and

- He escapes his fears and depression that crystallize in the presence of the dementors, revealing himself by his conjuring of the Patronus at book's end and by his defeat of the dementor host to be an advanced magician of no little power.

The first two of these escapes and revelations were discussed at some length in Part Two of this book. But Harry's battle to overcome the dementors is the larger part of the plot in *Prisoner* so it warrants interpretation.

Rowling has answered every question about the dementors with the same explanation: they are incarnations of depression and despair. She has, of course, given them a name reflecting their meaning: *de* is Latin for "from" or "out of", while *ment* comes from the Latin word *mens* meaning "mind". The dementors are literally the "drive-you-out-of-your-mind-ers". Lupin gives us some details about these guardians of Azkaban:

> "Dementors are among the foulest creatures that walk this earth. They infest the darkest, filthiest places, they glory

in decay and despair, they drain peace, hope, and happiness out of the air around them. Even muggles feel their presence, though they can't see them. Get too near a dementor and every good feeling, every happy memory will be sucked out of you. If it can, the dementor will feed on you long enough to reduce you to something like itself... soul-less and evil. You'll be left with nothing but the worst experiences of your life." *(Prisoner,* **p. 187)**

Hagrid was imprisoned in Azkaban at the end of **Chamber**. He tells Harry, Ron, and Hermione about it:

"Yeh've no idea," said Hagrid quietly. "Never bin anywhere like it. Thought I was goin' mad. Kep' goin' over horrible stuff in me mind...the day I got expelled from Hogwarts... day me dad died...day I had to let Norbert go....

"Yeh can' really remember who yeh are after a while. An' yeh can' see the point o' livin' at all. I used ter hope I'd jus' die in me sleep.... When they let me out, it was like bein' born again, ev'rythin' came floodin' back, it was the bes' feelin' in the world. Mind, the dementors weren't keen on lettin' me go." *(Prisoner,* **pp. 220-221)**

Dementors, then, crush their victims' humanity by feeding on their "hope, happiness, and desire to survive" **(p. 237)**. Lupin reports that "they don't need walls and water to keep the [Azkaban island] prisoners in, not when they're all trapped inside their own heads, incapable of a single cheerful thought. Most of them go mad within weeks" **(p. 188)**. But they have a "last and worst weapon.... The Dementor's Kiss":

"It's what dementors do to those they wish to destroy utterly. I suppose there must be some kind of mouth under there, because they clamp their jaws upon the mouth of the victim and — and suck out his soul."

Harry accidentally spat out some of his butterbeer.

"What — they kill — ?"

"Oh no, " said Lupin. "Much worse than that. You can exist without your soul, you know, as long as your brain and heart are still working. But you'll have no sense of self anymore, no memory, no... anything. There's no chance at all of recovery. You'll just — exist. As an empty shell. And your soul is gone forever... lost."
(*Prisoner*, p. 247)

The Kiss is Rowling's poetic expression of the human "consolation" found in despair: a living death, worse than physical death — only soul-less existence. The dementor's effect on Harry even without this kiss is remarkable enough. Just being near one, Harry experiences the live replay of his parents' murder by Lord Voldemort over his crib. Needless to say, this knocks him out and off his feet — and, at the climax of a Quidditch match, off his broomstick. The fall nearly kills him, and Gryffyndor loses the match.

This won't do. Harry needs a defense against these dementors and goes to the Defense Against the Dark Arts (DADA) teacher, Remus Lupin. Though Lupin protests that he is not "an expert at fighting dementors, Harry...quite the contrary" **(p. 189)**, he agrees to give Harry tutorials in how to dispel a dementor.

Rowling has said that Lupin is a favorite character of hers; his incurable werewolf condition is much like her mother's fatal Multiple Sclerosis, especially in how people are unable to see around it. She has promised he will return. What do we know about him?

Lupin has been a werewolf since childhood. Dumbledore allowed him into Hogwarts and created a place for him to weather his monthly, monstrous transformations. He would be taken to the Shrieking Shack through a passage guarded by the Whomping Willow, where he would stay until he resumed human form.

His best friends — James Potter, Sirius Black, and Peter Pettigrew — discover his secret and resolve to become animagi so they can spend time with Lupin when he transforms into a werewolf. In their animal forms, the four have great adventures outside the shack, all unbeknownst by Dumbledore.

When Pettigrew betrays the Potters to Voldemort, Black is accused of the betrayal and of murdering Pettigrew. He is thrown into Azkaban without a trial. No one except Lupin knows that Black is an animagus — and Lupin is not telling. He confesses he was afraid of losing Dumbledore's high opinion; only the Headmaster's kindness had let him into Hogwarts, and Lupin had repaid that kindness by irresponsibly romping through the countryside in his werewolf form with his animagi friends.

Lupin appears to be impoverished at his first appearance in *Goblet* on the Hogwarts Express, so we may assume it isn't easy for a werewolf to get on in the wizarding world. He has been given the DADA teaching job despite his lupine condition and (more importantly) despite his friendship with Black. Lupin and Snape (no fan of Black or his friends) are especially sensitive about this relationship and the corresponding possibility that Lupin is somehow aiding Black.

This last bothers Lupin because he is in some measure helping Black by keeping his animagus identity secret. Lupin has his job because Dumbledore believes in him; he is unwilling to test Dumbledore's good will and reveal the secret fellowship of Messrs. Moony, Wormtail, Padfoot and Prongs.

In **Prisoner**, Lupin acts as Harry's tutor and *de facto* Jungian analyst. He is not only coaching Harry in dementor defense, but in his repeated exposure to his parents' dramatic demise, Harry is also overcoming it as a trauma. This is an echo of Dumbledore's "minor work" in **Stone**, when he taught Harry that it won't do to stand before the Mirror of Erised and long for his dead parents. Harry relearns this critical lesson with Lupin. After one especially traumatic session, Harry reflects:

> He felt drained and strangely empty, even though he was so full of chocolate. Terrible though it was to hear his parents' last moments replayed inside his head, these were the only times Harry had heard their voices since he was a very small child. But he'd never be able to produce a proper Patronus if he half wanted to hear his parents again…
>
> "They're dead," he told himself sternly. "They're dead and listening to echoes of them won't bring them back. You'd better get a grip on yourself if you want that Quidditch Cup." **(p. 243)**

Chocolate, the ultimate comfort food, helps speed recovery from exposure to a dementor, but defense from these soul-sucking nasties involves what Lupin and Hermione both classify as extremely advanced magic. What Lupin tries to teach Harry is how to conjure a "Patronus" using the "Patronus Charm".

This is no easy feat, and Lupin is pained by the experience as well. When Harry says he heard his father speaking, Lupin almost loses it (p. 241). No doubt the analyst is experiencing some catharsis of the unresolved issues surrounding James Potter's death, namely, Lupin's still being Black's "secret keeper". He almost bites Harry's head off when he asks Lupin in all innocence if he knew Sirius Black (p. 242).

The Patronus Charm requires the wizard to say the words "Expecto Patronum" and to concentrate as hard as possible on a happy memory, to fill the heart with joy. At first, Harry is only able to conjure a thin, wispy Patronus when he practices with the boggart. The problem is he "half wants" to hear his parents even in their death throes. After he gives himself a stern talking to (quoted above), he finds he can do it. He conjures a magnificent Patronus while chasing the Snitch at his next Quidditch match, and dispels the dementor impersonators from Slytherin.

However, Harry struggles in later attempts to conjure the Patronus, and is only able to do it in the presence of the real thing after his remarkable experience in the Shrieking Shack. A closer look at the words of the charm reveals why — and the larger meaning of **The Prisoner of Azkaban** as well.

David Colbert has written a charming companion book for the **Harry Potter** books called **The Magical Worlds of Harry Potter** (for more on this and other books about Harry, see Appendix B). It's a hoot! But in one **Magical** section called "Latin for Wizards", there's a mistake. Mr. Colbert's Latin is probably in better shape than my own, but he blows the translation of the Patronus Charm. He says *Expecto Patronum* comes "from *expecto*, to throw out; and *patronus*, guardian" **(Magical Worlds, p. 125)**. It makes sense as a charm — "I throw forth a guardian" — but it's not what the Latin says.

Expecto is an ellision of *ek or e* ("out from, out for") and *specto* ("look, watch"). *Expecto*, consequently, doesn't mean "to throw out" (that would have been *expello* or *expelliarmus* — as in "I punched the teacher so they *expello*-ed me from school"). What it does mean is "to look out for, await, long for expectantly". In the Latin version of the Apostle's Creed, the "await, look for" conclusion ("*I look for* the resurrection of the dead and the life of the world to come") begins with the word *expecto*.

Patronus can mean "guardian". But in the context of **Prisoner**, it's good to realize the word *patronus* comes from the root *pater*, which means "father". *Patronus* means "little father" or "second father", which you can see in the English word that most obviously derives from it: "patron", the person who pays your bills like dad did while you work on a special project. The word can be used as "godfather" (especially as in the movie with Brando), "guardian", or "deliverer" (as in "from danger"). In this last sense, "savior" is not a bad translation.

Expecto patronum, consequently, can be interpreted a couple of ways. Because Harry's Patronus comes in the shape of his dad as animagus, you could say it means "I look for the figure or shade of my father". (Given the way many people feel about their dads, mustering up the height of happiness might be a real trick while saying these words.)

The way Rowling uses this phrase, however, echoes its use from the Apostle's Creed — "I long for my savior and deliverer". The charm is said in joyful expectation and in faith that deliverance is coming. I have three reasons for thinking this explicitly Christian meaning is the correct interpretation:

- Lupin is no great shakes at this charm. His haunting problem is not his trouble with lunar cycles, but his lack of faith in Dumbledore's love. Dumbledore has been his "second father" and "patron", but Lupin cannot sincerely say *expecto patronum* with joy and faith, because he doesn't trust that Dumbledore will love him if he were to know the truth about him.

- Harry's Patronus takes the shape of a stag that shines "as bright as a unicorn" **(p. 385)**. Both the stag and the unicorn are traditional symbols of Christ.

- Harry is only able to conjure his Patronus after the Shrieking Shack experience, and after seeing what he thinks is the ghost of his father conjuring a Patronus to save him from the Dementor's Kiss.

What is it about these experiences that create the breakthrough for Harry? The Shrieking Shack is an alchemical crucible with character catalysts for Harry's purification, dissolution, and perfection (as in **Stone**). At the side of the lake, he realizes his identity with his father, on earth as in heaven. That may be a reach for some of you, especially if you're stuck on the improbability of these being implicitly Christian books, so let's walk through it.

In the Shrieking Shack, Harry is surrounded by the four alchemical catalysts and the colors we learned in the discussion of **Philosopher's Stone**. Ron is still "red", passionate sulfur; Hermione is still "mercury" or "quicksilver". The black and white elements, however, are different (though Snape makes an appearance when Sirius is revealed to be not so "black"). Sirius Black, of course, takes the "black" part of unclean "guilt, origin, latent (hidden) forces". As Dumbledore did with the Mirror in **Stone**, Lupin this time performs the "white" initial or minor work, clearing away Harry's paralyzing longing for his parents. He has "flecks of gray" in his brown hair; my mental picture of a werewolf (unconfirmed by the text) is of a silver-gray, giant wolf. Close enough to "white".

Under these contrary influences, Harry's anger, misconceptions, and passion dissolve. He learns the identities of Messrs. Moony, Wormtail, Padfoot, and Prongs, along with the remarkable story of betrayal and escape surrounding the Fidelius Charm that protected Harry's family. He is transformed by these revelations, so he is no longer the out-of-control, angry young man that blew up Maggie Thatcher (I mean, Aunt Marge) on Privet Drive for carelessly insulting his parents. Harry has become a man capable of forgiving both Black for making Pettigrew the Potters' "secret keeper" and Pettigrew for betraying his family to Voldemort.

This last act is one of superhuman contranatural mercy, which no one else in the Shack is capable of. The "gold" purified soul does this in imitation of his father. As Harry puts it: "I'm not doing this [preventing your execution] for you

[Pettigrew]. I'm doing it because — I don't reckon my dad would've wanted them to become killers — just for you" (*Prisoner,* p. 376). This humility, compassion, and mercy is evidence that he has indeed achieved a degree of spiritual perfection; his will and his father's will are one and the same (see John 17:21 and Matthew 6:10, 26:39).

But Harry is just beginning to realize the identity between himself and his father. They leave the shack, and Lupin transforms in the light of the full moon. Black too becomes his animal form to protect everyone from the werewolf, and in the confusion Wormtail escapes. The children hear Black screaming and run to his aid at the side of the lake. Dementors! Harry struggles to conjure a Patronus but fails. He is saved, though, from the Dementor's Kiss by a spectacular unicorn-like Patronus, conjured from across the water by a figure which he thinks is his father.

Dumbledore sends Harry and Hermione back in time to rescue Buckbeak and Black. On this trip, Harry cannot help himself; he has to see if it was his father that saved him. He realizes at last he had not seen his father conjuring the Patronus — he had seen himself. He conjures the spectacular Stag Patronus, the image of his father as Prongs (and Christ) that saves Hermione, Sirius, and himself from the dementors.

Hermione is stunned that Harry is capable of this sort of advanced magic:

> "Harry, I can't believe it….You conjured up a Patronus that drove away all those dementors! That's very, *very* advanced magic…."

"I knew I could do it this time," said Harry, "because I'd already done it…. Does that make sense?" (*Prisoner*, **p. 412**)

It makes sense, Harry, but perhaps only if you look at this as a Christian familiar with the Gospel according to St. John. (See The Rev. Dr. John Romanides article, "Justin Martyr and the Fourth Gospel" at *www.romanity.org*, to understand how the depth of this gospel differs from the three synoptic gospels.)

St. John's Gospel tells us that the Son's relation to the Father, and ours to Him through the Son and His Spirit, are the essential relationships of Christian salvation. That Harry's father appears in the form of a Christ symbol (the son), and that Harry's deliverance (as son) comes at his realization that he is his father (in appearance and will), are Rowling's poetic expression of the essential union of Father and Son for our salvation.

In **Prisoner**, Harry at last comprehends his likeness with his father. By this knowledge he is able to summon a Christ-figure as his salvation, in hopeful, almost certain, and joyous expectation of deliverance. He yells "EXPECTO PATRONUM" without having to think a happy thought **(p. 411)**, because his expectation itself is one pure happy thought.

Sirius Black tells Harry in his last words before flying away from Hogwarts on the wings of a happy hippogriff: "You are — truly your father's son, Harry…" **(p. 415)**. Dumbledore tells him during their end of book consultation, "I expect you'll tire of hearing it, but you do look *extraordinarily* like James" **(p. 427)**. Harry at the end of **Prisoner** has realized his identity with his father.

What is Prisoner of Azkaban about?

I said at the beginning of this chapter that **Prisoner** isn't an easy book. It is a difficult read, and because of its subject matter, many people have told me they find it depressing — which I think is an understandable reaction. **Prisoner** is about how to combat the demons of the modern world: the depression and despair consequent to lack of faith.

Rowling's answer for this problem, though, is anything but depressing. Implicitly and almost explicitly, she tells us the answer is your ability to call on Christ in faith. Escape your ego attachments, and identify instead with your Heavenly Father as His sons in the Spirit.

She also seems to be suggesting that Jungian analysis and counseling may be helpful in this effort! But following Harry's path, she lays out these steps for success beyond analysis:

Understand yourself as son of God in need of patronage and savior.

Harry is a troubled young man when he arrives at Hogwarts this year. He enters counseling for tutorial help in understanding his problems. His enlightened counselor steers him toward the advanced magic of selfless and joyous expectation of a deliverer.

No humility, no grace.

Harry is not equal to this magic until his ego concerns have been purified and dissolved. Only when his family history is clear to him is he capable of the humility necessary to forgive and have mercy. It is a patristic formula — "No humility, no grace" — that explains Harry's new abilities to see and act after the Shrieking Shack.

In humility and joy, cry out in faithful expectation.

Consequent to his forgiveness and mercy in the Shack (in imitation of his father), Harry is able to see his likeness with this father and to cry out in confident (literally "with faith") expectation of his savior. This achievement is the cure for depression and despair.

Look for the Stag (Son of God) to expel the wraiths of despair.

Harry is saved by the Stag Patronus that he conjures, and Sirius is saved by the hippogriff Harry and Hermione ride to his tower window. In Christ, we, too, are delivered from death and from the shadows cast by death in this life: depression and soulless despair.

This may not be as simple a Christian morality play as the one acted out in **Chamber of Secrets**. But it reflects the Inkling themes, Christian symbolism, and doctrine that we have seen in all the **Potter** books.

What Rowling does for alchemy in **Philosopher's Stone** and religious faith in **Chamber**, she does for psychology and therapy in **Prisoner of Azkaban**. Each book reveals its chosen path or spiritual work as beginning and ending in the individual's communion or relationship with Christ.

That **Prisoner**, despite its complexity and profundity, did not derail or even slow the Pottermania juggernaut, speaks to both the hunger for this message and the art with which Rowling delivers it. If I prefer **Chamber** to all the other **Potter** books, it is **Prisoner** that I re-read most often. As a son, man, and daddy, its Christian meaning is especially helpful to me.

Chapter 14

The Meaning
of
Goblet of Fire

If you were on planet earth in July of the year 2000, odds are
good you remember the release of **Goblet of Fire**, the fourth
Harry Potter book. Ms. Rowling and her publishers managed
to get U.S. and U.K. bookstores to agree not to sell the book
until after midnight on July 8th. Amazon.com sold 350,000 copies
prior to release (six times their previous record), while Barnes
and Nobles sold more than 500,000 the first weekend to set
their all-time sales record — incredible for a non-holiday period.
Harry graced the covers of all the weekly newsmagazines, and
people talked of little else — really. I was in a crowded bookstore

at midnight with my kids in costume on July 8th; where were you? Were you the lady dressed as the Sorting Hat? Cute!

And the critical response? Again, no revelation of depth and meaning of the books and not a word about their Christian themes. The companion books began to come out, and two Christian books were released (one panning, one begging each side to respect the other — see Appendix B). Reviewers in the magazines and newspapers expressed delight with its story, the many literary references, and the enthusiasm with which children were reading it. (All together! Say "literacy tool"!)

All this publicity, greater than any book in the series had yet received, also generated continued disdain and protests from Christian groups and high brows, many of whom were quoted in Chapter 1 of this book. More interesting were new complaints saying the book was way too long, had too many new characters, included too many twists at the end, and was too broad in scope. Some folks missed the cozy Hogwarts intramural contests and "small town feel" of the first three books.

Those who complained about the "Big Changes" can't be faulted. Rowling said in every interview that I've read from that time (and she gave quite a few) that *Goblet* was the "turning point" in the seven book series. And she should know. *Goblet of Fire* is a transition novel from personal warfare and largely psychological drama to warfare and social drama on the world stage.

In the first three books, for example, the sports we follow are the Quidditch contests between the four houses at Hogwarts School. Students there have talked before about professional Quidditch teams and national programs, but it has never diminished the intensity or focus on the competition for the intramural Quidditch Cup.

Goblet opens on Privet Drive, but before you know it we are at the World Cup, and suddenly the Quidditch games at Hogwarts seem pretty pedestrian, almost amateur affairs. When Harry gets to Hogwarts, he learns there will be no Quidditch, for the international TriWizard Tournament is coming. First the World Cup, then the Olympics!

What is true of sports is even more true of the continuing war between Harry and Lord Voldemort. In *Stone*, *Chamber*, and *Prisoner*, Harry and Lord Voldemort (or his representative) duke it out, one on one, inside Hogwarts somewhere (even miles underground). While *Goblet* does feature another battle royale between Harry and He-Who-Must-Not-Be-Named, the fight is off-campus, fought in a crowd of Voldemort's supporters, and inconclusive. The reader realizes at the end of *Goblet* that the battle was just the opening engagement of what promises to be a World War.

And the flood of new characters! From the Ministry in London, we meet Bartimeus Crouch (Sr. and Jr.), Alaister "Mad Eye" Moody, Ludo Bagman, Rita Skeeter, and a gaggle of Death Eaters. From overseas come Viktor Krum, Igor Karkaroff, Madame Maxime, and Fleur de la Coeur. And a few new non-persons: Winky the House-elf, the Nifflers, and my personal favorite, the blast-ended Skrewts. I forgot Bertha Jorkins? Well, she never appears on stage except as an unhappy Dumbledore memory and as a shade from Voldemort's wand.

What is amazing about all these new characters, besides their diversity and sheer numbers, is that each one of them plays a major part in either the main drama of the TriWizard tournament or in one of the several themes and "side shows" not on center stage. Rowling introduces all these new players, and by the end of the book they are as believable and important to the storyline as, say, Professor McGonagall, who appears on the first pages of the first book.

The expansion of scenery and multiplication of stage sets are as astonishing as these many changes. Readers of the first three books knew the Hogwarts grounds, the Great Hall, the Gryffyndor Common Room, the Dormitory, and many of the class rooms. They felt right at home. *Goblet* introduces them in a rush to the much wider wizarding world at Hogwarts and abroad. Harry and readers get to see:

The Quidditch World Cup

Harry, Ron, and Hermione get tickets to the World Cup. On their walks through the international campsites, they learn that witches and wizards are in every country — not to mention that there are Hogwarts-like schools in these countries. In the time it takes to draw a wand, they see they are provincials on a world stage.

Hogwarts underwater

Harry dives into the Great Lake on his second TriWizard task. He does not meet the Giant Squid — but he does run into Moaning Myrtle, grindylows, and the mer people.

Hogwarts "True Romance"

Goblet features a yule ball; on promenade night, Harry learns about wizard dancing, rock music, ritual courtship, necking in the bushes, and no little heartache after being turned down by Cho — though Ron's feelings for Fleur and Hermione will probably be more important in the long run (see Part Four). Jane Austen lives!

Life under Voldemort

"Mad Eye" Moody gives Dark Arts lessons in his Defense Against the Dark Arts classes. As he sees and learns about the three "Unforgivable Curses", Harry finally has some real experience of what life was like during Voldemort's reign of terror.

Life with Voldemort today

The first scene of the book is of home life at the Riddle house. The barely human "baby" Voldemort lords it over Wormtail with threats of magical violence. Only Nagini, the enormous serpent pet, is at ease in this nightmare existence, to which scene we return for the "rebirthing party".

Wizard Courtroom

Harry "falls" into Dumbledore's pensieve of memories and has some experience of "wizard justice". He witnesses two trials of Death Eater suspects, both of which are "shadow trials". In the first Stalinist tribunal, no witnesses are called, the judge calls out his hatred for the defendants, and the Death Eaters are sentenced to life terms. In the second O. J.-style trial, popular sportsman Ludo Bagman is released with only the pretense of examination. Harry sees (one hopes) not to expect much from Wizard law-and-order types or magical courtrooms.

Azkaban

Sirius Black tells Harry, Ron, and Hermione what it is really like in the Wizard island prison-fortress. It is no less than an over sized torture chamber or concentration camp with cells.

Dementors as "Guards"? The dark, underside of the wizarding world is evident, and we learn why Dumbledore is so concerned at the end of *Goblet* about the "security" of such a place after Voldemort's return.

Rowling is no doubt a political liberal or "left winger". The sentiments that made her feel at home when she worked at Amnesty International (the international advocacy arm for political prisoners worldwide) are on display in her depictions of the justice system in the parallel magical world of Great Britain. However, her politics do not dull the sharpness of her observations and satirical portraits of our media, government, democracy, sports, international relations, courtship, education, and family life. Dickens lives!

Goblet is her most subversive picture of the modern world. It serves as an indictment of modernity's absurd and inhuman institutional injustice. Perhaps most readers overlook these criticisms because of the adventure and mystery tale they come wrapped in, but that's a little like reading *Gulliver's Travels* as a travelogue. *Goblet* is the longest book of the series and its most pointed collection of grand social and political satire. Rowling has made the move from interior to exterior work, from the personal and the psychological to Social Drama.

Sports

Beyond her satire (and as its vehicle), Rowling's *Goblet of Fire* is mostly about sports. This thought has caused a few members of my audience to laugh when I presented this chapter as a lecture. Afterwards a kind gentleman told me that following alchemy, a medieval morality play, and Jungian analysis, "sports" was a surprise topic — and a comic surprise at that. Okay, I can see the humor in this assumed contrast. But **Goblet** is at least as profound as the earlier three books. Let's look at sports as Joanne Rowling presents them in **Goblet.**

First of all, sports are supposed to be fun to play and entertaining to watch. The sports scenes in **Goblet** are no exceptions to this rule. From the roller coaster (without tracks) speed of the Quidditch World Cup match between Ireland and Bulgaria, to the three TriWizard Tournament tasks, sports in the wizarding world are about as exciting as sports can be — at least for the participants. I don't think Rowling cares much for spectator sports, because except for the Dragon task, spectators at the Cup and Tournament are obviously unable even to see most of what they're "watching". (Imagine watching the surface of a lake for an hour!)

Sports, too, are a great vehicle for political satire. Rowling is able to draw unflattering pictures of self-important Ministry figures taking their work (and themselves) very seriously at the World Cup. The several politicians, especially the Minister of Magic and Barty Crouch, Sr., aren't even there to watch the Quidditch match. But the politics of the TriWizard Tournament dwarfs the World Cup.

The purpose of the TriWizard Tournament is overtly political, very much as the modern Olympic Games are and were meant to be. (If you have any doubts, please read John MacAloon's **This Glorious Symbol** about de Coubertain and the genesis of the modern Olympic "Games".) We're told that Ministry officials spend months in international "deep waters" negotiating terms for the Tournament, for the sake of fostering good will and brotherhood among international wizardry. Baloney.

Everyone who comes to the Tournament comes to win and, in winning, to claim a victory for their school, nationality, and pedagogical theory. Is this unlike our world? Anyway, there are Ministry types all over Hogwarts, from the selecting of champions to the tragedy of the final task.

The Goblet of Fire has a meaning beyond sports (see the discussion of titles below), but here it is clearly a clever parody of the Olympic Torch as "magical, mystical object". It is able to discriminate among entrants and select each school's champion. I suspect Rowling is suggesting that our elevation of torch-carrying Olympians is on the ridiculous side of the spectrum — especially when someone the crowd thinks unworthy is selected. The bitterness experienced by Harry points to the whole Goblet/Olympic ritual as an orchestrated sham, rather than a measure of worthiness and glory.

But to Brits, sports have a greater political purpose, even an historical one. Those United Kingdom citizens I have met disagree with each other on just about everything, except for sharing a quasi-religious seriousness about sports. I'm not just talking about soccer and cricket — try to have a light-hearted dart game with a Welshman and you're in for a surprise. He may be smiling, but he's deadly serious.

The historical background is the English conviction that "the Empire was won on the playing fields of Eton". This means that Englishmen feel in their hearts and bones that competitive sports, played in youth and as adults (even if only experienced vicariously), are the surest forge for sterling character. The virtues of perseverance, pluck, and honor that distinguish these islanders in their grander moments — they attribute these vitues to their gaming. Is this quasi-religious seriousness really religious?

Leon Podles in his **The Church Impotent** argues that "because sports provide an initiation into masculinity, they can easily become a religion". He writes:

> For modern man, team sports are more transforming than religion because they provide a greater escape from the self. Paul Jones, a Dulwich boy who was killed in World War I, claimed that in the attempts to develop team spirit, "Religion has failed, intellect has failed, art has failed, science has failed. It is clear why: because each of these has laid emphasis on man's *selfish side*; the saving of his *own soul*; the cultivation of his *own mind*; the pleasing of his *own senses*; But your sportsman joins the Colours because in his games he has felt the real spirit of unselfishness, and has become accustomed to give all for a body to whose service he is sworn." Sports on this view are a better school of charity than religion, for the ultimate test of charity is the willingness to die in war. Not only were wars won, but souls were saved on the playing fields of Eton. **(Podles,** *Impotent,* **pp. 168-169)**

Podles thinks sports has become religion for many if not most American males because "as liberal Protestantism abandoned the Puritan message of death and transfiguration", sports have filled the void of masculine initiation in the male psyche. He traces the feminization of the Western church to innovations and departures from Orthodoxy by Saints Thomas and Bernard. He does this historical detective work to explain the documented absence of "real men" (and often "any men") from Christian congregations, Catholic and Protestant, in America and overseas (the notable exception being countries that are traditionally Orthodox Christian).

Many critics of the Narnia and Middle Earth books, friendly and hostile, have noted the absence of religion in these books by very religious authors, despite their not very well-hidden spiritual intentions in writing. There are sports and games in the **Chronicles** and *The Lord of the Rings*, but these sports are only props and preps for warfare. Because the theology of masculine service and virtue has been removed from the Western Church, it seems that sports and warfare have supplanted religion both in real life and in the literature written to prepare one for real life. Podles goes so far as to say that "Tolkien transmuted his war experiences at the battle of the Somme into fantasy in *The Lord of the Rings*" (*Impotent*, p. 188).

Joanne Rowling, through no fault of her own, differs from her Inkling forebears in not having been a World War I combat veteran. But she follows their lead in her books, which teach the masculine stock responses of virtue and bravery and the full-chested alignment of soul. *The religious moments in the **Potter** books are exclusively in Harry's Quidditch games, Tournament sports tasks, and combats with Voldemort.* Sports and warfare are ciphers for the spiritual combat. This is true throughout the series, but in none of the other books as clearly as in **Goblet**, Rowling's book on sports.

From the elation of victory Harry experiences when catching the Golden Snitch, to the selflessness he and his teammates exhibit in every game for the good of the Gryffyndor squad, everything that should be true of church life we see in Harry's life as a member of a Quidditch team. Community spirit isn't restricted to the team, of course; they are the extension of the House, which worries itself before, cheers itself hoarse during, and celebrates the victory after each match as the eighth member on the pitch.

But Harry's spiritual experiences in Quidditch are mostly in flying. His first time on a broom he has a "rush of fierce joy" (*Stone*, p. 148) which never leaves him. When he has to think an extraordinarily happy thought when facing a boggart-dementor in **Prisoner**, the first one that comes to mind is, not saving Ginny, not the Hogwarts victories in Quidditch and for the House Cup, not the Philosopher's Stone, but incredibly his first time on a broomstick (p. 237).

Harry doesn't pray. Not before bed, not before meals, never. Rowling to my knowledge only uses the word once in the series — during the first TriWizard Tournament task. Harry is in something like shock, dumbfounded before the Hungarian Horntail and the stands filled with spectators.

> "*Accio, Firebolt!*" he shouted.
>
> Harry waited, every fiber of him hoping, praying....
> (*Goblet*, p. 353)

I don't want to make too much of this exclusive usage (I do not have a **Potter** concordance and cannot be sure of it), but exclusive or not, its usage here points to the religious or spiritual experience Harry has on a broomstick. The poetry is fairly transparent. In defying the most deadening natural law, the gravity which keeps us "earth bound", Harry (a "damn good flyer" in the estimation of Moody and all others) is in the heavens, his natural element and birthright. How many times are we told his father was also a grand flyer?

And these games are not child's play. The TriWizard tasks all hold the strong possibility (I think "likelihood" in the maze) of death — and of course Cedric does die. Rowling is pointing to what these games should represent and support, rather than replace: the spiritual combat with principalities and powers, within and without the aspirant.

Harry's magical selfless times in the heavens pale before the drama and intensity of his combat with evil. In *Goblet*, this fight happens almost as the final task of the Tournament. Harry's one-on-one combat with Voldemort in the graveyard (as in the earlier books) is a textbook illustation of how a Christian should face his or her three enemies — the world, flesh, and the devil. Here's a closer look at the steps to face these enemies, with examples especially drawn from *Chamber of Secrets* and Harry's battle at the Rebirthing Party in *Goblet of Fire:*

Recognize and name the enemy.
> The thin man had stepped out of the cauldron, staring at Harry...and Harry stared back at the face that had haunted his nightmares for three years. Whiter than a skull, with wide, livid, scarlet eyes and a nose that was flat as a snake's with slits for nostrils...
>
> Lord Voldemort had risen again. (*Goblet*, p. 643)

Recognize your helplessness on your own.
> *Help me — help me —* Harry thought, his eyes screwed tight under the hat. *Please help me —* (*Chamber*, p. 319).

All that he had learned [in his one dueling club lesson] was the Disarming Spell, *"Expelliarmus"*... and what use would it be to deprive Voldemort of his wand, even if he could, when he was surrounded by Death Eaters, outnumbered by at least thirty to one? He had never learned anything that could possibly fit him for this. He knew he was facing the thing against which Moody had always warned... the unblockable *Avada Kedavra* curse — and Voldemort was right — his mother was not here to die for him this time.... He was quite unprotected.... (*Goblet*, p. 660)

Confess your loyalty to the good.

"You're not," he said, his quiet voice full of hatred.

"Not what?" snapped Riddle.

"Not the greatest sorcerer in the world," said Harry, breathing fast. Sorry to disappoint you and all that, but the greatest wizard in the world is Albus Dumbledore. Everyone says so. Even when you were strong, you didn't dare try and take over at Hogwarts. Dumbledore saw through you when you were at school and he still frightens you now, wherever you're hiding these days." (*Chamber*, p. 314)

"Harry crouched behind the headstone and knew the end had come. There was no hope... no help to be had. And as he heard Voldemort draw nearer still, he knew one thing only, and it was beyond fear or reason: he was not going to die crouching here like a child playing hide-and-seek; he was not going to die kneeling at Voldemort's feet... he was going to die upright like his father.... (*Goblet*, p. 662)

Look for the graces of the Trinity in the Holy Spirit.

A gleaming silver sword had appeared inside the hat, its handle glittering with rubies the size of eggs. (*Chamber*, p. 320)

And then an unearthly and beautiful sound filled the air.... It was coming from every thread of the light spun web vibrating around Harry and Voldemort. It was a sound Harry recognized, though he had heard it only once before in his life: phoenix song.

It was the sound of hope to Harry.... The most beautiful and welcome thing he had ever heard in his life...He felt as though the song were inside him instead of just around him.... It was the sound he connected with Dumbledore, and it was almost as though a friend were speaking in his ear....

Don't break the connection.

I know, Harry told the music, I know I mustn't.... (*Goblet*, p. 664)

And finally, work these graces to overcome the enemy.

The basilisk lunged again, and this time its aim was true — Harry threw his whole weight behind the sword and drove it to the hilt into the roof of the serpent's mouth — (*Chamber*, p. 320)

"Do it now," whispered his father's voice, "be ready to run... do it now...."

"NOW!" Harry yelled; he didn't think he could have held on another moment anyway — he pulled his wand upward with an almighty wrench, and the golden thread broke; the cage of light vanished, the phoenix song died — but the shadowy figures of Voldemort's victims did not disappear — they were closing in on Voldemort, shielding Harry from his gaze —

And Harry ran as he had never run in his life... (*Goblet*, p. 668)

Rowling uses combat and sports as metaphors for the spiritual warfare. She does so to initiate all her readers, male and female, into the martial virtues of selfless sacrifice, bravery, and courageous combat — the three virtues Voldemort tells

Harry his parents displayed at their death **(*Stone*, p. 294)**. I do not doubt that she does this because she is aware, as were Lewis and Tolkien, that sports and warfare have supplanted the Western Church in the hearts and minds of many, as places for masculine initiation and heroic virtue. Nonetheless, she points through these play and mortal battles to the truths of the Church, and to the greater battle against a foe who wants our spiritual as much as our physical deaths.

What is *Goblet of Fire* About?

Goblet of Fire is a big book, certainly the longest single book I have read out loud to my children, and it doesn't lack for events and meaning. Here's a quick survey in summary:

- There are important changes in Harry from the beginning to end of **Goblet**. He moves from being a spectator at the World Cup to a school champion to "shouldering a grown wizard's burden" **(p. 699)** against the Dark Lord. He matures from a teenager concerned about the opinions of others to a young man of integrity and self-confidence **(see Part Two for more on the changes)**;

- There is an expansion of the storyline and focus from wee Hogwarts and Harry's internal and external struggles, to the world stage and social drama of good versus evil. Rowling skewers not a few sacred cows in her satirical portraits of everything authoritative and institutional, from the courts and prisons to schools, the media, government, and sports;

- There is a continuation of the alchemy theme of purification and perfection by trial, both in the crucible of the phoenix song cage with Voldemort and in the Four Tasks of the TriWizard Tournament. In these tasks Rowling echoes the steps of purification before Harry gets to the mirror in **Stone**. The

Tournament tasks are keyed to the four elements of alchemy: air, earth, fire, and water. Each suggests classical or medieval tournament sport:

Air: fighting dragons (reference to knight's warfare);

Water: rescuing hostages (again, knight's work);

Earth: finding center of maze despite obstacles (Theseus' hero journey); and

Fire: combat of elect champion with Evil One in graveyard (morality play).

When I think of the fourth book, though, I am struck by the lessons Rowling teaches through sports competitions and the graveyard combat with Voldemort. For example, in the World Cup match, Bulgaria is overmatched by Ireland, whose Chasers score almost at will, soon amassing a lead that even catching the snitch would not overcome. Krum catches the snitch anyway in a diving race with the Irish seeker, and the match ends.

The Bulgarian Minister of Magic comments, "Vell, ve fought bravely" **(p. 114)**, and there was some bravery in what Krum did. His nose had just been shattered by a bludger when the Irish seeker dove for the snitch. But there is some nobility, too, in the way Krum ends the match. As Harry observes after Ron calls Krum an idiot:

> "He knew they were never going to catch up!" Harry shouted back over all the noise, also applauding loudly. "The Irish Chasers were too good.... He wanted to end it on his terms, that's all...."
>
> "He was very brave wasn't he?" Hermione said....
> (*Goblet*, **p. 114**)

This is Harry's kind of sports hero. Krum was interested in doing the right thing even if it meant losing. Honor, bravery, sacrifice — this is what you learn in sports, if your focus isn't only on winning and losing. We see it again and again in Harry's choices at the TriWizard Tournament:

- Task 1: Harry clues in Cedric that it's about dragons;

- Task 2: Harry saves more than just his hostage; and

- Task 3: Harry saves Cedric twice in the maze.

I would go so far as saying that Rowling offers Harry's charity and nobility in contests that are life and death battles, as really the reason he is able to escape Voldemort and live to fight another day. If that seems far-fetched, it should be recalled that Harry only does well in the Tournament because of "charity" he receives (from those who want him dead — Moody/Crouch, Jr. and Bagman), and only escapes Voldemort because of charity (from Voldemort's victims — those who are already dead).

Dumbledore tells us the explicit message of the various battles in **Goblet** at the Leaving Feast:

> "Remember Cedric," he says. " Remember if the time should come when you have to make a choice between what is right and what is easy, remember what happened to a boy who was good, and kind, and brave, because he strayed across the path of Lord Voldemort. Remember Cedric Diggory" **(Goblet, p. 724)**.

Harry made this same hard, right choice in the graveyard, "to die upright like his father, and he was going to die trying to defend himself, even if no defense was possible..." **(Goblet, p. 662)**.

Harry's choice is made after he witnesses and passively participates in something a little scarier than a bludger to the nose: the black mass that raises Voldemort's new body. A black mass is the demonic mockery or aping of traditional Christian liturgy. Everything that is sacred is inverted in a black mass; death and darkness trump life and light. In the magic potion and ceremony that Voldemort orchestrates as black magician-priest, all the Christian mysteries (sacraments) are turned on their head with demonic consequences:

- the Eucharist or life-giving body and blood of God are mocked in the potion's requirements of the blood of an enemy, flesh of the servant, and bone of the father (inverting blood of the Savior, flesh of the Master, and Spirit of the Father);

- the baptismal font and immersion in the name of Father, Son, and Holy Spirit are turned qualitatively inside out in the Voldemort baby's immersion in the cauldron with three magical, physical ingredients (and the "old man" rather than the new man or "babe in Christ" rising from the font);

- confession or the "sacrament of reconciliation" occurs after (instead of before) this black mass and "old man" baptism - and the Black arts priest neither forgives nor absolves the Death Eaters' sins and unworthiness;

- consecration of priests and disciples has its carnival mirror image in the blessing of Wormtail and the promised ordination and reward of Voldemort's true servants (and "excommunication" or murder of those who have broken faith with him);

- the "Liturgy of the Word" or sermon is mocked in Voldemort's edifying lesson and instruction to his disciples concerning his "passion and resurrection"; and

- the Mystery of Christian burial is turned on its head by the graveyard of a church becoming a birth place of devils rather than a resting place for those hopeful of an authentic resurrection from the dead.

Harry not only witnesses the death of his friend and this series of demonic desecrations of holy things, he is part of it because his blood, made magically powerful by the sacrificial death and love of his mother, is necessary to the potion (another inversion of the Eucharist). And yet Harry decides to stand and fight as the image of his father. This "steadfastness in faith", despite the darkness and perversion surrounding him, is the cause of Harry's consequent epiphany and Theophany in battle, and recalls his victory in the Chamber of Secrets. **(Thanks to Eileen Rebstock for her help in understanding** *Goblet's* **rebirthing party.)**

This courage in making a choice, wrapped up with the love of the father, invite the golden light and inspiring phoenix song that envelope him when he locks wands with Voldemort. Rowling tells us in *Fantastic Beasts* that phoenix song is "reputed to increase the courage of the pure in heart and to strike fear into the hearts of the impure" *(Beasts,* **p. 32)**. I said that in *Chamber* Rowling uses this song as a symbol of the Holy Spirit, and the Trinity is again evident in the Light cage: the association with Dumbledore and the voice from the phoenix song suggest words from above at Theophany, the phoenix feathers in the wand as a phoenix represent Christ, and the song with its effects point to the Holy Spirit.

Harry only experiences this symbolic epiphany of the Trinity because he is pure of heart. In every task of the Tournament, in every difficulty with close friends and media, he has been courageously on the side of the truth rather than "going for" the easy win, quick fix, or safe path. Rowling as Aesop seems to be telling us that it is not study, your special external preparations, or even your piety that save you in the end. Rather, it is your internal quality — the courage, love, and virtue within — that determines your receptivity to the graces that will save you in the spiritual warfare.

In this, **Goblet of Fire** is no different than the other books of the series; where it differs is in the breadth of the effect that Harry's purity of heart has. We have seen in each book how our preparations and personal choices shape the outcome of our personal struggles with evil; in **Goblet**, we can see the larger consequences of this personal struggle for our friends and the world. Harry has not only survived, but his victory in escape has mobilized and inspired all the white hats to take on Voldemort. So, too, our pursuit of spiritual perfection, however private and personal, ennobles and enlightens the world.

Chapter 15

The Meaning
of the
Harry Potter Titles

Joanne Rowling has been pigeonholed into two very unfortunate boxes: "welfare Mom lottery winner" and "writer of black magic texts". In interviews she seems to be pretty tired of both narrow slots. In *Newsweek*, she said:

> "With the people who wanted to accuse me of Satan worship,
> I was full on for arguing it out with them face to face. But
> you know you're not going to change their views. The only
> thing I have argued forcibly is that the idea of censorship
> deeply offends me." (*Newsweek*, July 10, 2000, p. 60)

About her welfare status, *Time* magazine reported:

> Rowling grew annoyed when newspapers played up this anecdote [of impoverished single mother] as a dominant chapter in her life. "It was a great story," she concedes. "I would have liked to read it about someone else." But the tale came to define her, the product of a middle class family and a university education, as a welfare mom who hit the jackpot. (*Time*, **September 20, 1999, p. 71**)

The tragedy and comedy of these depictions is that they obscure her genius and meaning almost entirely in the popular (and even the well-read) mind. It is very difficult for people with these mental pictures of Rowling to think of her as a Christian writer, not to mention one of Lewis and Tolkien's stature, or even of Austen's or Dickens'.

I have been asked by audiences this question again and again: "If she is writing Christian books, why is she being so secretive about it? Isn't she being deceptive by making it so hard to see what the books are about? Why doesn't she just tell us the books are Christian?" Well, she does. In the title of every book she says that it is about **Harry Potter and Christ**. Every one. Let's look at them if you don't believe me.

The Philosopher's Stone

What is a "philosopher's stone"? It is the product, really a by-product, of spiritual purification, dissolution, and perfection within a revealed spiritual tradition. It has the legendary powers of being able to turn lead to gold and give immortality to its owner through the "Red Lion" elixir available from it. However, the Stone itself is simply the symbol of the end of the alchemical process: divinization or theosis in Christ.

> From the Christian point of view, alchemy was like a natural mirror for the revealed truths: the philosophers' stone, which turned base metals into silver and gold, is a symbol of Christ, and, its production from the "non-burning fire" of sulphur and the "steadfast water" of quicksilver resembles the birth of Christ-Emmanuel. **(Burckhardt,** *Alchemy,* **p. 18)**

Alchemy is about the transmutation of the soul from spiritual lead or death, to gold or life in Christ. This is the Stone's power of granting immortality. It is no accident that the Stone in Rowling's book is blood red; we are meant to think of Christ's blood as the Elixir that bestows immortality in Communion. ***Harry Potter and the Philosopher's Stone,*** then, is about Harry and Christ. As we have seen in the discussion of the meaning of ***Philosopher's Stone,*** the title points to the meaning of the book.

Chamber of Secrets

To see through this title, you have to remember the morality play that takes place inside the Chamber of Secrets. What happens there? The Phoenix or "resurrection bird", traditional symbol of Christ, saves faithful Harry and restores his "Ginny" or innocence. He does this by helping Harry defeat the giant serpent and Tom Riddle (both satanic figures). The play ends with all the surviving human players miraculously ascending to the world of light and laughter on the wings of the Phoenix.

The Chamber in one sense stands for "the World", because it is the place where Harry and the Phoenix do battle with the prince of this world and his deadly servant. But why is it called the Chamber "of Secrets"? Secrets are hidden things, and this chamber acts as an alchemical crucible of the hidden or spiritual things in our hearts. The Chamber, then, is more like an "inner temple" where the hidden things are kept, the secret spiritual battlefield.

Rowling uses the word "chamber" to push us to this interpretation because the spiritual battlefield and inner temple of the human person reside in the heart, an organ of chambers. It is not too big a leap from inner temple to "throne of God", and to an understanding that the secret here is Christ, Who sits on this throne.

The Prisoner of Azkaban

Azkaban is a magical word combining Shazam, Abracadabra, the "-stan" ending names of Soviet Republics, and Alcatraz — adding up to an apt description of the Wizarding world's island gulag. The words in this title do not point us to their meaning, but to the person whom they describe: Sirius Black. Given the book's revelation of Harry's "son-ship" with respect to his earthly and heavenly fathers (see Chapter 13), it is appropriate that the title be about Harry's *God Father*.

Sirius, though, is only a stand-in for another more famous martyr here. He is after all an "Unjustly Condemned Man" who "Rises from the Dead" of Azkaban and is "Hated by the World" (muggle and magic, ministry and media). He is revealed in the end as a "sacrificial savior" and "loving defender of

God-son". Patronus means both godfather and savior, so this title, ***The Prisoner of Azkaban***, points to Sirius Black, and through him to Christ.

The Goblet of Fire

> Dumbledore now took out his wand and tapped three times upon the top of the casket. The lid creaked slowly open. Dumbledore reached inside it and pulled out a large, roughly hewn wooden cup. It would have been entirely unremarkable had it not been full to the brim with dancing blue white flames. (*Goblet*, p. 255)

Dumbledore tells us that "The champions will be chosen by an impartial selector: the Goblet of Fire". Moody later describes it as "a very powerful magic object" (p. 279). Is this a clever invention of Rowling's?

Well, yes and no. No, it has a referent in medieval legend, but, yes, Ms. Rowling has changed it a bit to suggest a specific meaning to that legendary piece. In Arthurian Legend, the magical object that selected champions worthy to behold it was the Holy Grail.

The Holy Grail, however, isn't just a magical object like a Sneak-o-scope or Foe glass that detects defects in people. It has its power because it is the Communion Cup of Christ's mystical Last Supper. Legend has it that it was brought by Joseph of Arimethea to England, at that time the most distant outpost of the Empire. Readers of the Arthurian tales know that it could only be found by the most pure of heart (notably Sirs Perceval and Galahad).

Rowling has made some interesting changes. The Grail of legend is silver, and it is sometimes represented more as a platter than what we would call a goblet. Her "large, roughly hewn wooden cup" is the Grail from *Indiana Jones and the Temple of Doom.* (Do you remember how Harrison Ford picks it from a room full of ornate chalices, because a wooden cup is what a carpenter would drink from?)

But the more interesting changes are the casket and the flames. The flames might be a touch to satirize the Olympic Torch, but the casket makes me think she is referring to what is inside a Communion Cup: the body and blood of Christ. Pre-Communion Prayers said by traditional Christians refer to their savior's life-giving body and blood as fire:

> If thou wishest, O man, to eat the Body of the Master, approach in fear, lest thou be scorched, for it is fire. **(Didactic verses)**

> Let the live coal of Thy Most Holy Body and Blood be for the sanctification and enlightenment and strengthening of my humble soul and body... **(First Prayer of St. John Chrysostomos)**

> And rejoicing and trembling at once, I who am straw partake of fire; and strange wonder! I am ineffably bedewed, like the bush of old.... **(Prayer of St. Symeon the New Theologian)**

> Behold I approach for Divine Communion. O Creator, let me not be burnt by communicating, for Thou art fire which burneth the unworthy; but purify me from every stain. **(St. Symeon Metaphrastes)**

> Thou hast ravished me with longing, O Christ, and with thy divine love Thou hast changed me. But burn up with spiritual fire my sins and make me worthy to be filled with delight in Thee... **(Communion Troparia)**

The Goblet of Fire in the fourth book title is a fictional Holy Grail which held in legend the Body and Body of Christ. Rowling's title until shortly before she went to press was "The Doomspell Tournament". I think she changed it so the Tournament would have a more Trinitarian feel — and the title would again be a reference to Christ.

The strangest characteristic of the Fire in this Goblet is that it is a non-consuming fire. Applicants throw pieces of parchment into these flames, and the fire does not burn them. Though it may seem a stretch to modern Americans, no citizen of Medieval Europe (or medievalist in the academies) would fail to note its parallels with the non-consuming fire of the burning bush on Mt. Sinai, the purifying flames of Catholics' Purgatory, and the Glory or Love of God, His Energies (which the Orthodox claim everyone will experience at death, as seen in the iconographic "halo" of Saints). All these are signatures or correspondences with God's Word, Who became man as Christ.

The Order of the Phoenix

The working title of the fifth book (not in print at this writing) is **Harry Potter and the Order of the Phoenix.** In Part Four, I will boldly predict what will happen in this book; here I will just try to explain the title.

We drew long ago a Ring Map of Harry Potter *Dramatis Personae* and their relationships (see **Chapter 2**). Good guys and bad guys fall into generational rings, some on the Gryffyndor side, the rest on the Slytherin end. The sides balance neatly: for every Dumbledore, there's a Voldemort, for Harry, a Draco, etc. There is no balancing group for the Death Eaters at the end of **Goblet** — or is there?

Dumbledore, after his confrontation with Fudge, starts making plans for the coming war with Voldemort:

> "Now I have work for each of you. Fudge's attitude, though not unexpected, changes everything. Sirius, I need you to set off at once. You are to alert Remus Lupin, Arabella Figg, Mundungus Fletcher — the old crowd. Lie low at Lupin's for a while; I will contact you there." **(Goblet, p. 713)**

"The old crowd", along with the Hogwarts regulars and the Weasleys, will be the Order of the Phoenix. By gathering around Dumbledore, they compensate for the magical weight of the Death Eaters around Voldemort. "Order" suggests Medieval groups of knights (for example, the Order of the Knights of Malta), which in turn point to "religious orders" within monasticism — both groups representing "soldiers of Christ".

You are probably tired of hearing how the Phoenix or "resurrection bird" is a traditional symbol of the Christ, so I won't mention it. Suffice it to say, **Order of the Phoenix** will not be a departure from Rowling's practice of titling each book **Harry Potter and the Christ.**

Chapter 16

The Meaning
of Harry's Name

Conclusion to Part Three

Ms. Rowling, then, is not being secretive, deceptive, or even especially subtle — every book title in the series proclaims the books are about **Harry Potter and the Christ**. To blame her for our thickheadedness is to compound the injury done her.

Has any author, not to say "any bestselling author", ever been so misunderstood and neglected? If nineteenth-century newspapers had been dim-witted enough to try to convince the public that Harriet Beecher Stowe's **Uncle Tom's Cabin** was a pro-slavery, secessionist propaganda piece — that would be comparable to Rowling's treatment by her 21st century critics.

I was taught that a grand exposition should always have three parts: saying what you are going to say, saying it, and finally saying what you've said. Let's recapitulate what we've said in this "book by book" look at *Harry Potter*:

- Book 1 is about purification and perfection of soul in Christ, so that at death it experiences God's glory as joy not agony;

- Book 2 is about the right place of books and literature in preparing us for life and salvation — and a response to Christian critics about the real enemies of the Church hidden in textbooks and popular fiction;

- Book 3 is about defeating depression and despair by escaping the ego and identifying with the heavenly father (by summoning the savior in joyful expectation);

- Book 4 is about love and courage being sufficient preparation for spiritual warfare, because it invites the golden light and phoenix song that protects the worthy champion; and

- The titles all are symbols or reminders of Christ.

If you want an easy way to remember what the books are about, just think of their subject matter as "methods that modern people use to transcend themselves", and add "through Christ":

- *Stone* is "Personal Transformation (here, Alchemy) through Christ";

- *Chamber* is "Conventional Religion through Christ";

- *Prisoner* is "Psychology through Christ"; and

- *Goblet* is "Sports through Christ".

Rowling is showing book by book how the various paths of contemporary popular spirituality are effective and lasting only when working in Christ.

I never did get through to those sixth graders in Port Townsend what *Harry Potter* was about. However, one thing I said that kept them quiet for a minute (I thought I had a beach head; they were in fact only reloading) was a discussion of the names of the two principal families in the book: the Potters and the Malfoys. I'll conclude this chapter with that discussion.

Almost every person in Rowling's series has a meaningful name. We've already dissected the names of Albus Dumbledore, Sirius Black, Remus Lupin, Peter Pettigrew (poor guy!), Severus Snape — and you'll have to believe me that the other characters also have names that throw light on their nature and role in the drama. No writer since Dickens has named her characters with such care — and high good humor!

I propose that Joanne Rowling is an Inkling writer whose books, besides teaching us the "Stock Responses" of good behavior and the right alignment of our souls, also prepare us for a life as Christians by showing us the traditional doctrines and symbols of that faith in story form. One piece of evidence for this hypothesis is the names she gives the Good Guys and the Bad Guys.

The wicked family in *Harry Potter* is the Malfoy clan. The father's name is Lucius, the mother's Narcissa, and their little boy, the darling of Slytherin House, is Draco — the Latin word for "Dragon" or "Serpent". The serpent is a traditional Christian symbol for the Devil, because the evil one takes the form of a snake in the Garden of Eden. C. S. Lewis, in his book *The Voyage of the Dawn Treader*, depicts a really nasty little boy much like Draco named Eustace Scrubb, who turns into a dragon. Rowling may be acknowledging both her debt to Lewis' Narnia books and how nasty Draco is by giving him this name. (See Part Four for another reason.)

Lucius, the Daddy, is perfectly wicked. He mistreats his servants, patronizes to everyone because of his "pure blood" and wealth, and is rather impatient and nasty to his own boy. He gave Riddle's diary to Ginny Weasley, which almost resulted in more than a few deaths. In *Goblet of Fire* he reveals himself as a Death Eater, a servant of Lord Voldemort. That is no surprise if you look at his name; *Lucius* suggests "Lucifer", which means "light carrier" in Latin. The angel named Lucifer, sadly, turned on God and became the Devil or Satan ("the deceiver"). Like his son, Lucius Malfoy has a satanic name.

Mom Malfoy's name is not another name for the devil, but it's pretty bad. Narcissus is a young man in Greek mythology who was very aware of his own good looks. He thought so much of himself that he rejected the love of the nymph Echo; he spent so much time admiring his reflection in a pond that some stories say he drowned, and better ones say he became the beautiful narcissus plant. A narcissist, consequently, is anyone of self-importance and ego (usually a self-loving monster). "Narcissa" is not a nice name — and it has enough sibilants in it that you sound like a snake saying it.

But the worst part of being a Malfoy is that last name. It is French for "bad faith" or "faith in evil". This can mean anything from "untrustworthy" to "Satan worshipper". I might move if the family next door was named "bad faith"! All the Malfoys are branded as Black Hats by their first and last names.

Let's look at the names for the Good Guys, by whom I mean the Potters. Harry Potter's late parents were named James and Lily. These have meanings, as you've probably guessed, quite different than the Malfoys.

James, for instance is the name of the disciple of Christ who was also his older brother (Joseph had several children before his marriage as a widower to the Mother of Christ). This brother was the only sibling to recognize Christ as the Messiah; he became (after the Resurrection, Ascension, and Pentecost) the first Bishop of Jerusalem and the first leader of the Church, the man in charge at the Council recorded in the Book of Acts.

You may not be familiar with this connection between "James" and "Christ", but be sure that the English are. Ambassadors from foreign countries to the British government are said to be going to the Court of St. James; another name for the British royal court contains "St. James".

Lily was the name of Harry's green-eyed mother. Lilies are magnificent, showy flowers of various colors and usually have a trumpet shape. They are symbolic of Spring, though many people associate this flower with death; a white lily is often put in a corpse's hands before its funeral. This is done because the lily as symbol of Spring is also the flower of Easter. Corpses are given a lily in hope of their Resurrection with Christ. "Lily", then, like "James", is a name with strong ties to Christianity.

Which leaves us with "Harry Potter". What does Harry's name mean?

Harry can literally mean "to harass, annoy, or disturb". Usually someone described as "harried" is run down by too much work and distractions. I don't think that's what our Harry's name is meant to imply, even though he does lead an exciting life.

Harry is also the familiar form of the names "Henry" and "Harold". More than one Shakespeare play is about "Harry Hotspur" (the Prince of Wales) and his wild life before becoming King — and his heroic life thereafter. Not a few critics have suggested this is a clue to what our Harry's future has in store. Given the royalty hint in James, this is a real possibility... **(Again, see Part Four for my guesses about Harry's future.)**

I think, though, that the Cockney and French pronunciations of Harry's name tell us what his name means. These pronunciations are made without aspirating or breathing through the "H". Instead of pronouncing the name as if you were saying he were hirsute (covered with hair), say it as if you were calling him an air-head: "airy". *Arry* with a long "A" suggests the word "heir".

The heir is the male person (heiress for a women) who stands to get what someone — usually a parent — will leave behind at death. It is usually used to describe someone who will inherit a great deal of money or a position. A prince, for example, is heir to the king's throne. When the king dies, the prince gets the throne and becomes king.

If *Harry* means "Heir-y", then what is our Harry "Heir to" or "Son of"? I think the answer to that is in the biblical use of the word "Potter". For this job you might want to get a concordance of the Bible.

This book lists every word used in the Bible and tells you where each word is found. The better ones also tell you the original Greek or Hebrew words beneath the translation. Looking up "Potter" in the concordance, we find references to its use in the Prophets Isaiah, Jeremiah, and Zechariah, the Book of Lamentations, Saint Paul's letter to the Romans, and in the Book of Revelations.

Because Tupperware wasn't available in biblical times, it shouldn't be surprising to find mention of potters in scripture. Pots held everything not kept in baskets. But to what are these Bible references alluding when they mention "potters"? Do they mean human potters?

Please get a concordance sometime if you haven't got one in hand now, and check up on what I'm about to say. When Bible scholars cite similar references to these "potter" passages, they often refer to God's creation of man as recorded by the prophet Moses. "And the Lord God formed man of the dust of the ground, and breathed into his nostrils the breath of life and he became a living soul" (Genesis 2:7).

Sometimes these scriptures refer to human potters. But even then, they point to the potter's craft of "shaping a vessel" to indicate God's activity in shaping us, creations or creatures in his image. Let's look at a couple of these "potter" references to see what I mean.

In Isaiah 64:8, the prophet says, "But now, O Lord, thou art our father; we are the clay, and thou our potter; and we are all the work of thy hand."

Jeremiah says, "Then the word of the Lord came to me saying, O house of Israel, cannot I do with you as this potter?

saith the Lord. Behold as clay is in the potter's hand, so are ye in mine hand, O house of Israel" (Jeremiah 18:5-6).

St. Paul rebukes the stiff-necked Romans by writing, "Nay but, O man, who art thou that repliest against God? Shall the thing formed say to him that formed it, Why hast thou made me thus? Hath not the potter power over the clay, of the same lump to make one vessel unto honour, and another unto dishonour?" (Romans 9:20-21).

God is thought of as a potter, from the beginning of the Bible to the Epistles of Christ's Apostles. Is there any reason to think this biblical usage survives to our times? Yes, there are reasons to believe that.

Orthodox Christians claim that they God in the same way the Apostles did, keep the same feasts and fasts, and say prayers that have been said by holy men for centuries. During Great Lent, the time of special prayers and fasting to prepare for the celebration of Christ's Resurrection (they call it "Pascha" rather than the Druid word "Easter"), the Great Canon of St. Andrew is recited.

These prayers, said around the world by Orthodox Christians, call on God in repentance for their sins. One of these prayers says, "In molding my life into clay, O Potter, Thou didst put into me flesh and bones, flesh and vitality. But, O my Creator, my Redeemer and Judge, accept me who repent" (Canon of St. Andrew, 1:10). *Potter* is here the equivalent of Creator, Redeemer, and Judge in referring to God.

You may never have heard of the Orthodox or seen an Orthodox Church (I hadn't until after graduating from college). You probably have heard of and used the Internet, though. If you don't think *Potter* means "God" to living, breathing

Christians — do a search of the World Wide Web for "Jeremiah Potter" or "Potters House".

What you'll find is several sermons on the passage from Jeremiah cited above. You may find a few angry notes about *Harry Potter* in there. And you will find web sites that are about sharing the gospel of Jesus Christ. Some of these are college missions, two I found were for rock musicians. One church (some say "cult") calling itself "The Potter's House" has 1000 churches, they say, in 73 countries. (I do not advise going to their web site, judging from another site that helps people wanting to escape and deprogram from this group.) In my first search, I found ten different evangelical groups with names about God using "Potter".

It is not off-the-wall, then, to suggest that *Potter* can be used as a synonym for "God" — and thus *Harry Potter* means "Heir to" or "Son of God". I rush to say this does **not** mean Rowling is offering Harry as a symbol of Christ, or as the Anti-Christ, or even as an allegorical Christ (which is how some people view C. S. Lewis' Aslan). Harry Potter is not the Son of God as Jesus Christ is, but in the manner that you and I are sons of God.

St. Athanasios the Great, a hero and confessor of the early Church, said that God became man that man might become God. He believed that by means of His incarnation, sinless life, and resurrection from the dead, Christ made it possible for human beings to share in His resurrection and become "little Christs within Christ" (a phrase attributed to St. John Chrysostom).

When Rowling calls Harry a name that means "son of God", she is teaching what the saints have taught for two thousand years. We are to love God not in fear as slaves, or in hollow obedience as servants, but we are to love God as dutiful sons created in His image, who live in joyous expectation of our inheritance — albeit at *our* deaths, if not before (paraphrasing St. Dorotheos, "On the Fear of God", *Dorotheos of Gaza*, Cistercian Publications, 1977, pp. 110-111).

Harry Potter as "son of God" is not a symbol of Jesus Christ, but of humanity pursuing its spiritual perfection in Christ. Harry Potter is "Every Man" hoping to live as God's image *and* likeness, now and in joy for eternity.

A review of the **Harry Potter** books — one by one, their titles, their themes, even their key names — all indicate that they are profound, edifying Christian morality tales. This is their secret, and this is the foundation of their powerful grip on readers. Their popularity results from the vicarious joy we experience with Harry as he seeks his symbolic perfection in Christ.

In the remaining chapters, I'll predict what will happen in the remaining **Potter** books. Stay tuned!

Part Four

What Will Happen With Harry?

Part Four

What Will Happen
With Harry?

As we've seen, the otherwise-mysterious popularity of the *Harry Potter* books can be understood in light of these "secret" ingredients:

Our Modern Thirst

C. S. Lewis has described the aims of education in modern times as "irrigating a desert", in contrast to the popular belief that it serves "to cut down jungles" or clear away delusions (as alluded to in *The Abolition of Man*, p. 24, and as illustrated in *The Silver Chair*). The desert Lewis thinks needs water is both spiritual and mental. Soft heads and hard hearts long for truth, beauty, and goodness, even though they have been taught to despise or disregard these qualities as subjective or sentimental. Abraham Maslow said "a capacity is a need"; our denied or misdirected spiritual capacities have created a nigh-on irresistible craving and need for Inkling quality reading.

A WOW! Story

Whatever the demand for edifying literature, it cannot have the desired effect if it isn't engaging and entertaining as story. Ms. Rowling's detailed, magical world allows and invites head-first immersion and suspension of disbelief. Her readers identify with Harry and are rushed to a catharsis in spirit with their hero via their imagination. Consciously and unconsciously, they absorb just sentiments, heroic virtue, and Christian doctrine — while loving the adventures in which this moral education is wrapped.

The Christian Meaning

The *Harry Potter* books do not offer a generic "good over evil" message. Ms. Rowling writes the powerful spiritual answer to mankind's larger questions in the only language even a post-Christian culture can understand: the symbols and doctrines of the Christian faith. *Harry Potter* fans enjoy a resurrection experience in every book, awash in word pictures of Christ and souls in pursuit of perfection in Him. Without this specific meaning, Rowling could not have achieved her unprecedented popularity in a culture that only knows of God in these forms.

Past Watchful Dragons

Lewis was aware of how repugnant anything "churchy" is to most people, and especially to children. He once explained that his *Narnia* books were written to sneak "past the watchful dragons" that guard our hearts against the Christian meaning of life. *Harry Potter* is so popular precisely because no one has stirred these dragons. By means of her Cinderella story, her cover of being anti-Christian, our cultural misogyny, and the condescension that she is writing only harmless children's fantasy, Rowling has been able to bypass the much more ferocious and watchful dragons of our day. Her disguise (as welfare mom Wicca cultist) does the concealment job more effectively than wearing Frodo's ring or Harry's Invisibility Cloak.

Having cracked the hidden meaning to the books, individually and as a series, and having explained the enigma of Pottermania, the only mystery remaining is what will happen in the final three books. The fun in that is only matched by its folly!

My older children and I have been discussing for the better part of two years now "what happens next" — thereby keeping the books' characters alive in our hearts, inviting second readings and frantic searches for evidence to support our guesses. This has meant quite a few grins and giggles for my family on car rides and walks.

But the folly of printing such guesses is as plain as the proverbial nose (and I have a big nose): not only can the guesser be sure that at least some of the guesses will be wrong, but a worldwide audience will always have evidence of just how wrong and far off the guesses were. Unlike Jeanne Dixon, the prospect of humiliation via failed predictions is not appealing to me.

Nonetheless, by popular demand (and by keeping my guesses fairly reasonable), here goes...

The three subjects to be treated in these last chapters are:

- What we cannot know about upcoming books;

- What we can know and can try to figure out; and

- My best guesses.

Asking your kindness when the fifth **Potter** book is released, let's begin.

Chapter 17

The Folly
of
Prediction:

What We Can and Cannot Know

W**hat we cannot know**

Just think about all the new things and new people that Rowling introduced in **Goblet of Fire**. Anyone crazy enough to have made predictions about that fourth book before its publication would have proceeded in ignorance of the World Cup, the TriWizard Tournament, Moody, the Crouches, Bagman, Skeeter, Krum, the Pensieve — do I need to go on?

What we cannot know — and I won't predict — are any new characters, new situations, or new events that Rowling may be cooking up in her creative cranium. I am not a mind reader, lurker in *Harry Potter* chat rooms, book industry spy, or personal friend of Ms. Rowling's.

Consequently, I'll refrain from imponderable specifics, and restrict my guessing to what we do know and have some prospect of figuring out.

What we do know

We know quite a bit about these books that can guide our guesswork about what is to come. We know, for instance:

The books build on one another

The *Harry Potter* books are accumulative in detail. Though Rowling gives us new characters, magic, and scenes in each book, when we get new stuff we lose nothing. Even though we have not seen Aragog since Book 2, if he reappears in Book 5 driving Mr. Weasley's Ford Anglia, we should be no more surprised than when we discovered polyjuice potion (last seen in Book 1) to be the key to the mystery in Book 4. We have been warned: forget nothing when guessing. (So what happened to Hagrid's umbrella? Arabella Figg, Moaning Myrtle, or Argus Filch may have it...)

The books follow a formula

Sports teams scout each other for a reason. The good teams won't — and the bad teams can't — reinvent themselves week to week. If you want to know what teams will do against you in the future, it's a good bet you'll see it when you scout their previous games.

It's easy to scout *Harry Potter*. Through her first four books, Ms. Rowling has followed her "hero journey" formula without exception from Privet drive to Platform Nine and

Three-Quarters pickup (though it seemed incredible after *Goblet* that Harry returned to Privet Drive). She certainly could abandon this formula — but it plays such a large part in the meaning of her books that I doubt very much she will. For the sake of guessing, the smart money is on the formula.

This is a big help — bigger than you might think. For example, I can be pretty sure I know a lot about the ending of *Order of the Phoenix*, because Rowling has a formula. The ending will be a shocker, for sure. It will reveal a good guy to be a bad guy and a bad guy to be a good guy. It will almost certainly feature Harry confronting Voldemort or a Death Eater against impossible odds, losing, then rising from the dead. And it'll conclude with Harry catching the southbound train from Hogwarts.

These aren't off-the-wall shots in the dark, because each shot has been on the mark for every previous *Harry Potter* book ending. Rowling's adherence to her formulas is our best guide in guessing.

The books are a series of stories within a larger story

Each book is the account of an adventurous year in the life of Harry Potter and company at Hogwarts. As each year is recounted, we learn more of the larger story of Harry and Voldemort. We are already aware of long strands of this enveloping story, so our guesses have to include both what we know so far and what we have to figure out. We know what questions the next books have to answer, and Rowling has given us some clues.

Keeping in mind that the books build on one another, that Ms. Rowling writes within several formulas, and that the books are only part of an encompassing story of Harry's beginnings and identity, let's quickly review what we know about the:

- Hero's Journey formula;

- Structure of relationships;

- What we know about Harry; and

- What the books mean.

Hero's Journey formula

As we've said, Harry travels in every book from the Dursley home on Privet Drive through a heroic adventure at Hogwarts back to King's Cross Train Station, Platform Nine and Three-Quarters, where the Dursleys are waiting behind the barrier to pick him up. Readers can expect the same cycle with differently detailed component parts in the next three books. Look for a magical, even explosive departure ("escape!") from Privet Drive en route to Hogwarts, a mystery to solve there, a crisis of some proportion, Harry's descent into battle, a fight against all odds, losing, rising from the dead in victory, a conference with Dumbledore to figure out what happened, and fun on the train home. (See Chapter 2 for a longer discussion and for a map.)

Structure of relationships

The relationships in the **Harry Potter** books can be imagined as generational rings. Each generational ring has a north and south side. The northern side consists of those characters in each generation that have some connection or kindred feeling with Godric Gryffyndor. Those in the south are characters that side with slippery Salazar Slytherin.

In the first ring in from these founders are the elder disciples of Gryffyndor and Slytherin, Albus Dumbledore and Tom Marvolo Riddle, also known as Lord Voldemort. Filling out this ring are the pets and followers of these towering figures. The next ring holds James Potter and Lucius Malfoy (and their respective wives and sidekicks). Harry, Draco, and their friends are at the center of all these relationships. They are the present representatives of this tradition of friction between Gryffyndor and Slytherin descendants. (Again, see Chapter 2 for the detailed map.)

Understanding this map is helpful for our guessing because Rowling observes a balance in the rings. If Dumbledore has a pet phoenix look for Voldemort to have a pet snake in the next book. If Voldemort has a group of followers around him, expect a group parallel to the Death Eaters to form around Dumbledore, namely the "Order of the Phoenix".

What we know about Harry

Every new chapter of the *Potter* saga has proven to be a continued clarification of "Who Harry Is" and "Why Voldemort wants him dead". Voldemort stages a battle between himself and the Harry at the end of *Goblet* to demonstrate to the Death Eaters that he is more powerful than this helpless adolescent. Why he needs to do this (in other words, why and how Harry keeps beating him) is at the heart of the coming war between his Death Eaters and Dumbledore's Order of the Phoenix. Our guesses should assume that Rowling will tell us more about Harry's background — then take a stab at explaining this background beforehand based on the clues already available.

What the books mean

As I hope the first three Parts of this book have demonstrated, Joanne Rowling is an Inkling author writing books that are edifying preparation for one's life in Christ. The **Potter** books are also jarring satires of the institutions and absurdities of modernity. I see no evidence or reason that the next books will not be of this same quality; my guesses will assume continuing instruction about the true, the good, and the beautiful — in order to purify, dissolve, and reshape us in God's image. And need I add — because confounding our rush to judgement is a prime theme — there will be surprise, after surprise, after surprise?

So we know a lot to guide our guesses, and we know what we cannot know. Let's jump into some serious speculation!

Chapter 18

Who is
Harry Potter?

We dissected Harry's name in Chapter 15, looking for clues about who he is, concluding that "Harry Potter" is best read as "Heir-y Potter" or "son of God". This does not mean that Harry is another Christ symbol. It seems instead that Harry is an "Every-man" character born to inherit, as an image of God, the Kingdom of Heaven. In this perspective, his years at Hogwarts are symbolic poetry of the soul's purification and perfection, in pursuit of claiming this divine inheritance.

Voldemort wants Harry dead, then, as a representation of the Evil One's desperate struggle to deny Every-man his salvation. These symbols have real referents and remain valid above and beyond any other interpretation made of Harry's story.

For within the story, Harry is much more than an Every-man stick figure. Voldemort may want him dead as Satan wants each of our souls dead — but I suspect that as Heir of Slytherin, Voldemart's motivation centers on Harry's secret identity: *Harry is the sole Heir of Godric Gryffyndor, rightful ruler and king of wizards.*

My reasons for believing this are twofold: the model of the Inklings and the rather heavily-drawn King Arthur parallels throughout the storyline. Inklings Lewis and Tolkien were both royalists who believed in the divine right of kings (even if each had reconciled himself to the realities and virtues of democracy). Narnia is a kingdom ruled by Aslan-blessed kings from creation to apocalypse. *The Lord of the Rings* is largely the story of the return of the true king Aragorn to Middle-earth — a king by blood, by trial, and by spiritual accomplishment. If Harry were not a king, Rowling would be stepping away from her Inkling mentors.

The King Arthur parallels in the *Harry Potter* storyline are more compelling evidence than Rowling's kinship with the Inklings. Harry's hidden childhood, education directed by a master wizard, and the manner in which his royal identity is revealed — these are all hand-in-glove matches with the Arthurian legend.

Hidden Childhood

Arthur is born son and heir to Uther Pendragon, the first king to unite Britain under one sovereign. Merlin convinces Uther that the king is about to die and that Arthur must disappear as a newborn for safety's sake and not be known to the world. Uther agrees, Arthur is placed with Sir Ector the Trustworthy, and Pendragon dies soon after, as Merlin had foreseen. Arthur grows up as the esquire to Sir Ector's son, Sir Kay, unaware of his true lineage.

Harry is born in Godric Hollow, the son of James and Lily Potter. His parents are hunted down and murdered by Lord Voldemort, the most evil wizard of his time. In his attempt to kill Harry (his primary target at the Potter house), Lord Voldemort is foiled by the love of Harry's mother. He disappears, seemingly destroyed, and the orphaned Harry is placed by the good wizard Albus Dumbledore in the care of his muggle Aunt and Uncle. Harry grows up as the whipping boy of his spoiled cousin Dudley, unaware of his lineage or wizard abilities.

Education and Direction by a Master Wizard

Arthur grows up oblivious to his destiny, but he is carefully watched over by Merlin in secret. He reaches his majority in good health and of sterling character, largely due to Merlin's protection and the humility fostered by his lowly position. When the right time comes for Arthur to know his identity, the son of Uther Pendragon has been groomed to take his rightful place on the throne.

As Arthur was by Merlin, Harry is both protected and groomed by Albus Dumbledore. His protective measures so far have included:

- The "old magic", the alchemy of Calvary, which protects Harry from Voldemort's unblockable curse as an infant and continue to protect him from Voldemort's touch until his rebirthing;

Even though Harry's mother had to die to make it work, we know this is Dumbledore's doing, judging by his ready explanation of Quirrell/Voldemort's inability to touch Harry at the end of *Stone* (p. 299), and also by Dumbledore's reaction at the end of *Goblet* when he learns that Voldemort can now touch Harry:

> For a fleeting instant, Harry thought he saw a gleam of something like triumph in Dumbledore's eyes..... "Very well," he said, sitting down again. "Voldemort has overcome that particular barrier." (p. 696)

In *Chamber*, Tom Riddle calls the protection furnished Harry's mother by sacrificing herself, "a powerful counter charm" (p. 317). In *Goblet*, he again says, "the traces of her sacrifice ... provided him with a protection I admit I had not foreseen ... This is old magic. I should have remembered it. I was foolish to overlook it" (pp. 652-653).

Voldemort's foolishness is, as Dumbledore explains, because "if there is one thing Voldemort cannot understand, it is love" (*Stone*, p. 299). I believe Dumbledore booby-trapped Harry's mom to exploit Voldemort's blind spot, shielding Harry from later attacks as well. That Voldemort called this an "old magic" is a tip of the hat to "the deeper magic before the dawn of time" — Aslan's loving self-sacrifice in the first *Narnia* book, which itself refers to Calvary. Whenever Dumbledore or Voldemort refer to old, ancient, or deep magic, think of God's mercy and love for us in the sacrifice on Calvary, and more often than not you will have Rowling's meaning.

- Harry being left as a baby at the home of blood relatives with an explanatory letter that shapes their treatment of him;

Dumbledore tells Professor McGonagall in the opening of *Stone* that he is leaving Harry in the care of "the only family left him", both because they will be able to explain what had happened to him when he grows up, and because it is best that Harry that grow up out of the limelight **(p. 13)**. Voldemort tells the Death Eaters that there was more to Harry's placement than concern about Harry growing up with a swollen head:

> "But how to get at Harry Potter? For he has been better protected than I think even he knows, protected in ways devised by Dumbledore long ago, when it fell to him to arrange the boy's future. Dumbledore invoked an ancient magic, to ensure the boy's protection as long as he is in his relations' care. Not even I can touch him there...." **(Goblet, p. 657)**

And the letter? Well, more on the letter later. It had to have been some letter.

- Arabella Figg's proximity to the Dursleys' home to watch over Harry;

Sirius Black is dispatched by Dumbledore at the end of *Goblet* to round up the "old crowd" **(p. 713)**. One member of this trustworthy bunch of tried and true Voldemort resistors that Dumbledore mentions by name is Arabella Figg — a name known to Harry. On Dudley's birthday "every year, Harry was left behind with Mrs. Figg, a mad old lady who lived two streets away" **(Stone, p. 22)**.

Mrs. Figg makes him play with her four cats and look through "photographs of all the cats she'd ever owned". Harry may have hated her house and its smell of cabbage (see the two references to Mrs. Figg in *Goblet*, pp. 79-80 — does she have a friend at the Ministry?), but it's not rocket science to see that Dumbledore left a cat lady watchdog to look over Harry at the Dursleys. Look for a bizarre reunion in *Order of the Phoenix.*

• Dumbledore's appearance at Quidditch matches in which Harry's safety is an issue;

When Harry's broom goes out of control at his first Quidditch match, Snape volunteers to referee the next game, and Dumbledore is in visible attendance to everyone's surprise and relief (*Stone*, p. 222). Dumbledore attends Harry's matches in *Prisoner*, and it's a good thing; he saves Harry from dying in a fall from his broom in the first match by dispelling the crowd of dementors with a Patronus (p. 181). In Harry's next match, Dumbledore is there to witness Harry's own stag Patronus (p. 263). Dumbledore is nowhere noted to have taken such cares for the life of another student, but Harry's life, it seems, is especially precious.

• Dumbledore's invisible supervision and voice;

The headmaster reveals to Harry in their first conference in front of the Mirror of Erised that he had been present, but not visible, when Harry had come to look at the Mirror with Ron the previous night. Harry hadn't seen Dumbledore and doesn't understand how he could do it — but "I don't need a cloak to become invisible", said Dumbledore gently (*Stone*, p. 213).

During Harry's graveyard fight to the death with Voldemort, his wand "connects" with the Dark Lord's, generating a Phoenix song and a cage of golden light. When Harry thinks of Dumbledore, a voice comes from the music that tells him to hold on (*Goblet*, p. 664). Dumbledore isn't there, so he has to download Harry's experiences later — or was that only therapeutic (see p. 695)? But he seems to have an "Obi-Wan" like presence around Harry, visible and invisible.

Do you think I'm making too much of Dumbledore's invisibility? Neville Longbottom is awarded the critical ten points by Dumbledore that give Gryffyndor the House Cup in Harry's first Leaving Feast, because of Neville's courage in standing "up to his friends" (*Stone*, p. 306). But no one was in the Gryffyndor common room when Neville did this — at least no one *visible*.

- Dumbledore's continuing refusal to let Harry know why Voldemort wants him dead.

Harry asks Dumbledore point blank why Voldemort wants to kill him at the end of **Stone**. The big man balks. "Alas, the first thing you ask me, I cannot tell you. Not today. Not now. You will know one day... put it from your mind for now, Harry. When you are older... I know you hate to hear this... when you are ready, you will know" (p. 299). Harry has not yet asked him again.

The mention of being "ready" suggests that Harry is both being protected from knowledge that may hinder or hurt him — and that Dumbledore is in some way responsible for bringing Harry to a condition of "readiness" for some position or trial. Dumbledore's grooming of Harry in the first four books is evident in his refusal to answer this question, as well as in:

- Dumbledore's conversation and debriefing at the end of each book;

Coaches of football teams analyze the film of last week's game and review it with their team, seeing what was done right and what needs work. Dumbledore would have been a great football coach, for he never lets Harry leave Hogwarts without a one-on-one conversation to review his "last game", explain what really happened, and spell out the lessons he needs to take with him for the next game. Nobody else gets these tutorial talks, and no one is allowed to sit in with Harry.

- Dumbledore's preparation before the Mirror of Erised;

Dumbledore is the white element in the alchemy of the first book. He is responsible for the "minor work" or preparatory stage of the process. This he does by explaining to Harry what the Mirror of Erised is and what desires must be transcended to "be prepared". As Dumbledore says: "The Mirror will be moved to a new home, tomorrow, Harry, and I ask you not to go looking for it again. If you ever *do* run across it, you will now be prepared" **(Stone, pp. 213-214)**. The headmaster seems to have a plan that Harry will run the gauntlet to get to the Stone and face the Mirror.

- Dumbledore's hurdles and trials for Harry to endure and overcome.

Harry thinks Dumbledore has him in training, too. Ron and Hermione explain to the hospitalized Harry what happened to them after Harry left to fight Quirrell:

> "Well, I got back all right," said Hermione. "I brought Ron round — that took a while — and we were dashing up to the owlery to contact Dumbledore when we met him in the entrance hall — he already knew — he just said, 'Harry's gone after him, hasn't he?' and hurtled off to the third floor."
>
> "D'you think he meant you to do it?" said Ron. "Sending you your father's cloak and everything?"
>
> "Well," Hermione exploded, "if he did — I mean to say — that's terrible — you could have been killed."
>
> "No, it isn't," said Harry thoughtfully. "He's a funny man, Dumbledore. I think he sort of wanted to give me a chance. I think he knows more or less everything that goes on here, you know. I reckon he had a pretty good idea we were going to try, and instead of stopping us, he just taught us enough to help. I don't think it was an accident he let me find out how the mirror worked. It's almost like he thought I had the right to face Voldemort if I could..." **(Stone, p. 302)**

As discussed in the book-by-book look in Part Three, the obstacles to be surmounted in the first and fourth books amount to trials of Harry's spiritual worthiness. Rowling uses Dumbledore as her symbol of "perfect man/alchemist" (looking like an "ancient of days" Father Time or conventional depictions of God the Father), which makes Harry's suspicion that the Head Man is quasi-omniscient seem plausible. Dumbledore certainly seems to give Harry just enough rope and knowledge to survive these tests. Bagman and Moody/Crouch Jr. help Harry in **Goblet** to win the Tournament and get a free trip to Voldemort. Is Dumbledore coaching Harry via full-contact scrimmages every year for the Big Game to come, when Harry is revealed as Heir of Gryffyndor? I think so.

Though Dumbledore may have been as surprised as anyone when Harry's name popped from the Goblet of Fire, and he could hardly have laid out the TriWizard tasks with Harry in mind, note that if Dumbledore had wanted Harry out of the contest, magical contract or no, it is unlikely anyone in that conference of International Headmasters would have overruled him. Dumbledore lets Harry go ahead because he thinks it will prove a fine workout for him — which, of course, it is. Like Merlin with the young King Arthur, Dumbledore is there to protect and prepare Harry for the battles and responsibilities in his future.

Sword in Stone, Sword in Hat

While fighting in the Tournament celebrating the magical sword placed by Merlin in an anvil (a stone in other versions), Sir Kay's sword breaks. His esquire Arthur runs back toward their pavilion to get another sword, when he sees the sword in the anvil. Arthur pulls it from the anvil unaware of what he has done; pulling the sword from the stone demonstrates that he is right regent and king of Britain, heir to Uther Pendragon.

Likewise, while in the Chamber of Secrets facing Tom Riddle, Harry is sent Fawkes the Phoenix and the Hogwarts Sorting Hat by Dumbledore. Riddle summons the Basilisk

and the battle begins. Fawkes helps by blinding the Basilisk —
but what help is the hat? Harry puts it on, cries for help, and
(voila!) a silver sword falls from inside the hat to bonk him on
the head. Harry kills the giant serpent with the sword and
lives happily ever after (until the next book).

Dumbledore in the post-battle review let's Harry in on
the sword's secret:

> Dumbledore reached across to Professor McGonagall's
> desk, picked up the blood stained silver sword, and handed
> it to Harry. Dully, Harry turned it over, the rubies blazing
> in the fire light. And then he saw the name engraved just
> below the hilt.
>
> *Godric Gryffyndor.*
>
> "Only a true Gryffyndor could have pulled *that* out of the
> hat, Harry," said Dumbledore simply. (*Chamber*, pp. 333-334)

It is not until Book 4 that the reader learns whose hat the
Sorting Hat is (get it? "Sword -in' Hat"?). Sure enough, the
Hat tells us that Hogwarts' founding four put brains in *Godric
Gryffyndor's* hat to sort new students (*Goblet*, p. 177). For whom
comes Gryffyndor's sword from Gryffyndor's hat? Harry
thinks Dumbledore's explanation means that he really does
belong in Gryffyndor House. Yes, Harry does — but there
are two larger meanings.

Why does Voldemort want Harry dead (even as baby)?

Harry asks Dumbledore at the end of *Stone* why Voldemort
wants him dead. The Headmaster demurs, saying only that
Harry will know when he's ready. However, Voldemort knows

now; he gives us a big clue at his Rebirthing party when he tells the Death Eaters:

> "You see, I think, how foolish it was to suppose that this boy could ever have been stronger than me," said Voldemort. "But I want there to be no mistake in anybody's mind. Harry Potter escaped me by a lucky chance. And I am now going to prove my power by killing him, here and now, in front of you all, when there is no Dumbledore here to help him, and no mother to die for him. I will give him his chance. He will be allowed to fight, and you will be left in no doubt which of us is the stronger." (*Goblet*, **p. 658**)

Voldemort is obviously concerned that his followers believe Harry is the stronger wizard of the two of them. Perhaps they have heard of the battle for the Philosopher's Stone? It is unlikely any except Malfoy knew about Harry's victory in the Chamber of Secrets. But even so, doesn't it seem ludicrous that Voldemort thinks he needs to prove his power greater than this teenage boy's? Or greater even than Harry as an infant? Why would anyone believe otherwise?

The only answer that makes sense to me (and, boy, my daughters have made up some doozies!) is that the fight between the original Gryffyndor and Slytherin has become a legacy. Professor Binns, late and current Professor of Magical History, tells of the original disagreement:

> "For a few years, the founders worked in harmony together, seeking out youngsters who showed signs

of magic and bringing them to the castle to be educated. But then disagreements sprang up between them. A rift began to grow between Slytherin and the others. Slytherin wished to be more *selective* about the students admitted to Hogwarts. He believed that magical learning should be kept within all magic families. He disliked taking students of Muggle parentage, believing them to be untrustworthy. After a while there was a serious argument on the subject between Slytherin and Gryffyndor, and Slytherin left the school." *(Chamber,* **p. 150)**

Dumbledore all but tells Harry that he is Heir of Gryffyndor when he tells him pulling the sword from Godric's hat is something only a "*true* Gryffyndor" could have done. But so what?

Well, if this original fight between Slytherin and Gryffyndor (and Gryffyndor's evident victory) is a legacy battle among their descendants, then Harry has "got to go" in Voldemort's eyes. As Heir of Slytherin, Riddle/Voldemort must eliminate the Heir of Gryffyndor, preferably in combat, to claim the right to rule all wizards. This illumines why the Dark Lord had to find and execute James Potter, and why he tried to kill Harry even as an infant: if a descendant of Godric Gryffyndor remains, wizards and witches may wonder if their top man is really boss, especially if he is Heir of Slytherin. The top man should wonder, too.

Remember the meaning of the House founders' names. Godric Gryffyndor, you'll recall, means "Godly Golden Griffin" and is a cipher for Christ. Salazar Slytherin, the sound of which is a snake speaking and moving through the grass, is another name for Satan, the deceiver, who was a serpent in the Garden. These two powers, Christ and the devil, are not equal (except in the popular mind); one is God, the other His servant, an angel (albeit a fallen angel). The devil may hate and oppose Christ, but he has no power over Him; he has only an influence on those who do not choose to live in Him and His victory over death.

Voldemort's attempt to kill Harry as a baby powerfully recalls Herod's equally satanic and pointless slaughter of all the two years old and under "in Bethlehem and in all the coasts thereof" to get the Christ child (St. Matthew 2:16). Voldemort "has doubts" whether he is Harry's master — and worries about his followers — because he knows he is not Harry's master. Harry Potter, "son of God", born in Godric Hollow, is Heir of Godric Gryffyndor and destined to defeat Voldemort, Heir of Slytherin, just as light shatters darkness. It doesn't matter how big or old the light is, only that it be light.

"Do you realize who this is?"

A critical part of the whole *Harry Potter* series will fall into place when Harry is revealed as the King Arthur of the Wizarding World. Certainly part of that world is already aware of it: Dumbledore and Voldemort know, of course, and comments by Fudge, Snape, and Malfoy suggest they too may be aware of Harry's lineage. The house elves already adore and serve him as savior and deliverer (see Dobby's speech, *Chamber*, pp. 177-178). Perhaps most tellingly, though, the Centaurs know who Harry Potter is — and they think he's important.

No small thing, that. As Hagrid puts it, the Centaurs are "not interested in anythin' closer'n the moon" (*Stone*, p. 254). They are otherworldly creatures above passion and concerns other than seeing the divine patterns in the heavens. The Centaurs are symbols of Christ (see Chapter 9), but their divine apathy can also be almost Nietzschean; one of the Centaurs, appropriately named Bane (meaning "cause of death, destruction; deadly poison"), talks as if they must not act for the good because they are "beyond good and evil". His exchange with Firenze is instructive:

> "Firenze!" Bane thundered. "What are you doing? You have a human on your back! Have you no shame? Are you a common mule?"

> "Do you realize who this is? " said Firenze. "This is the Potter boy. The quicker he leaves the forest, the better."

> "What have you been telling him?" growled Bane. "Remember, Firenze, we are sworn not to set ourselves against the heavens. Have we not read what is to come in the movements of the planets?"

> Ronan pawed the ground nervously. "I'm sure Firenze thought he was acting for the best," he said in his gloomy voice.

> Bane kicked his back legs in anger.

> "For the best! What is that to us? Centaurs are concerned with what has been foretold! It is not our business to run like donkeys after stray humans in our forest!"

> Firenze suddenly reared on his hind legs, so that Harry had to grab his shoulders to stay on.

"Do you not see that unicorn?" Firenze bellowed at Bane.

"Do you not understand why it was killed? Or have the planets not let you in on that secret? I set myself against what is lurking in this forest, Bane, yes, with humans alongside me if I must." (*Stone*, p. 257)

The Centaurs know the whole story (even though there seems some proscription against telling Harry). Voldemort is coming back and resuming power, but Harry Potter is the obstacle to his final victory. Bane's response to this knowledge is fatalistic: "kicking back" in anger, figuratively "doing nothing". By contrast, Firenze heroically rises up in front (elevating his human half above the animal), proclaiming his kinship with the murdered unicorn (Christ) and his enmity with Christ's enemies. He considers carrying Harry Potter to safety an expression of that kinship and enmity.

The Centaurs will return. The passage above can be interpreted in terms of its place within **Stone**, but the far-sighted Centaurs are clearly talking about the eventual return of Voldemort that takes place in **Goblet** (and a return which will probably not be complete for two more books). What is relevant here is Firenze's exclamation: "Do you realize who this is?" The familiarity of the three stargazing Centaurs in **Philosopher's Stone** with this "son of God" and Heir of Gryffyndor hearkens to the three Magi astrologers with foreknowledge of Jesus Emmanuel's birth.

However, the rest of the world will not learn Harry's royal destiny until the end of the next book. I believe it will be revealed during the next fight with Voldemort, at

Dumbledore's death, or (very likely) both. Now that Harry has been prepared, either Dumbledore or Voldemort or both will give Harry the news of his birth right when he is forced by Dumbledore's demise to lead the forces resisting the Dark Lord.

Yes, Dumbledore must die — and soon! My reasons for suggesting this unpopular idea are three:

- Defeat, departure, or death is what happens to great wizards and God-figures in traditional fiction (Merlin), Inkling literature (Gandalf — and Aslan), and even popular movies (goodbye, Obi Wan!);

- Rowling observes the conventions of the Hero's Journey, a staple of epic poetry and fairy tales, wherein heroes almost inevitably face their greatest, final trials independent of their otherworldly guides (remember, Dumbledore is absent from Hogwarts during Harry's battles in *Stone* and *Chamber*); and

- Harry will never be the True King of Wizards in his subject's eyes, or even the focus of the Godric Gryffyndor squad, until Dumbledore exits and Harry defeats Voldemort on his own.

This last point needs some explanation. Albus Dumbledore has protected and guided Harry through soul-perfecting trials to ready him for his place as Heir of Gryffyndor. Dumbledore acknowledges that Harry "has shouldered a grown wizard's burden and found [himself] equal to it" (*Goblet*, p. 699). But as it stands, the "white hats" all look to Dumbledore to lead them against the Heir of

Slytherin; the consensus is summarized by Hagrid's comment: "'S long as we've got him, I'm not too worried" (*Goblet*, p. 719).

Therefore, for Harry to be king or even much of a leader, Dumbledore must die. The final step in Harry's formation as King will be as a leader of the frightened and confused good guys against Voldemort in the wake of Dumbledore's death.

Chapter 19

Is Snape With Us
or
Against Us?
And Other Questions That Need Answering

"Who is Harry Potter?" is far and away the most important question to be resolved in the upcoming books. It is remarkable that Rowling has come this far without telling us — and perhaps it will be another book before we have the final answer. There are other questions, though, that need a guess before I hazard the folly of suggesting what the coming book titles and their subject matter will be. Here are the best answers my home grown team of Harry sleuths and I could come up with to these subsidiary questions.

Why are the Dursleys so afraid of Magic?

Vernon Dursley and his wife Petunia do not have a healthy respect for "magic". Their response to even the mention of magic is horror and rage. This makes sense on two levels, but is really queer on another.

First, it creates a great foil between the magic and muggle worlds. If Harry came from a happy, supportive, loving home (or even a sane one), what joy would he feel at Hogwarts? He'd be homesick. No matter how bad life gets at Wizarding School, Harry is never homesick for the Dursleys. This could just be a necessary plot device to keep things moving along. But I doubt it.

Second, the Dursley's nastiness bolsters Ms. Rowling's point about the modern world: those who are the archetypes of the materialist outlook have to be monstrous to foster sympathy for the alternative, symbolist perspective of the magical world. Therefore the Dursleys are cartoon figures; they represent the knee-jerk fear and dismissal of anything greater than "the realm of the physical sciences" in the modern academy, media, and government (and of anything spiritual not conforming to mechanical ideology tests from Scripture).

The portrayal of The Dursleys has grown even nastier, perhaps, as Rowling uses them to vent her feelings for the lack of thoughtful review of her work by the *literati* and certain fundamentalists. The smugness, self-importance, and meanness on Privet Drive towards Harry's "abnormality" look a lot like the Low Road responses her books have received.

Having said that, the Dursleys are the only characters in the series that are unbelievable; they're ridiculous to the point of burlesque. Given Ms. Rowling's ability to draw characters that are simultaneously fantastic and believable, together with her penchant for springing surprises to confound the rush to judgment in her readers, I think it more likely that the Dursleys have a reason to be paranoid about magic. "Reason to be paranoid", of course, points to traumatic experience.

We know the Dursleys have some experience of magic. Petunia Dursley does not have fond memories of her sister Lily Potter; she recalls Lily coming "home every vacation with her pockets full of frog spawn, turning teacups into rats" (*Stone*, p. 53). It seems their Mom and Dad were very proud of lovely Lily the Witch and not as fond of plain Petunia the Muggle.

This experience might explain the Dursleys' familiarity, resentment, or even contempt of all that is magical, but not their blind fear and rage about "being different". The Dursleys were this way well before Hagrid confirmed their exaggerated opinion of magic by putting a pig's tail on Dudley; their unbalanced beliefs shaped how Harry was "raised". Beneath the Dursleys' neurosis and phobia lies some much more traumatic experience, or the threat of trauma, or both. I think it's "both".

Lily and James were probably never kind to the Dursleys. If Lily was turning her teacups into rats, it is easy to imagine James and Sirius playing more serious pranks. However, I suspect this mischief only laid the foundation for an experience of dark wizardry that would haunt anyone in their right minds: a visit from Voldemort and the Death Eaters.

The Dark Lord wanted the Gryffyndor line extinguished to cement his right to rule. But James and Harry were concealed from him by the Fidelius Charm. Before Voldemort learned from Pettigrew where the Potters were hiding, is it not likely that Voldemort had taken steps to find them on his own? As torturing Muggles was a delight to Voldemort and his followers, I suspect they found the Dursleys and tortured them for whatever knowledge they could extract about James and Lily's whereabouts.

A visit from Voldemort could make you hate and fear the magical forever — especially if the Dark Lord seemed a logical progression of your patronizing and prank-loving in-laws. But the Dursleys' dread of seeming out of the ordinary is peculiar, *unless they've been warned to prevent Harry having a free rein with his magic so as not to draw unwanted attention from evil wizards.* A warning to lie low or at least not flaunt his powers could have triggered the traumatized Dursleys into fearing any show of the peculiar from Harry.

"We swore when we took him in we'd put a stop to that rubbish," said Uncle Vernon, "swore we'd stamp it out of him! Wizard indeed!" *(Stone, p. 53).* Dumbledore's letter may simply have been misunderstood. His kind admonition to keep Harry in check for the boy's good and safety may have caused them to fear the reappearance of the Death Eaters. This fear might easily have become a mania for appearing normal and loathing the different — for Harry's good as well as their own. The Dursleys may have felt that it was no kindness to raise Harry to become a wizard, as their only experiences of wizards ranged from uncomfortable to life threatening.

Harry's real surprise when he finally gets to read Dumbledore's letter to the Dursleys (probably in Book 6 or 7) will be that the Dursleys were trying to protect Harry from this evil "magic disease" when they kept him in the dark about his heritage, either out of misunderstanding — or perhaps at Dumbledore's very suggestion! His letter may have only explained how Harry was orphaned, that the Dursleys were Harry's only protection from Voldemort, and that Arabella Figg would be watching them as Dumbledore's contact person. Perhaps he mentioned that the Ancient Magic protected Harry while in the care of his relations.

Or maybe he didn't. Dumbledore's comments to Professor McGonagall at the time imply that he thinks Harry's growing up with difficulties is much preferable to growing up comfortable and famous. Might he not have asked them to raise Harry as a "normal" boy and discourage him from using magic? Whatever he wrote, he left Uncle Vernon with the conviction that Dumbledore was "a crackpot old fool" (*Stone*, **page 59**). I suspect his note was the cleverest kind of reverse psychology to get the Dursleys to raise Harry with little reason to think himself special.

What is marvelous is that the Dursleys agreed to raise Harry at all. There is no evident advantage in it for them (except perhaps the psychological jollies from torturing a helpless boy?). Either Dumbledore gave them an incentive, or else the Dursleys raised Harry despite their ill feelings about his kind. I suspect it is the latter, so that Harry will come to a sort of grudging gratitude to the Dursleys after reading the letter. I would not be surprised if Harry has to save the Dursleys from the Death

Eaters, perhaps at the cost of his own freedom (look for this at the end of Book 6 or 7).

Why does Professor Severus Snape hate Harry so?

Rowling has trimmed back the "hedge of history" concealing Snape's hatred for Harry enough to reveal that:

- Snape and James Potter hated each other at school;

- While students together, Sirius once sent Snape to see Lupin in his werewolf form — a recipe for almost certain death or infection with the werewolf curse. Harry seems to remind Snape of this incident in the Shrieking Shack, when James Potter prevented Snape's death; and

- Their hatred springs from Gryffyndor/Slytherin rivalry. Snape was notorious for his familiarity with the dark arts, and is obviously the ideal Slytherin wizard. Sirius as Gryffyndor-ite seems to hate Snape as much as Snape hates Harry and Sirius.

But really, as Fudge observes, Snape is "quite unbalanced" when it comes to Harry (*Prisoner*, **p. 420**). The venom he feels comes right to the surface whenever he sees Harry; he delights sadistically and melodramatically in punishing and provoking the boy. Childhood rivalries seem insufficient to explain Snape's visceral hatred for the Potters.

A better reason (or two) is suggested by what we know about Professor Snape beyond his relationship with Harry. For instance, we know that Snape was a Slytherin as a student, and that he is the Slytherin House Master (the only time he is not in black is at events he is obliged to wear Slytherin green). Dumbledore has also revealed (in person and in the Pensieve memory Harry visits) that "Severus Snape was indeed a Death Eater. However, he rejoined our side before Lord Voldemort's downfall and turned spy for us, at great personal risk" (*Goblet*, **pages 590-591**). He dispatches Snape at the end of *Goblet* to Voldemort to resume this dangerous work (and what one assumes cannot be a warm welcome, given Snape's scrutiny of Quirrell in *Stone*).

The Sorting Hat tells us that Salazar Slytherin was "power hungry" and "loved those of great ambition" (*Goblet*, **p. 177**). He also "started all this pure blood stuff" (as **Ron put it in** *Chamber*, **p. 152**) because he disliked accepting students who were not from pure-blood Wizarding families. Severus Snape, whose name shares initials and a slippery assonance with the original Slytherin, should likewise be ambitious and concerned about blood purity, as leader and archetype of Slytherin House.

Snape is ambitious, at least in one sense of that word. The Greek word usually translated from Attic texts as "ambition" is *philotime* or "love of honor". As Fudge had observed, Snape comes unglued and unbalanced at the end of *Prisoner*; this is not because of blood lust for Black but due to the repercussions of Black's escape on Buckbeak, whereby Snape lost the honors and fame promised him by Fudge for his part in catching the escaped prisoner (such as receiving the Order of Merlin, getting a write-up in the *Daily Prophet*, seeing Harry humiliated, and so on). As Dumbledore puts it, Snape has "suffered a great disappointment" (*Prisoner*, **p. 420**). He seems in the days that follow to be close to a nervous breakdown.

Snape's "love of honor" seems a more plausible explanation for his hating Harry, especially in light of his clandestine heroism against Voldemort. Remember that Snape changed sides at great risk before Voldemort "died" in the attempt on Harry's life. By his cradle victory over Voldemort, Harry deprived Snape of the honor due him for the risks he took as a spy against Voldemort, as well as trapping him in the low profile role he has at Hogwarts. Snape is unable to reveal his heroism lest he be attacked by his fellow Death Eaters, with whom he remains on good terms (if his favor with the Malfoys is any measure).

Here is Snape's real reason for hating Harry, the famous boy who conquered the Dark Lord. *By no virtue of his own, Harry commands the adoration of magical folk worldwide for the very deed which the forgotten Snape had worked to achieve at great risk of his life. Harry is a walking, talking reminder of Snape's "nobody" status, his forced isolation, and of the honor he deserved but will never enjoy.* No wonder Snape considers it his personal mission to "treat [Harry] like any other student" *(Prisoner, p. 387)* — its a great cover for acting out his inner rage and frustration.

And the Slytherin concern for purity of blood and disdain for mudbloods and muggles? I'll go out on a limb here and say that part of Snape's hatred for Harry has to do with his green-eyed mother Lily.

We know very little about Lily Potter beyond her sacrifice which saved Harry's life and her green eyes (Harry looks like the clone of his father except for having his mother's eyes, a quality mentioned in each book). Hagrid also says that she and James were "head boy an' girl at Hogwarts in their day" *(Stone, p. 55)*.

The only clue as to what Lily's green eyes might mean is that Slytherin's house colors are green and silver. Hanging on this thin strand, I suggest the following scenario. Lily Potter was in Slytherin House and was very successful and popular there, though a mudblood. Snape, likewise a Slytherin prefect, loved her from afar and hoped to "win her hand". But she "betrayed" him: first by becoming Head Girl and surpassing him in honor (James having been selected as Head Boy), but more importantly by falling in love with his arch rival and *Gryffyndor* stalwart, James Potter.

Snape is such a melodramatic figure, recalling for Joan Acocella the 19th century caricatures of "the rapacious Jew" (*New Yorker*, **July 31, 2000, p. 76**), and for others the cartoon Snidely Whiplash who opposed Dudley Doright. I have no qualms imagining Snape descend year by year into deeper bitterness for the love he lost as a young man. There is even something noble in his "remaining true", despite her not having proved equal to his unrequited love (perhaps attributed to her mudblood unworthiness).

How will Snape turn out in the end? Almost certainly he will play a heroic part on behalf of the "white hats". His courage and love of honor will bring him to turn on Voldemort in the end (probably resulting in his own death). I imagine that reversal will happen to save Harry, whom Snape will then tell of his great love for Lily. Think of Harry's surprise at the bond he has with Snape.

Before this dramatic disclosure, look for Snape to act as a double agent, serving neither side sincerely but his own interest above all. At Dumbledore's death, Malfoy will again pressure the school governors, this time to make Snape the Headmaster (or possibly the vampire Dark Arts teacher predicted in

Chapter 20). The "white hats" will then recognize Snape's duplicity and forsake him — only to be surprised and saved by this tortured man and hero when he sacrificially betrays Voldemort at the last possible moment.

What role must Neville Longbottom play?

Outside of "the dream team" of Harry, Ron and Hermione, the one student at Hogwarts whom Rowling has taken the most care in shaping and revealing is Neville Longbottom. He will be critical to the final drama, perhaps playing the decisive role.

What we know about Neville is:

- His parents, Frank and an unnamed mother, were aurors. They are clinically insane after having been tortured via the Cruciatus Curse by Death Eaters looking for the departed Lord Voldemort. Neville was raised by his grandmother because his parents are unable to care for or even recognize him;

- The Longbottoms are a respected, old wizard blood family. His parents were very popular, and Neville's grandmother is very conscious of the family honor (and that Neville is not being a good representative);

- He is anything but a promising wizard. He says of himself "everyone knows I'm almost a squib" (*Chamber*, p. 185). Witches don't consider him a great date for the Yule Ball in *Goblet*, and little wonder. He is homely and overweight. He has a memory that fails him constantly, and he is inept in the class room. His capabilities on the broomstick are such that "when Neville flies for England in Quidditch" is a school euphemism for "never";

- His greatest fear is Professor Snape, who enjoys belittling him publicly; and

- He does quite well in Herbology, his favorite subject.

Neville's name points to his "nobody" status. Neville breaks down to *ne*, meaning "no" or "not", and *ville*, "villa" or "village", for a sum of "no-place" or "no-where". Longbottom gives us *long*, "big in size or duration in time", and *bottom*, "butt" or "lowest place", for a composite of either "big butt" or "long time at bottom of heap". Every day he answers to a name meaning "nowhere-man big-butt/low caste". How appropriate that Harry tells Stan Shunpike while hiding on the Knight bus that his name is Neville Longbottom **(Prisoner, page 34)** — it's a great name for an unassuming alias.

When Harry learns about Neville's parents from Dumbledore in *Goblet*, he is moved to a new appreciation for his peer:

> "He imagined how it must feel to have parents still living but unable to recognize you. He often got sympathy from strangers for being an orphan, but as he listened to Neville's snores, he thought that Neville deserved it more than he did." **(p. 607)**

Perhaps Harry will soon realize that Neville is to his generation what Peter was to his father's.

Harry notices that Peter and Neville resemble each other physically **(Prisoner, p. 213)**, as one would expect from our relationships map, where generational rings balance within one side to another and from generation to the next. James Potter had two close friends and a hanger-on, Peter. So in the generational ring that follows, his son Harry also has two close friends and a hanger-on, dear old Neville.

The love and masculine virtues of the elder Potter's threesome (we could say "Trinity") were insufficient to redeem or initiate Peter Pettigrew and secure him against the fear and temptations of Voldemort. Will Harry, Ron, and Hermione be able to save Neville from Peter's fate of cowardice and betrayal? This may be the pivotal question of the Potter books, and I have to think the answer is "yes".

Dumbledore awards 10 points to Gryffyndor House at the end of *Stone* in recognition of Neville's courage in standing up to his friends **(page 306)**. These few points put them over the top and win Gryffyndor the House Cup over Slytherin. I think that Rowling is foreshadowing here in the first book the climactic battle in Book 7. This near squib and plant authority, Neville Longbottom, by his courage in the face of bullying Snape or patronizing friends, will tip the balance for Gryffyndor's heir, perhaps at the cost of his life. Look for Neville with Trevor (another animagus?) on his broomstick in the last battle, "flying for England". The "last" and long-at-bottom will be "first" in the end — the critical, proverbial straw and mensch that break Voldemort's back.

Is Wormtail Harry's Ace in the Hole?

Sirius Black wondered at the end of *Prisoner* why he hadn't suspected Pettigrew of being Voldemort's spy. As he tells Peter, "I'll never understand why I didn't see you were the spy from the start. You always liked big friends who'd look after you, didn't you?" **(p. 369)**. No doubt Rowling will give us more information about Pettigrew's childhood that explains his weakness and cowardice, but his name tells us much. As we have seen, his names *Peter Petttigrew* and *Wormtail* both break down to "little penis". Lacking the manly courage and necessary integrity necessary, this "Mr. Penis-not-so-big" fails his three school friends and becomes Voldemort's henchman.

Harry is distraught about showing mercy to Pettigrew, who afterwards escapes to help Voldemort. But Dumbledore consoles Harry with a prediction that Wormtail may turn out all right in the end:

> "Pettigrew owes his life to you. You have sent Voldemort a deputy who is in your debt....When one wizard saves another wizard's life, it creates a certain bond between them ... and I'm much mistaken if Voldemort wants a servant in the debt of Harry Potter. ... This is magic at its deepest, its most impenetrable, Harry. But trust me... the time will come when you will be very glad you saved Pettigrew's life." (***Prisoner***, p. 427)

At the beginning of ***Goblet*** (pages 8-9), Peter does show some eagerness to escape Voldemort and find a substitute for Harry in the Dark Lord's plan. Peter is not gentle with Harry in the graveyard Rebirthing party, but neither is he cruel; he is ashamed enough of what he is doing never to be able to look Harry in the face. I think it may be assumed that Pettigrew's "negligence" in allowing Barty Crouch, Sr., to escape was a Wormtail stab at freedom. Voldemort certainly considers his service unwilling and suspect, just as Dumbledore assumed.

If Peter does become a mensch in the end and find the courage to turn against Voldemort, it will be an echo of Gollum's "service" to Frodo and Sam on Mt. Doom at the end of **The Lord of the Rings**. Gandalf told Frodo not to regret Bilbo's having shown mercy to Gollum (which mercy Frodo later shows himself), just as Dumbledore counsels Harry.

These echoes are so loud and Peter's conformity with Dumbledore's prediction so uniform that I am suspicious. The point's been reached where it wouldn't even be very surprising if Peter becomes a hero! And I confess to expecting only authentic, unheralded surprises from Ms. Rowling. Look for Peter perhaps to make a feint for freedom and to do the right thing — and fail.

Or maybe Peter will never do anything but what Voldemort wants; now that would be surprising! "Wormtail" may be a Tolkienesque echo not of Gollum and his good/evil schizophrenia so much as of Grima "Wormtongue", servant (and slayer) of the Dark Wizard Saruman.

Why is Harry so Rich? What is the source of the Potter fortune?

If I am right in speculating that Harry is Heir of Gryffyndor, then perhaps his extraordinary fortune in a vault under Gringott's Bank is no mystery. Maybe these are the trappings of royalty, the Gryffyndor family jewels. If the Potter wealth is inherited, James' ability to afford an invisibility cloak while a student makes sense, since "they're really rare, and *really* valuable" (*Stone*, p. 201).

I don't doubt that the Potters never wanted for money, but there are reasons to think Harry's wealth came from commerce more than inheritance. I think Sirius Black and James Potter made a lot of money inventing products for Zonko's joke shop. Before you close my book with derision, hear me out!

Sirius Black is rich, too. He has enough money in Gringott's to be able to buy Harry the most expensive broomstick made, a Firebolt. To whom does Hagrid liken Sirius and James as troublemakers (*Prisoner*, p. 204)? Who "inherits" their Marauder's Map? The answer is Fred and George Weasley, the twin brothers who dream of opening a joke shop and spend all their free time inventing devilish toys and treats, from fake wands to canary creams and tongue ton toffees.

However, it is Snape who points the finger at Sirius and James as "joke shop" toy manufacturers. He discovers the Marauder's Map in Harry's pocket, and gets insulted in writing by the map's four authors when he commands the Map to reveal its secret. Snape calls Lupin immediately and asks for an explanation. Lupin is one of the Map's authors, but Snape doesn't accuse Lupin of this outright. He seems instead to be looking for a confession.

> "Full of Dark Magic?" [Lupin] repeated mildly [to Snape]. "Do you really think so, Severus? It looks to me as though it is merely a piece of parchment that insults anybody who reads it. Childish, but surely not dangerous? I imagine Harry got it from a joke shop -"

"Indeed?" said Snape. His jaw had gone rigid with anger. "You think a joke shop could supply him with such a thing? You don't think it more likely that he got it *directly from the manufacturers*?" (**Prisoner, p. 288**)

Snape seems well aware of the real identities of the four map makers including Lupin, whom he may be accusing of helping Harry off campus despite the threat of Sirius Black (whom Snape does know is Lupin's old buddy). His "manufacturers" line moves me to think Snape also was aware of how Sirius and James made their money: as Zonko suppliers.

Harry has a real admiration for George and Fred. He gives them his TriWizard Cup winnings to help them start their joke shop. Laughter and a Weasley joke product will play no small part in the finish (see **Chapter 20**), and I think Harry realizes this in his bones. After all, his father may have been a professional.

What's up with Ludo Bagman?

Fred and George Weasley at the end of **Goblet** explain that Ludo Bagman, the lovable head of the Ministry department for magical sports and games, welched on his World Cup bets. The Weasley twins had bet all their savings on Ireland winning but Krum getting the snitch. Bagman had given them good odds on such a long shot, which came in. He paid them in leprechaun gold and then refused to pay up when that money disappeared.

Fred and George believe that Ludo leaves the TriWizard Tournament on the lam at its shocking conclusion to flee the

Goblins. They heard he was in real debt to the Goblins and placed a bet on Harry to win outright. Harry's tie meant he was in even more debt and trouble, hence his departure in haste after the third task. I think the whole story unlikely, even if it appears to explain why Ludo was eager to help Harry with each task.

First, the bets. Ludo is supposed to be afraid of the Goblins and to be betting on Harry against them to gain his freedom. If so, why do the Goblins sitting with Ludo allow him to leave for a private conversation with Harry when he appears in the Three Broomsticks for a Butterbeer? They know that Ludo knows the coming tasks; isn't it incredible the Goblins would allow him to cheat in his bet right in front of them? Hermione say Goblins are more than capable of taking care of themselves and wizards (see *Goblet*, p. 449) — there is something askew here.

Next, the evidence of a shady past. Harry sees Bagman on trial as a Death Eater in the Pensieve. Ludo ducks the charge in O. J. fashion by playing the part of a harmless, great athlete persecuted by overzealous Ministry officials. Crouch is outraged by his escaping punishment, and Winky tells us in real time at Hogwarts that "Mr. Bagman is a bad wizard! A very bad wizard! My master isn't liking him, oh no, not at all!" (*Goblet*, page 382). Though Dumbledore tells Harry that Bagman "has never been accused of any Dark activity since" his trial (page 603), there is obviously more to him than meets the eye.

His name, for instance. *Ludo* sounds harmless and fun, perhaps, as in "ludicrous". But *ludo* is the Latin word for "I play, I am playing a game". *Bagman* is the male equivalent for "bag lady", I suppose, but its slang usage is for the toughs who collect dues and such for mafiosos. Brits use *bagman* to describe traveling salesmen. *Ludo Bagman,* then, means either "I am playing the part of village idiot or itinerant salesman" or "I am having a great time as a mafia bully".

It could mean both these things, because Ludo does have a great front as an aging jock "hit too many times by a bludger" and he may very well be a Death Eater who escaped punishment. I think he was in The Three Broomsticks hanging with Goblins who are also old friends of Lord Voldemort. Ludo and the Goblins wanted Harry to win the Tournament for the same reason Moody/Crouch, Jr., wanted him to win: to speed the return of the Dark Lord.

Bagman flees away after the third task (leaving the false trails of gambling debts) to get to where he could disapparate and return to Voldemort, apparating being impossible while at Hogwarts. He may also have been concerned that the miraculously-returned Harry knew Ludo had "helped" him in the manner of Moody/Crouch, Jr. Either way, look for Bagman to be on the Dark Side in the coming books, openly or undercover, and to be the Wizard leader of a Goblin Revolt in either **Order of the Phoenix** or the book following.

What role will Hagrid play in the Final Act?

Hagrid will play a BIG role, of course! This Falstaff figure has played the buffoon on the periphery of each novel, good for laughs, theme development, and plot movement. Unlike the original Falstaff, who fell to the sidelines when Harry Hotspur

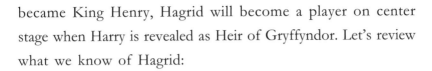
became King Henry, Hagrid will become a player on center stage when Harry is revealed as Heir of Gryffyndor. Let's review what we know of Hagrid:

- Hagrid is a contemporary of Tom Riddle/Voldemort and among his first victims (Hagrid was expelled on Riddle's testimony for something he hadn't done);

- Dumbledore kept Hagrid from Azkaban at that time, got him the gamekeeper job, and in Harry's third year appointed Hagrid to teach "Care of Magical Creatures". Hagrid has a nigh-on ferocious loyalty to Dumbeldore, and the Headmaster has been heard to say "I would trust Hagrid with my life" (*Stone*, p. 14);

- Hagrid is a half-giant whose father died in Hagrid's second year at Hogwarts, and whose giantess mother Fridwulfa (whom he does not know) may still be alive; and

- Hagrid has a remarkable taste and affection for the monstrous. He is quite capable with any magical creature, but has a gift with fantastic and dangerous ones from Acromantulas (Aragog!) to Blast Ended Skrewts. His life dream is to raise a dragon as a pet.

Dumbledore's fifty-year project as stepfather to Hagrid will pay royal dividends in the books to come. This half-giant with a taste for monstrous pets will play the decisive role both in negotiations with his Mom and her fellow giants, and with Madame Maxime, the Headmistress of Beauxbatons Academy.

This would be enough to earn Hagrid hero status in the war on Voldemort, but there will be more. Look for his entry or return at the end of one of the next three books, as the Cavalry used to ride in to save the day in serial Westerns. He won't be riding a horse, though — I picture him on Norbert the Norwegian Ridgeback leading Aragog's family, Fluffy, and a skrewt or two in a horrible charge on Voldemort's dark legions. The Malfoys' unkindness to Buckbeak and Voldemort's lies about the boy Hagrid will be repaid handsomely and with interest by this adopted son of Albus Dumbledore.

Chapter 20

What Happens Next
Book by Book

Answering questions about the major story line ("Who is Harry Potter?") and lead characters is one sort of foolishness; trying to guess what Rowling will actually do in the three books remaining is greater foolishness by far. It's still fun, though, so let's see what we can come up with. Anyone reminding me years from now what I predict here (should I be wrong...) will be answered only be glares and denials.

Book	Way To God	Means to God	Battlefield
Philosopher's Stone	Alchemy	Philosopher's Stone	Obstacle Course
Chamber of Secrets	Religion	Phoenix & Trinity	Chamber
Prisoner of Azkaban	Psychology	Stag & Hippogriff	Shrieking Shack
Goblet of Fire	Sports	Grail: Goblet & Cup	Graveyard
Order of Phoenix	*Love Relation-ships*	*Phoenix*	*King's Cross Station*
Wounded Unicorn	*Eastern Religion*	*Unicorn*	*Forbidden Forest*
Centaur's Choice	*Combat*	*Centaur*	*Godric Hollow*

Book	DADA's Secret	Obstacle or Distraction	Key to Victory
Philosopher's Stone	Possessed	House Cup Points	Alchemical Process
Chamber of Secrets	Fraud	Self Image	Loyalty, Faith, Works
Prisoner of Azkaban	Werewolf	Personal Fears	Identification with Father
Goblet of Fire	Death Eater	Others' Opinions	Goal ↦ Personal Victory
Order of Phoenix	*Spy*	*Romance*	*Love ↦ Personal Love*
Wounded Unicorn	*Vampire*	*Esoterism*	*Humility, Obedience*
Centaur's Choice	*Auror*	*Self-Importance*	*Martial Virtues*

In the chart above I lay out both my picture of what Rowling has done in the first four books and my guesses (*in italics*) for the next three. Before going into more detail about my guesses, let me explain each chart column and note the patterns and models which I am trying to follow.

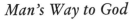

Man's Way to God

Rowling explores a different path that modern people take to find God in each of the *Harry Potter* novels. Book by book she has shown us the landscape of traditional transformation (alchemy), conventional religion, psychology, and sports. Given the trajectory of Rowling's storyline, I chose Eastern religion, love relationships, and warfare as the most likely follow-up paths — out of a list of transcendence that also included family, work & business, social causes (SPEW!), and "Sex, Drugs, & Rock 'n' Roll".

Man's Means to God

Each book has a Christ symbol or "Resurrection Vehicle" that saves Harry and others in their moment of greatest need. Harry achieves the Philosopher's Stone after five trials, and this achievement saves him in his first adventure. It is the Phoenix in *Chamber*, the Stag and Hippogriff in *Prisoner*, and the Grail/TriWizard Cup Portkey in *Goblet* that raise Harry and friends from the dead. For the rest, I chose the remaining Christ symbols from the chart of these symbols in Chapter 9. As I predict no little time in the Forbidden Forest for Harry in the remaining books, the Centaur and Unicorn from that forest seem credible guesses.

The Underground Battlefield or Battle Within

Rowling's hero journey formula includes a "descent to do battle" in each book. This "trip down" is a symbol of the movement inward we take to do battle. Harry and companions jump through the trapdoor to face the soul trials of their worthiness and receptivity for the Philosopher's Stone. Harry does battle with satanic forces in the heart of Hogwarts' secret chambers. The Shrieking Shack is where Harry and company do a little group therapy (and primal scream) in the psychological *Prisoner*.

Harry faces down Voldemort in a graveyard in *Goblet* in sympathy with those having already died. I think the next two books will end at King's Cross — the "underground" — and in the Forbidden Forest. Having come full circle, the Last Battle will take place in Godric Hollow.

Defense Against the Dark Arts Teacher Secret

Every Defense teacher so far has had a surprise to share at book's end. A man possessed, a fraud, a werewolf, and a Death Eater have startled us. Look for the trend to continue with a spy, vampire and auror teaching Defense (assuming the Hogwarts curriculum continues during the war to come). The spy could be Snape, becoming DADA teacher at last, if he teaches more about Dark Arts than Defense. The auror could be from the Department of Mysteries, an "unspeakable". The vampire has been predicted several times, and there is no "vampire" entry in *Fantastic Beasts*; how will she cover for his sleeping all day? (Something only a Potions Master could conceal...)

Distractions or Obstacles on the Way to God

Every path has its obstacles and distractions. I matched up the obvious ones for my guesses of the three books to come.

Key to Victory on the Way to God

Each path also has its key to overcoming the obstacles and achieving communion or transcendence. The keys in this column are again a match with my guesses for the way.

Rowling Formulas

Every book so far has been a hero's journey from the Dursley's to King's Cross. Expect that to stay the same — believe it or don't! — though the Dursleys may have to leave Privet Drive, and King's Cross may become the magical battlefield in one book. And as usual expect a surprise revelation at the end of each coming book, with an apocalypse and "end of the world or age" to close the series.

Meaning of Books

Rowling is writing edifying Christian novels to teach us the Stock Responses and Right Alignment of soul. Her books baptize the imagination in traditional Christian symbols and doctrines as well as preparing us for a life in Christ. This ongoing meaning will not change in future books. Expect Harry to make the hard choices, be transformed by his experiences, and to die and rise again as a cathartic model for us of the heroic Christian life.

Inkling Models

Tolkien and Lewis end their own seven-book series with dispiriting pictures of the decadence of a world on its last legs — and its glorious death and rebirth due to those who resist evil and darkness, even when there seems no hope for their cause. These apocalypses feature a battle of all living characters, good and evil. Because of her intellectual kinship with the Inkling pair, my guesses presume that Rowling will follow their model.

Without further ado, here are my prestidigious prognostications:

What Will Happen in Book 5: *Harry Potter and the Order of the Phoenix?*

Order will begin as if nothing has changed (a "sitzkrieg"), but the war has begun and with it the "End of Life as We know It".

The Dark Side will rise with a rush and a few surprises. Azkaban will be opened to return the LeStranges to Voldemort, and the Dementors and Death Eaters will be free to play. This they will do in the wake of the Goblin revolt and takeover of Gringotts. The Ministry will be ineffectual in putting down the rebellion staged by Voldemort and Bagman, but the Death Eaters ride to the rescue. Public acclamation for the "black hats" is inevitable; the Ministry follows *Daily Prophet* editorial advice and begins to negotiate a pact with Voldemort.

The Order of the Phoenix sees through this charade. This secret society of Voldemort resistors will have a roll call list that reads: Dumbledore, Figg, Fletcher, Diggle, Black, Lupin, the Weasleys (aside from trouble with ambitious Percy), Snape, the Hogwarts staff, Harry, Ron, Hermione, Hagrid, Krum, Fleur, and assorted Gryffyndors, house elves and friends. Being "white hats" they will be poorly organized, hesitant "to pull the trigger", and easily penetrated with spies.

They will have limited engagements with the Death Eaters and always come out losers (in fact or in the press copy). The *Daily Prophet* will color them as extremists, outlaws, even terrorists; Ministry persecution will follow soon enough to seem to be "doing their duty". The fact that Hagrid is discovered to be talking with the giants brings out the heavy artillery from the Ministry: the Unspeakables, many of whom are Death Eaters. (Look for fallout and major marketing damage control because of the terrorist thing; it may be one reason this book has been delayed so long…)

Life at Hogwarts goes on superficially as always with the war being reported from the periphery. The romances suggested in **Goblet** (Harry and Cho, Victor and Hermione, Ron and

Fleur) take flight; via the agonies of these first loves and the effects on the individuals and friends, Rowling will move "Romantic Love" front and center as this book's "way to God". Hermione comes into her own in this book; mercurial, passionate, blunt and brilliant. I can hardly wait to see her juggling Ron and Victor.

If you doubt the Rowling-Austen connection, re-read *Emma* and *Pride and Prejudice* or just *Sense and Sensibility* while you can for a preview of the romantic coming events. Austen always has the obvious love match fail in the end before the claim of the old steady hand. Cho, Viktor, and Fleur as exotic foreigners have little chance to win Harry, Hermione, or Ron in the Austenesque world of Hogwarts.

The surprise ending is that the Defense Against the Dark Arts teacher is a spy/double agent who betrays the Order of the Phoenix. They are compelled to battle on poor ground (King's Cross: appropriate for the revelation to happen here) against superior forces convinced they are winning a war against terrorism. Dumbledore will die in combat with Voldemort, but not before protecting Harry's escape (in Obi Wan Kenobi fashion). On his deathbed or by owl post, the wizard will tell Harry who he is and all Dumbledore has done to prepare him for what he must now do. Harry at last is revealed as Heir of Gryffyndor, and Fawkes the Phoenix helps him escape to fight another day.

What Will Happen in Book 6: *Harry Potter and the Wounded Unicorn?*

Unicorn will be the darkest and most difficult (can you say "least popular"?) of the series. The war ends with Voldemort victorious and the unrestricted Reign of Death Eaters in the magical world. The way to God here throws conservative Christian groups into a tailspin for its new age associations (albeit again implicitly about the Way, the Truth, and the Life in Christ).

The New World Order that begins subsequent to Dumbledore's demise is applauded by our friends at *The Daily Prophet*. Voldemort is no longer He-Who-Must-Not-Be-Named but de facto regent or king, hailed as hero and liberator, the Heir of Slytherin. Dumbledore and the Order of the Phoenix will be crucified figuratively as history is re-written to document their terrorist activity and cruel subjection of the Dark Lord and the Death Eaters. The Ministry becomes a carbon copy of Vichy France and its infamous collaboration "for survival". The Dark Arts rule Hogwarts under new Headmaster Lucius Malfoy.

The Order of the Phoenix post-Dumbledore stumbles badly, of course. Their lack of confidence in Harry, their child king, results inevitably in bungling and tragic failures. They survive despite the infighting that makes them seem leaderless. Hagrid finds them a safe place to hide: in the Forbidden Forest with Aragog and the Acromantulas. And then, the Pyramids? Persecuted, in hiding, confused more often than not, the Order begins to take shape as a force under Harry, their Robin Hood leader.

This book's way to God will be some secret martial arts or yoga-like training the Order receives (from Cho's parents?) to parallel the Way or Tao of many Eastern Religions which western people choose to follow in the modern world. Schooling at Hogwarts continues in the castle for non-combatants, but the real study takes place in the forest and desert. Look for extensive work with the Patronus Charm and a way to block the unforgivable curses, especially *Avadra Kedavra*. Initiated in this martial art, Harry will rally the Order to do battle with the Death Eaters. Cho dies or her relationship with Harry changes from romantic to professional; Harry looks to Ginny for support and affection through his dark times.

Their new Defense Master (an old hand?) is revealed to be a vampire and the Order is ambushed in the Forbidden Forest. Things go badly despite heroic aid from the Unicorns and giant spiders. The Death Eaters have the Dursleys as hostages, so Harry attempts their rescue; he is wounded and captured in the heroic attempt. Ron and Hermione escape with most of the Order in their darkest hour.

What Will Happen In Book 7: *Harry Potter and the Centaur's Choice?*

Rowling has said that Book 7 will be encyclopedic in length because she will be saying goodbye to her characters. I expect an ending of surprises and turnabouts a la Austen — and a combination of *The Return of the King* and *The Last Battle*. Harry returns to lead the Order of the Phoenix and the forces for good against Voldemort — winning a triumph against all odds, but at the cost of the world as he knows it.

Look for Snape or Pettigrew to free Harry and pay for this betrayal with his life. I expect it will be Snape, and we will learn at last the reason for his hatred and double life throughout the series. Perhaps the scene we will most remember: Snape as the good thief on the Cross serving Harry and the Gryffyndors at the very end — when it counts.

The only sure thing in the final book is that there will be Surprise after Surprise! Here are a few I'm anticipating:

- Harry risking all to save poor Dudley — or vice versa;

- An air force of dragons featuring Norbert, Charlie, and Hagrid;

- The Flying Ford Anglia, the pink umbrella, and Trevor the Toad redux;

- Percy Weasley leaving the Ministry or serving as double agent;

- Epiphany of Centaurs, hippogriffs, phoenixes, and unicorns;

- Reappearance of Hagrid, Mom, Norbert, Aragog Jrs., and giants — to save Harry;

- Dobby and Winky leading House elves against the Goblins; and

- Crookshank's identity revealed! Is he Dumbledore's brother Aberforth?

The biggest surprise, though, will be the conversion of Draco Malfoy. Perhaps as a generational balance with Snape and Lily, we will learn of Draco's love for Hermione the mudblood. Unwilling to kill her or her friends, he forsakes the Dark Side and his family to join the Order (albeit as a pariah to each side — and earning only a cold shoulder from Hermione?). Draco's change will echo the conversion of Eustace Scrubb from human dragon to real dragon to Aslan-baptized Christian in Lewis' *The Voyage of the Dawn Treader*. Harry's attempts to befriend this painful figure and honor him will be among the most heroic things he has ever done (just as Edmund Pevensie's conversation with Eustace on the beach is a pinnacle of the *Narnia* books).

The way to God in this last book will be the way of combat. Rowling will orchestrate a paean to the martial virtues of bravery and selflessness in the last battle. Look for Draco and Longbottom as the flying tiebreakers in this match.

And the "Killer Ending"? Voldemort will win the match and last battle, only to self-destruct in the end by forgetting the "old magic" of sacrificial love. He dies because of overconfidence or pride; his hubris (I want to say "in front of the Mirror of Erised") makes him mistake a Weasley "Joke Wand" for the real thing. This mistake results in Harry's escape and Voldemort's eventual demise. (If I were a graduate student looking for a thesis topic, it would be "The Place of Humor in the Fight against Evil in Joanne Rowling's Harry Potter Novels".) If Pettigrew/Wormtail is to "do a Gollum or Wormtongue", it will be here.

The Centaurs are a force to be reckoned with — and their unexpected choice to intervene sweeps the field of Death Eaters. Firenze meets Voldemort again, and Fawkes takes on Nagini in the battle royal and finale at Godric Hollow. Look for a series of *Iliad*-style one-on-ones to highlight the "way of combat": the virtues of bravery, loyalty, perseverance, discipline, obedience, selflessness, sacrifice, you name it. The one fight you won't want to miss is Draco versus Lucius Malfoy after Lucius kills Lupin, Draco's only friend in the Gryffyndor camp.

And, of course, the feature steel-cage payback grudge match at Godric Hollow will be the Heir of Slytherin versus the Heir of Gryffyndor, for all the marbles. Come early for good seats.

The Inklings end their books with apocalypse and farewells. Rowling has said there will be no sequels to the *Harry Potter* series; I think she is so sure of that because the price of victory over Voldemort will be at least the destruction of Hogwarts castle and perhaps of the entire magical world. (Who knows what the Department of Mysteries has in its bandolier? A neutron bomb to take out witches and wizards?)

The finale may be baldly Christian to reveal at last Rowling's secret. For this reason and its length, don't expect the last book to appear for years! I wouldn't be surprised if the movies catch up with the books for a stunning simultaneous release. It will take some remarkable real world magic to keep the lid on the secret ending if that's the case — but what a finish it would make to the Pottermania phenomenon.

Epilogue: Who ends up with whom?

I don't know, of course, who survives all these battles. I expect the bodies will stack up pretty high by the end. However, among the survivors, there will be a lot of couples, if only for the proper Austenesque/alchemical finish (*conjunctio oppositorum*). I would not be surprised to see:

- Harry with Ginny after romancing Cho;

- Ron with Hermione after romancing Fleur;

- Krum with Fleur after romancing Hermione (if either survive…);

- Hagrid, of course, with Madame Maxime (I don't think she'll make it…);

- Dobby & Mrs. Winky Dobby as paid servants to Hermione;

- Dursleys repentant, redeemed, and even "abnormal"; and

- the Death Eaters dead or banished after Battle in Godric Hollow.

Conclusion to the guesswork

I hope you had a fifth of the fun reading these guesses that I had in writing them. I hope too you remember that Rowling may employ certain formulas when she writes, but only to focus her inventive powers. None of the books will be what I have predicted because I cannot imagine the new books' creations and fresh characters — which I expect will be their most delightful and challenging quality!

Having excused myself with a "Please don't hold me accountable for being wrong in these predictions", let me rush to add a "Please give me credit if I score any hits with my buckshot approach"! I hope you are inspired to read the books again to hunt up the clues that demonstrate how wrong I am and how right your theories are. Rowling's books are tightly woven tapestries: the secrets are all revealed in the weave if you look long enough and hard enough.

Expect to be delighted with the new characters and situations she weaves into her formulas, but anticipate as well that some will be disappointed with the coming books. There will be deaths of major characters, and the victory of the Dark Lord will be depressing, to say the least. At last folks will realize she is not writing children's books, and her popularity will fade (to the delight of her critics and perhaps eventually to her relief) from the height of the mania it has presently reached.

My hopeful last prediction is that the success of the *Potter* books and movies will generate a new genre of Inkling literature. The unprecedented sales Ms. Rowling's books enjoy are largely due to the great need in the hearts of readers growing up in an anti-traditional world on fast forward. It may also be explained by the profound way she has met this poignant need — accompanied by entertaining stories, engaging characters, and powerful themes artfully presented for the elevation and experience of real virtues.

But her popularity is also understandable only in light of the dearth of competition. Are there no other authors schooled in the Classics and the Christian tradition? There are thousands. Are there any of Ms. Rowling's particular wit and genius? I doubt it very much. Nonetheless, the "best possible ending" I can imagine to the Harry Potter craze is that authors with the necessary background will attempt to recreate her success by writing edifying fiction that baptizes and sustains our imaginations and hearts.

Thank you, gentle reader, for traveling this far with me. I hope you will contact me with any questions at my snail mail address: 231 South 7th Street, Port Hadlock, WA 98339 (or e-mail me at john@zossima.com). I would love to have your feedback on what you've read, and any suggestions for ways to improve the next edition of this book (which, God willing, will be written soon after *Order of the Phoenix* is published). If this book has been of any help to you in understanding Ms. Rowling's imaginative masterpiece and the Christian path to which she points, I shall be gratified.

The remainder of this book is a short epilogue on literary criticism along with a collection of appendices — things I wanted to include without disrupting the main argument of the book, or matters that belong in one place for easy reference. Browse and enjoy!

Epilogue

Modernist Criticism
of
Traditional Literature

Epilogue

Modernist Criticism
of
Traditional Literature

Epilogues I enjoy reading are the ones in which the author finally lets go and says why she wrote the book in the first place. That being the case - and my wanting you to leave with a pleasant experience - let me tell you at last why I wrote this book.

I haven't lied to you when I said that I wrote it largely in response to off-the-wall criticism (see Appendix A) or to fill a gap in current critical responses (see Chapter 1). But I haven't told the whole truth. The reason I wrote **The Hidden Key to Harry Potter** (even before all the books of the series were available) was to anticipate and break the spear tip of the modernist literary interpretation of Joanne Rowing and authors like her. Modern tools of analysis have a limited value in unwrapping works that don't share or actively oppose modern conventions. I hoped to demonstrate that traditional (which is to say "anti-modern") fiction can be discussed and understood more clearly by thinking differently than the habits of mind that these books are criticizing.

Before you give me a "thumbs up" or "thumbs down" on my attempt, please read through my survey of current literary schools and ask yourself, "If John is right and Rowling is writing a Christian attack on the foibles of modernity, what good is the highbrow approach to a work such as hers which critiques their mistakes?" After that, I hope you will reflect a moment on what *Hidden Key* is about and whether it succeeds or fails in its attempt to open up the meanings both of *Harry Potter* and of Rowling's success.

Here is my roller coaster survey of modern literary criticism:

- Neo-Historicist - Critics of this school examine the text as an historical artifact in which its contemporary cultural ideologies and taboos are crystallized. The neo-historicist traces the determining influences of history on the work to reveal its meaning.

- Marxist - Marxist literary critics understand books as material products manufactured by the dominant forces and ideas of the generating culture; these material products in turn act as passive indoctrinators of their readers into the culture's prevailing, unexamined ideology. The meaning of the work is teased out in the exposition of the determinist forces and ideas of the culture.

- Cultural Criticism - Something like "interdisciplinary Marxists", the cultural critics examine books (cartoons, movies, events, etc.) in light of the forces - economic, artistic, media, audience response - active in the creation of the text. "Meaning" or "freedom" (or hegemony) is only possible by being conscious of and resistant to these ideological constraints and forces.

- Feminist - Feminist literary critics explore neglected works by women or interpret texts from an exclusively feminine perspective (by employing litmus test readings of authors' sensitivity to women's issues). Meaning is the relative freedom or slavery of the author with respect to the dominating patriarchal culture.

• Reader Response - Critics of this school follow Stanley Fish (hence this subjectivist camp being called "the school of Fish") by believing that a written work is best understood in light of what it does to the person reading it. What a book means cannot be objectively understood except in terms of the questions, thoughts, or feelings it raises in many of its readers.

• Psychoanalytic - Psychological readings of books (if Freudian) look to interpret the author's instinctual repressed selves and desires, or (if Jungian) aim to read the collective unconscious restricted by the cultural mores of the author. Every book is something of a Rorschach test, whose personal or cultural meaning is learnt by uncovering what is struggling to surface from the unconscious mind of the author.

• Structuralist - Structuralist critics read a text linguistically and systematically as a collection of signs to reveal a grammar behind its forms. This semiotic approach reveals contextual meaning by isolating both the binary oppositions comprising a work's structures, and the resolution of these structures by a third term. Really.

• Post-Structuralist & Deconstuctionist - All the folks who disagree with the structuralists.

I think these various schools can be categorized into three schools of thought:

(1) Outside Readers - folks that see the meaning of books in understanding the forces outside the author which create the book's characters, plot, and conclusion (namely, the artistic culture, the economic system, dominant ideologies, and sexual taboos shaping the author from the outside).

(**2**)Inside Readers - readers that see the meaning of books in understanding the forces inside the author which create the book's characters, plot, and conclusion (namely, the repressed instincts, sublimated desires, and urgings of the collective unconscious that shape the author from the inside).

(**3**)Scientistic Readers - academics pursuing the authority of their counterparts in the physical sciences by breaking a text down to its linguistic molecular structure and tracking its reaction with another chemical reagent (the reader).

All of these schools neglect the possibility that an author's meaning may transcend historical, personal, and biological bipolarity (!) to describe a supernatural verity or contranatural reality. If critical interpretation is a house, then the "inside readers" are in the cellar digging into the unconscious dark spots; the "outside readers" are in the closets trying to determine how expensive the clothes are and what they reveal about the cultural mores and taboos; and the "scientistic readers" are testing the air coming from the vents for a sign of the relation between the air breathed in and the breathers. No one is looking out the window from which the poet himself looked, nor is anyone attempting to see what the inspired poet saw and tried to describe.

C. S. Lewis grouped this collective blindness to the possibility of objective reality and meaning into one fault that he labeled "The Personal Heresy". Lewis thought this personal heresy or theory neglected the obvious relationship of reader and author, as well as what causes pleasure or pain in the reader. First of all, the reader as a reader experiences the world through the writer:

> [T]he thing presented to us in any poem is not and cannot be the personality of the poet. It is the liquid movement of silk, or the age and mystery of man, or a particular man escaping from a long period of restraint - never

Wordsworth, or De la Mare, or Herrick.... [I shall be told that] it may be true that what I am aware of in reading Herrick's poem is silk, but it is not silk as an object *in rerum natura*. I see it as Herrick saw it; and in so doing, it may be argued, I do come into contact with his temperament in the most intimate - perhaps in the only possible - way.... Let it be granted that I do approach the poet; at least I do it by sharing his consciousness, not by studying it. I look with his eyes, not at him. He, for the moment, will be precisely what I do not see; for you can see any eyes rather than the pair you see with, and if you want to examine your own glasses you must take them off your own nose. The poet is not a man who asks me to look at *him*; he is a man who says "look at that" and points; the more I follow the pointing of his finger the less I can possibly see of *him*.... To see things as the poet sees them I must share his consciousness and not attend to it; I must look where he looks and not turn round to face him; I must make of him not a spectacle but a pair of spectacles....

(C. S. Lewis, *The Personal Heresy*, pp.11-12)

This being the case, the author's meaning is not in the author or poet's cultural or psychological determinants - but in the veracity and beauty his writing demonstrates about something outside him and these influences. The work of the poet is an act of transcending personality:

A poet does what no one else can do: what, perhaps no other poet can do; but he does not express his personality. His own personality is the starting point, and his limitation: it is analogous to the position of the window or the degree of courage in the scout. If he remains at his starting-point he is no poet: as long as he is (like the rest of us) a mere personality, all is still to do. It is his business, starting from his own mode of consciousness, whatever that may happen to be, to find that arrangement of public experiences, embodied in words, which will admit him (and incidentally us) to a new mode of consciousness.... [T]he result, when it comes, is for him, no less than for us, an acquisition, a voyage beyond the limits of his personal point of view, an annihilation of the brute fact of his own particular psychology rather than its assertion. **(Lewis, Personal Heresy, p. 26)**

Lewis attributed the victory of the personal heresy in the interpretation of literature to two things. First, there is the fallen human preference for gossip and slander over meaning and truth. Second (and more important to the victory of determinist criticism) is "that the typical modern critic is usually a half-hearted materialist" **(Heresy, p. 28)**, who is unwilling or unable to grapple with either existential despair on the one hand or meaningful existence and its responsibilities on the other.

This last is crucial because Lewis contends that good writing is inspired or transpersonal. Critics who are half-hearted materialists, unwilling to take the plunge into either nihilism or faith, create a natural or restricted-to-the-personal way of approaching great literary works - "giving them their due" without daring to embrace their spiritual source and meaning as guides in their own lives.

Lewis clearly was alarmed by this trend (and its complementary tendency for literature to become a religion with artifacts, relics, dogma, and revered saints). So was his fellow Inkling, J. R. R. Tolkien, whose great fear about the reception of *The Lord of the Rings* (beyond that it might never be published!) was that it would be interpreted as allegory. He was haunted by concern lest his mythopoetic and linguistic history of the Third Age be reduced to a tit-for-tat concealed story within a story or clever representation of World War II. Perhaps it is just as well that he never lived to see his marriage, sexuality, and supposedly chauvinist politics and misogynist leanings put under the microscope - even offered up as the causes and greater meaning of his artistry!

J.K. Rowling has not yet completed her *Harry Potter* series. Even with three books remaining, the Academy sharks are circling to feed on this feast of material for analysis and conjecture. Jack Zipes' book on children's literature was first out of the blocks in 2002 to explain the Potter phenomenon as indoctrination into the predominant mores of our desire-driven consumer culture (*Sticks and Stones: The Troublesome Success of Children's Literature from Slovenly Peter to Harry Potter*). Andrew Blake, a British professor of Cultural Studies, has blessed us with *The Irresistible Rise of Harry Potter: Kid-Literature in a Globalised World*. And the first collection of academic approaches has just been released with insights from Native American sources, sociologists, and feminists (*Harry Potter's World: Multi-disciplinary Critical Perspectives*). Don't look for the tide to go out anytime soon.

This reductionist or naturalist school of literature, what Lewis called "the personal heresy", presupposes four remarkable conditions in its approach to *Harry Potter* specifically and to literature in general:

(1) That writers are unconscious of the predominant ideologies of their times and unaware of the influence these ideas (along with their own psychological history and make-up) might have on their work;

(2) That critics as such stand above these influences and (as if at the end of times) speak to us groundlings with a semi-divine objectivity;

(3) That their view-from-Everest objectivity and clarity enable them to approach texts the way a physical scientist examines a specimen (without any of the scientific method's self-restriction and humility concerning the effect of the observer on the observed); and most important,

(4) That muse-inspired writing does not exist.

In this view, muse-inspired writing cannot exist because of the unexamined but adamantine "given" or premise behind naturalist interpretation: that supernatural or contranatural realities do not exist, so the borders of reality are bounded by what can be measured in physical or energetic quantities. This naturalist restriction upon all things includes man, of course, whose supposed formation in the image of God and life in Christ are necessarily delusions springing from anthropomorphic identification with religious totems.

However, the naturalist position is absurd in each of its four presumptions as well as its one major premise. Point by point refutation looks like this:

(1) Artists and writers are of all people perhaps the most aware of the predominant ideologies of their environment and era - and they are at least as likely to be exploring or critiquing these cultural positions in their work, as they are to be acting as unconscious front men or doctrinaires;

(2) Critics, who are uniformly creations of the modernist academies and naturalist world view, are much more likely to be creatures of ideology than the creative persons they critique;

(3) The similarity of modern critical scholarship to reductionist science and scientism reflects the influence of ideological naturalism on its supposed objectivity;

(4) Muse-inspired writings cannot be demonstrated to be non-existent without starting from the premise that nothing supernatural or contranatural exists.

This essential naturalist premise cannot be demonstrated. The idea that the only things existent are matter and energy contradicts itself and confesses its limitations even as an ad hoc tool, for nature cannot be offered as the criterion or bounds of truth without asserting something existent outside of natural matter and energy (if only the concept of "truth" itself). And how does the naturalist critic himself escape from the naturalist world into objectivity and freedom? When the naturalist asserts the truth of naturalism, s/he necessarily asserts with the same breath that this claim is made with reference to non-existent reality and that the claim cannot be believed as objective because of the ideo-materialist determinants shaping the claimant.

Leszek Kolalowski, the Oxford sociologist, has said of the naturalist view in politics that "the materialist interpretation of history is either nonsense or a banality". This is at least as true of the critiques of literature cooked up by the "half-hearted materialists" in our academies. That great writers (as all people) necessarily reflect in some fashion the ideas of their time and the details of their upbringing tells us nothing. That these influences determine their viewpoint and are the larger part of their meaning is nonsense.

And in certain cases, perhaps it attains a state beyond satire and nonsense (if this is possible). I think of unselfconscious papers written to critique poets and writers - who are themselves artfully criticizing the perspective of these academic critics and the culture that gave birth to cultural studies departments. Here the dwarf feigns a larger view than the giant he hopes to instruct. The cultural study or personal analysis or critical biography which examine the creators of such thoughtful artistic pieces as *The Chronicles of Narnia*, *The Lord of the Rings*, or the *Harry Potter* books necessarily become something ludicrous and pathetically comic, evoking images of third graders writing teacher evaluations, chemists analyzing scripture by burning it in an autoclave for a caloric reading of ink and paper, and miniature dogs yapping heroically while chasing their own behinds.

The Hidden Key to Harry Potter has several times descended to speculation about Ms. Rowling or referred to her background as inductive evidence for my theories. I regret these descents, even if in a popular work such gossip seems more appropriate than in a formal treatise. I have tried, despite these failings, to take the **Harry Potter** books seriously and explain their remarkable, even unprecedented, popularity in terms of the genius and artistry of the author. Consequently, **Hidden Key** is heavy on the symbolism within the books, their active and passive critique of modern institutions and ideologies, and their debt (consciously acknowledged by the author) to the English Christian literary tradition.

In so doing, my hope has been to write in respectful kinship with this tradition and to create a foil for the naturalist fare already coming from the academy. **Hidden Key** is an attempt to demonstrate that traditional (which is to say "anti-modern") fiction can be discussed and understood more clearly if one refrains from thinking in the ways such works are criticizing.

I leave it to you to judge the value of my attempt to employ traditional tools to lay open a traditional work for better understanding of its meaning and the genius and muse of its author. I am grateful for whatever thoughtful response or reflection my book may have inspired in you.

Cordially,

John Grangser
john@zossima.com

Appendices

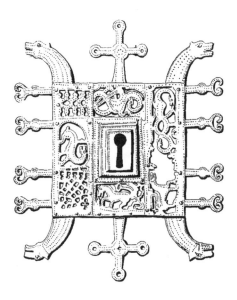

Appendix A

Inkling Similarities
and
Differences

The Hidden Key to Harry Potter is that Joanne Rowling is writing edifying Christian fiction. I have suggested that she is following in the tradition and conventions of Inkling writers C. S. Lewis and J. R. R. Tolkien. This Inkling connection is not essential to grasping the key to understanding the Potter books, but I do find it helpful. Pointing to the common ground in intention, design, and symbolism (shared by the Potter series with *The Chronicles of Narnia* and *The Lord of the Rings*) has made it easier to see Rowling as a Christian writer despite her occult-laced reputation.

I am not denying that there are obvious differences between the books and the authors. Lewis and Tolkien inhabited a world that no longer exists, which world fostered their peculiar genius. Oxford dons, trench warfare combat veterans, sacramental Christians at war with the spiritual vacancy and decadence of modern times, Medievalists fluent in the mythologies of the Mediterranean and Far North, men who lived almost exclusively in the company of men (and scholarly men like themselves to boot) — no, I don't mean to suggest that Rowling is an Inkling clone. Polyjuice Potion, complicated surgery, and a time machine would be necessary for that.

Nonetheless, having said that the authors and their works spring from different worlds and have different emphases (perhaps as true between Lewis and Tolkien as between them and Rowling), I rush to emphasize that their similarities are greater than their imagined differences. It is not sloppy thinking or failed memory that has led so many critics and casual readers to remark that while reading about Harry, they experienced again the feelings and challenges they remembered from Narnia and Middle-Earth. These books are trying to do the same thing and use many of the same tools, which together produce effects of remarkable resemblance.

I have tried to show how Ms. Rowling has written novels laden with Christian themes, doctrine, and images "to baptize the imagination" of her readers through an imaginative experience of the truths of the Christian faith. This book is perhaps too full of references and explanation of her training us in the so-called "stock responses" of moral virtue and "right alignment" of the soul's faculties. These are the signature purpose and means of edifying fantasy fiction according to C. S. Lewis — and both his work and J. R. R. Tolkien's reflect this conviction.

I have also attempted to reveal that Ms. Rowling is writing a broadside attack on the materialist worldview that is the predominant feature of life in the modern world. The scientistic focus on matter and energy as reality is the *de facto* state religion of the West, with a stranglehold on conversation in the academy, media, and government. Ms. Rowling asks us to think with an anti-materialist perspective, "magically", if you will, and to look "diagonally" at things to see their *eternal* qualities in addition to their ephemeral quantity and mass. She has sub-created a magical diagonal world — sans technology, but rich in virtue and vice — which points to belief in the traditional truths as more satisfying and ennobling than modern superstitions.

In this vein, it is also an acerbic satire of the absurdities and cruelties of "real world" institutions and conventions, recalling the darker Narnia of Lewis' *The Silver Chair* and *The Last Battle*. Lewis fans will be reminded more forcefully of the last novel in his *Space Trilogy*, *That Hideous Strength*, in which he paints a similarly dark picture of the self-impressed, small-minded world of our times. And even though the good wins out in the end in these books and *The Lord Of the Rings*, it is always only a small, temporary victory achieved by heroic individuals amid ages of corruption and dissolution — the best of this world has passed to a better place, and the good are left here to fight on despite the downward turn of the times.

Given the powerful similarities in the books by these authors, I am always surprised by those vehement defenders of Lewis and Tolkien who believe Rowling is certainly no good and probably a satanist. No matter that Lewis and Tolkien were criticized in their day as moral relativists teaching prohibited magical arts in their writing — these Inkling fans know it was not true the first time around, but assume it is true of Rowling today.

I do not wish to patronize people who want to shield themselves and their families from pernicious occult influence and "unbiblical" spirituality. I am one of them. Unlike most of them, I take my Defense against the Dark Arts seriously enough that we don't own a teevee or VCR, and our children are not allowed on the internet. While not wanting to sound condescending, I do think that those who shield themselves from the *Potter* books reveal convictions about Rowling and the Inklings that are more ignorance than informed opinion.

For example, nearly everyone with whom I have discussed the *Potter* books, from the most excited fan to the most concerned Christian parent, carries the same media-inspired picture in their mental wallets of Ms. Rowling as a poor single mother who won the lottery by writing books Christians hate. For the concerned parents, this meant simply being careful not to read the books.

So when confronted with the assertion that Rowling is a Christian writer akin to the Inklings, these people necessarily argue from ignorance of at least one half of the equation. Sadly, more often than not, they argue from ignorance both of Rowling and of Lewis and Tolkien. No matter — in order to brand Rowling as an occultist and satan worshipper, the kinship even casual readers see between her work and the Inklings' must be stamped out.

Richard Abanes has written a *Potter*-bashing book titled ***Harry Potter and the Bible: The Menace behind the Magick.*** He has read each book of the Rowling oeuvre carefully (I would say "under the microscope"), to detail for his readers every possible occult association. He asserts that the many look-alike associations he finds demonstrate "a *direct* link to paganism/ witchcraft" (p. 241, his emphasis) in Rowling's work.

Looks like a witch, must be a witch. Not only is this illogical *prima facie*, it is horribly unsympathetic to the text. In his zeal for uncovering the similarity between subjects taught at Hogwarts and obscure magical books from cults, he fails to mention anything of the prevailing traditional Christian themes, symbolism, and doctrines presented in each **Potter** book. He overlooks each and every satirical treatment of the modern outlook, misses all the Resurrection experiences and edifying changes in the characters, and condemns Rowling for "unkind prejudices" evident in her treatment of fat people and Muggles, among others.

I once read that quite a few of the 18th century readers of Swift's **Gulliver's Travels** thought that Lemuel Gulliver was one unlucky sailor and his book an argument against traveling on the water. Swift was not writing for these *yahoos*, though, but about them.

It will not surprise you to learn from the back cover of **Magick** that Mr. Abanes, in addition to having "produced two full length CDs of original contemporary music", has written "nearly a dozen books on cults, the occult, and world religions". The reason he does not suspect that Ms. Rowling's "prejudices" might be part of her conscious treatment of the theme of prejudice — is that his own well-intended concerns about the occult amount to a prejudice that blinds him to any larger or Christian meaning present in the **Harry Potter** series.

I am discussing Mr. Abanes not just to revel in another man's failings (you are probably more aware of my own at this point than I am). He turns out to be an admirer of Lewis and Tolkien. He devotes an entire chapter of his philippic against Ms. Rowling to the cataloguing of differences between her books and the good stuff: **Narnia** and **The Lord of the Rings**.

I have listed all the differences he discovered — let's take a quick look at each:

Difference: *"The fantasy tales of Lewis and Tolkien fall within the category of mythopoetic literature, meaning that they take place in worlds disassociated from the real world in which we live."* **(Abanes, *Magick*, p. 230)**

Hogwarts is very much situated in our world, albeit invisible to non-magical people like ourselves. But this does not make it different than Narnia and Middle-Earth. Narnia and our world meet in many places aside from the back of a wardrobe; Aslan even shows himself here in ***The Silver Chair***. We learn at the end of ***The Last Battle*** that Narnia and Earth are reflections of the same place and share this greater reality as our real home. Lewis does not create Narnia to take you elsewhere, but to point to that reality reflected in our world through Narnian images.

Tolkien, too, is writing about Earth in his Middle-Earth. ***The Lord of the Rings*** is set at the end of the Third Age, our earth's "middle age". Plato and the Vedas talk about the Four Ages (in the reverse action of alchemy, the ages move from gold to lead). Tolkien's Middle Earth is his imaginative (and philological) history of what our world may have been like in mythological times. He and Lewis did not think myth was fantasy, but revelation of truths greater than visible, measurable ones. Remember that to both Inklings, Christianity is primarily true myth and, astonishingly, also true in history.

Abanes' failure to understand Inkling fiction as symbolist literature moves him to disparage Ms. Rowling. She, however, both understands it and is writing it.

Difference: *Tolkien has "an expansive imagination and brilliant mind"; Rowling has written books that "are little more than occult* *glamorizing, morally bleak, marketing sensations filled with one dimensional characters and a hero who is, to borrow the words of Rowling's Professor Snape, 'a nasty little boy who considers rules to be beneath him.'"* **(Abanes, *Magick*, p. 233)**

This is a combination of the popular misconception of Ms. Rowling as a Wicca-Welfare Mom, misogyny, and an inability to read with discernment or sympathy. I doubt Mr. Abanes was a Classics or Literature major in school (a quick check of *www.abanes.com* confirms this; Mr. Abanes was a Communications major).

> **Difference:** *"The struggle between good and evil in **The Hobbit** and **The Lord of the Rings** trilogy relies heavily on, and is rooted in, Tolkien's devout Christian faith. His good characters are truly good. His evil characters are truly evil .... In Rowling's novels, however, moral ambiguity and relativism abound, while at the same time no one really seems to know who is and who is not evil."* **(Abanes, *Magick*, p. 234)**

Ms. Rowling is assumed not to be a Christian. Consequently, her surprise endings cannot be a way she shows her readers their unloving and unfounded rush to judge (that is, their prejudice). This supposed difference is ironically evidence of Mr. Abanes' inability to discern and of his prejudices against those who are not public Christian apologists. Until Tolkien's **Silmarillion** was published and before Lewis revealed his faith in radio lectures, few even among professional reviewers guessed their works were Christian. It should be little surprise that Ms. Rowling too is misunderstood.

> **Difference:** *"The 'magic' most often seen in Tolkien's novels is not the kind of occult based/contemporary pagan magick Rowling employs....'[M]agic' in the context of Middle-Earth does not include any kind of supernatural power. It is a natural ability given only to Elves."* **(Abanes, *Magick*, p. 235)**

> ***Difference:*** *"[Magical objects] on the Harry Potter series are bewitched or enchanted. However, the objects in Tolkien's fantasy receive special qualities through 'lore,' which Tolkien likened to technology and science. They are created in accordance with the laws of nature as found in Middle-Earth."*
> **(Abanes, *Magick*, p. 236)**

Again, Mr. Abanes has no idea that Ms. Rowling's magical world might be a counter spell to the enchantment of modernism (paraphrasing Lewis), used to forcefully condemn the materialist and anti-traditional worldview that undermines Christian belief. That the supernatural (or magical) and natural were not distinct or separate realities to beings living in Tolkien's Third Age makes no impression either.

Though I am sure these are not his conscious beliefs, it is tragic that Mr. Abanes seems to be calling for an ideologically pure fiction where the supernatural is distinct and apart from the natural world. Sadly, this is the materialist rather than the Christian view; it seems Mr. Abanes drifts into a den of tigers and atheists while trying to swat a mosquito in witch's garb.

> ***Difference:*** *"Rowling's wizards are human, whereas Tolkien's 'wizards' are not human at all.... In Tolkien's writings, Elves, the Maiar and Valar are simply exercising their God given abilities when they do 'magic', either for good or evil. In J. K. Rowling's world, however, wizards are human and their magickal powers are tapped/increased through occultism."* **(Abanes, *Magick*, p. 237)**

Mr. Abanes forgets that the angelic character of Tolkien's wizards was not public knowledge until after his death and is nowhere discussed in the storyline of ***The Lord of the Rings***. Consequently, the great majority of his readers and movie fans would be unaware of this — and that did not bother Tolkien. There is no God or Religion as such in Inkling fantasy; Rowling observes this ground rule for not "disturbing watchful dragons". Inkling fiction "smuggles theology" — and smuggling is undercover work.

Hogwarts, too, is not an occult academy. They learn magic there the way conventional muggle students learn conventional subjects in our schools. (**Or as Tolkien's Elves learnt magic in Faerie? See** *The Hobbit*, **chapter 8.**) There are no invocations of occult or satanic powers. Harry is actually considered rather dull as a student, and his success against Voldemort is never attributed to his magical abilities. If Mr. Abanes would think of Hogwarts as satire on public education in modern times, he would see something of what Ms. Rowling is about, and why her books are so popular with the inmates of our schools.

Difference: *"Furthermore, there is no Iluvatar (i.e., God) overseeing the battle between good and evil. This is by far the most profound difference between Rowling's books and the works of Tolkien.... The most critical difference between Rowling and Tolkien is the spiritual perspectives from which they created their stories. Tolkien was unabashedly Christian."* (**Abanes,** *Magick,* **pp. 237, 239**)

Again, there is no Iluvatar in *The Lord of the Rings* either — to the reader not schooled as well in the *Silmarillion*. Mr. Abanes also assumes, incorrectly, that Ms. Rowling's books are not shaped by a Christian perspective. A reader of Dickens, Austen, and the Inklings recognizes the spiritual perspective of Rowling as that of her favorite authors.

Difference: *"The 'Christian theology' in Lewis' fantasy is veiled beneath various characters (e.g., Aslan the Lion). Consequently there is no* <u>direct</u> *association that can be made between the books and any contemporary religion. In Harry Potter, however, a* <u>direct</u> *link to paganism/witchcraft is made via the presentation to readers of current occult beliefs and practices."* (Abanes, **Magick**, p. 241)

Anyone not able to make a direct association between Narnia and the Christian faith is a little dull; these veils are meant to be transparent, and they are. The direct links between **Harry Potter** and paganism/witchcraft, on the other hand, are anything but self-evident; they exist only in the occult-focused mind of Mr. Abanes and like-minded critics. Look-alike associations are not demonstrations of identity or direct links. To those not already familiar with their occult usage, the magic in **Harry Potter** is an entertaining back drop for the stories, rather than an invitation to Satanism.

> **Difference:** *"There is indeed a witch in the Narnia series, but she is evil and based on age-old and widely accepted illustrations of evil. In contrast, the witches and wizards in Harry Potter are children who share numerous characteristics in common with young readers.... Consequently, Rowling's line between fantasy and fiction is extremely thin."* (Abanes, **Magick**, p. 241)

Mr. Abanes neglects to mention the kind and noble magicians Coriakin and Ramandu in Narnia, and that Aslan is not distraught with Lucy practicing magic over Coriakin's book (see **The Voyage of the Dawn Treader**). He also does not remark on "the age-old and widely accepted" symbols of Christ and Christian theology prevalent in Ms. Rowling's books. Consequently, the line between criticism and "witch hunting" here is extremely thin.

More than a few critics have rightly observed, I think, that the children of Hogwarts are the most un-childlike children since the Pevensies. If Harry Potter were a real boy, the books would have to be about his recovery from the abusive upbringing he endured at the Dursleys. As it is, he is something of a Superboy when, if Rowling were a realist author, he should be a Neville.

> *Difference:* "*Lewis does not present a conflict between good and evil based on any 'dark side' concepts of power... In the Chronicles of Narnia series, the conflict involves two opposing forces (i.e., kinds of magic) of entirely different origins.*" **(Abanes, *Magick*, p. 242)**

> *Difference:* "*Lewis' good characters...do not overcome witchcraft by learning more witchcraft. Instead they respond to evil by becoming servants of the good character, Aslan....Rowling's good characters, however, seek to overcome evil by using the same dualistic magical power employed by Lord Voldemort and his Death Eaters.*" **(Abanes, *Magick*, p. 242)**

Mr. Abanes accuses Ms. Rowling of a kind of Manichean heresy with George Lucas' face superimposed on it. She does have wizards talk about the "dark side" and the dark arts but, significantly, there is no "force" or neutral power of which there are light and dark sides. Because no one invokes occult forces or God in her books, a sympathetic reader of Mr. Abanes' bent might suggest that the **supernatural** or even **contranatural** is **natural** to these humans and "going to the dark side" little different than "going bad" (i.e., selfish, materialistic, or criminal) is to us.

But there is no charity or sympathy in Mr. Abanes' reading, which is what tells against him in the end, more than any of his failed points of argument. His cannot be the Christian interpretation, however well intended and closely argued, because there is no love in it.

> *Difference:* "*Rowling's works...are completely dependent on magick. It is central to her story, whereas Lewis uses magic*

sparingly and in a highly stylized manner that does not connect with the real world." (Abanes, *Magick*, p. 243)

Magic is the background or scene of the *Harry Potter* novels but, as with the smell of salt in the air by the sea, after a few minutes the reader is unaware of it. Rowling writes like her heroes, Austen and Dickens, Sayers and Lewis, so that one is much less focused on the magic than on the concerns of the people, their relationships, and struggles.

In this I think she is the better writer than Tolkien or Lewis (albeit an apples and oranges comparison). Only the "magick" consumed person could read these books and think they are "completely dependent" on occult magic — their power is not in the magical stage props, which are usually entertaining and often distracting, but in the relationships and changes of the lead characters.

Difference: *"The ultimate meaning of the works"; "Rowling's novels seem to have no grander purpose than to 'provide a rollicking good time'" while "Lewis' novels... offer an immeasurably deeper gift to readers", namely an introduction to Christ through Aslan.* (Abanes, *Magick*, p. 243)

Wait a minute! I thought there was no direct link between Narnia and Christianity.

Consistency is the hobgoblin of little minds, I guess. Rowling's novels have been shown to be of the same "ultimate meaning" as the *Narnia* books, so let's move on to Mr. Abanes' last point.

Difference: *"In the works of Tolkien and Lewis issues of 'morality and integrity are at stake and dealt with as important and significant concerns'....In the Harry Potter series, however, morality is presented inconsistently....Rowling's moral universe is a topsy-turvy world with no firm rules of right and wrong or any godly principles by which to determine the truly good from the truly evil."* **(Abanes, *Magick*, pp. 243-245)**

In books which are about the war of good and evil — and where the good only prevail by way of their virtue and dependence on figures representing Christ and the Holy Trinity, only the clueless or willfully blind reader is unable to discern the truly good from the truly evil. That good people sometimes do bad things and the bad some good does not make the ***Harry Potter*** world "topsy-turvy", but much like our own.

What is edifying in this alternate universe parallel to our own, is that we are able to experience in our imagination both love and life after death in Christ, because of our identification with Harry's loyalty and courageous faith. Mr. Abanes' blindness to this is no fault of Ms. Rowling, but testimony of his ideological and jaundiced reading of her work.

I have fallen to the failing of which I accuse Mr. Abanes: a lack of charity in reading and a lack of love for the writer I criticize. Mr. Abanes certainly feels he is doing God's work protecting innocents from satanic influence, and he should be applauded for that intention. It is unfortunate that his abilities to interpret literature of quality are limited to reading interpretations made by others, because the virtue of his intention will be forgotten as ***Harry Potter***'s Christian meaning becomes clear in the last books.

Then I hope those Christian critics of the same mind as Mr. Abanes who wrote articles, gave sermons, and spoke to friends about the dangerous demonic forces at play in ***Harry Potter***, will realize their error and what damage they have done to the faith and the Church in the eyes of unbelievers. Already the schools and media portray faith in Christ as a confession of ignorance and weakness. Imagine the field-day these self-appointed enemies of delusion will have because of the evangelical rush to brand as "evil" and "witchcraft" what is Christian and spiritually edifying. Certainly it will be a good time for humility from the pulpit and written apologies to Ms. Rowling by owl post.

Could I be wrong? If I thought I was wrong, it would have been fraudulent for me to write this book. Please be sure I am convinced that Harry Potter is a Christian hero. But, yes, I could be wrong. You have my word that, if I am, I'll send a long note of apology to Mr. Abanes for him to include in the next edition of his book (and I'll eat my hat).

Appendix B

Guide to the Guides

Books About Harry Potter

Seven books about **Harry Potter** of some value are currently in print, and four more are about to be released as this book goes to press. I have enjoyed each and every one in print — and I learned quite a bit along the way. Fellow students of the **Potter** books (those who like them and those that don't) have asked for my opinion of these guides and companion pieces. I am happy to oblige this request with thumbnail sketches of each book's more obvious virtues and deficiencies.

Companion Texts:

Because the medieval and magical world of Hogwarts is populated with people, animals, and language unfamiliar to most modern readers, Harry's popularity has created a market for companion texts. The following two books explain many of the historical and literary references Ms. Rowling makes in her stories. They are not infallible guides (see Chapter 13 for a notable gaffe in the meaning of the Patronus Charm) but on the whole they are dependable, delightful, and a definite plus in coming to a better appreciation of Ms. Rowling's knowledge and craftsmanship.

1. David Colbert, *The Magical Worlds of Harry Potter: A Treasury of Myths, Legends and Fascinating Facts*, Lumina Press, Wrightsville Beach, NC, 2001.

Virtues:

(a) Encyclopedic — You have to love the careful research and consequent trivia that constitute this guide. Who was to know that "Avada Kedavra" is Rowling's adaptation of an Aramaic spell to cure disease? Who would have tracked Aragog the Acromantula and his wife Mosag's names to the Biblical Gog and Magog?

(b) Sense of Humor — Colbert was once the head writer of teevee's *Who wants to be a Millionaire?*, and he keeps his treatment of this material light. All of his answers to his *Jeopardy*-like questions are entertaining as well as informative.

Deficiencies:

(a) Organization — *Magical Worlds* is annoying in that it is alphabetically organized, but the chapter titles are in the forms of questions. This makes the table of contents effectively useless for quick skimming.

(b) Syncretic — Colbert delights in the incredible wealth of medieval and magical allusions to be found in Rowling's *Harry Potter*. He certainly is aware of many Christian symbols therein and the scriptural references Rowling makes. But he misses the boat on "Alchemy" and other Christian allusions because the treasury sees no pivotal meaning in the books.

2. Allan Zola Kronzek and Elizabeth Kronzek, *The Sorcerer's Companion: A Guide to the Magical World of Harry Potter*, Broadway Books, New York, 2001.

Virtues:

(a) Organization — Strictly alphabetical, this *Companion* is simple to use. If you want to find "Alchemy", you might be disappointed not to find it with the "A"s, but a quick check in the table of contents reveals "Nicholas Flamel" (and a decent discussion of alchemy).

(b) Seriousness — The Kronzek's take their history and magic seriously. Consequently, their book doesn't have the grins and giggles of Colbert's book. It does have greater depth in its entries and more references, however, which are this book's real strength.

(c) Magic entries — This is indeed a "**Sorcerer's** Companion". There are entries about the fantastic beasts and the like, but the value of the Kronzeks' book is in the articles on magic and magicians: 15 pages on the history of magicians alone and more on witches, wizards, etc.

Deficiencies:

(a) Entry Selection — I enjoyed reading the selections on Demons, Circe, Gnomes, Morgana, Palmistry, and Zombies, but really, they aren't part of the Hogwarts world. Colbert is more Harry-focused than the Kronzeks.

(b) Naturalism — For all their great love of the mantic arts and magic, the Kronzeks don't want anyone to think that they believe the history of magic is anything but "bad science", ignorance, and superstition. Alas, they are naturalists; distancing themselves appropriately from the occult, they also are skeptical about the existence of a supernatural or contranatural realm. Expect a patronizing historical "explanation" for much of what medieval men and women believed to be true and beautiful — and no mention of Christianity apart from its supposed persecution of all magicians.

Critical Reading:

The great success of the *Potter* series has spawned a few books exploring their meaning. For example, Scholastic, Inc., has put out Reader's Guides for each book with study helps for use in the classroom. I review below the two books for adult readers by other publishers.

3. Philip Nel, *J. K. Rowling's Harry Potter Novels: A Reader's Guide*, Continuum Books, New York, 2001.

Virtues:

(a) Brevity — Mr. Nel's book is less than one hundred pages long, packed with the best life of Rowling, survey of influences, and discussion of themes available (besides this book!). He is succinct and on-target.

(b) Clarity — Mr. Nel writes excellent expository prose. He has the evidence from the texts and the critics to make his points, and he uses this evidence elegantly in a short space.

(c) References — Mr. Nel's research, especially of criticism of the Rowling oeuvre and her many interviews in England and America, is a gold-mine for both the casual reader and the serious student.

Deficiencies:

(a) Grapeshot — Mr. Nel covers a host of influences and themes, but won't commit to identifying the principal or most important ones. If you expect to find answers about the meaning of the books themselves or why they are so popular, you will be disappointed.

(b) Information before insight — There are some jewels in here! I had not noticed, for example, that all the numbers on Diagon Alley are prime numbers. Mr. Nel reveals that — but doesn't explain it except as a number game along the lines of Lewis Carroll. When Mr. Nel does share his insights (his rebuke to her jaundiced critics is excellent), the reader only wishes his *Guide* had less information and references, and more of Mr. Nel's discernment.

4. Elizabeth D. Schafer, Ph.D., *Beacham's Sourcebooks for Teaching Young Adult Fiction: Exploring Harry Potter*, Beacham Publishing, Osprey, FL, 2000.

Virtues:

(a) Coverage — Almost 500 pages in length, Dr. Schafer touches on almost everything imaginable about *Harry Potter*. She has written the unrivaled source book for the *Potter* series.

(b) Gateways — Food in *Harry Potter*? Geography? Mythology? If a homeschooling parent wanted to write a "Unit Study" using *Harry Potter* to create a curriculum for an enthusiastic child, Dr. Schafer's *Sourcebook* has all the subjects, references, and internet sites necessary.

Deficiencies:

(a) Depth — The book is written at the third grade reading level, and while the references are encyclopedic in number, they are also usually superficial. A great resource for brainstorming but not for serious study. Nel's *Guide*, though only one-fifth the length, is the more stimulating and challenging "trot".

(b) Insufficient Charity — Dr. Schafer does not respect Christian objections to the *Potter* series. She is uncharitable and condescending to parents with occult concerns.

Christian Reflections:

Because a large part of the media storm surrounding *Harry Potter* has been generated by the controversy about whether Ms. Rowling's works lionize forbidden occult practices, several books have been written within the "Christian Ghetto" to answer that question. Though they may be of little interest to readers who are not "heart, soul, mind, and strength" Evangelical-believers, these books are the only ones that examine the books as to their meaning, good or bad.

5. Richard Abanes, *Harry Potter and the Bible: The Menace behind the Magick*, Horizon Books, Camp Hill, PA, 2001

Virtues:

(a) Intention — Mr. Abanes is a real-life "Ghost Buster" of sorts, who has written many books on cults and their heresies (his latest book is on the Latter Day Saints). He wrote this book because he knows that playing with spiritual powers outside an authentic revelation is not fun-and-games, but a life-and-death matter. His intention, protecting the innocent from corruption, is outstanding.

(b) Organization — *Bible* is meticulously organized. Mr. Abanes reviews each book and discusses its failings. He then offers his commentary on why the books are dangerous and should be avoided.

(c) Thoroughness — Nothing escapes Mr. Abanes's microscopic examination of the books in his search for what is wrong with them — except, of course, their larger meaning and great value. That Mr. Abanes misses the boat was not for lack of effort and "close reading".

Deficiencies:

(a) Ideological faith — Mr. Abanes's faith is one of litmus tests and proof texts. In brief, he reads the Bible as a Muslim reads the Koran: as an ideological guide and work of jurisprudence, rather than the voice of tradition understandable within that tradition. Ms. Rowling as a traditional and orthodox Christian is of an incomprehensible worldview to Mr. Abanes. It is difficult to read his book after the first few pages, because it descends into a diatribe and harangue.

(b) Insufficient Charity — Mr. Abanes has written a 275 page book without saying a single kind word about Ms. Rowling, her books, or anyone stupid enough to read or enjoy them. How is this possible for an author claiming to be writing a Christian book? Only someone of the author's black-and-white world view "looking for ammunition" could find this book helpful or insightful.

6. Connie Neal, **What's a Christian to do with Harry Potter?**, Waterbrook Press, Colorado Springs, CO, 2001.

7. Connie Neal, **The Gospel According to Harry Potter**, Westminster John Knox Press, 2002

Virtues:

(a) Intention — Mrs. Neal's books on **Harry Potter** have been written to bring peace to Christian communities divided by Pottermania. **Christian** argues that Potter-bashers and Potter-lovers can both be earnest Christians; **Gospel** demonstrates how the novels can be read as lessons in Bible teachings and Christian morality.

(b) Organization — Mrs. Neal's books are a model of clear organization and thoughtful arguments. No "lost asides" or "straw men" here.

(c) Clarity — Mrs. Neal is the best writer commenting on the **Potter** books except Mr. Nel. Her prose is written at the level of popular magazines, and her points are always well made.

Deficiencies:

(a) Thesis — Mrs. Neal argues that the books *can be read* as if they were Christian by the Christian reader trying to make the best of this cultural phenomenon. That the books are *in fact* Christian and only understandable in light of their Christian symbolism, morality, and meaning escapes her.

(b) Excessive Charity — Mrs. Neal is very sensitive to those Christians who insist that reading *Harry Potter* novels amounts to sinful disregard for scriptural injunctions against the occult. Her charity is admirable but excessive; these Christians are well intended in their caution and obedience — but they are wrong. Mrs. Neal seems afraid to say this, though she has come as close as one can in *Gospel*.

(c) Faint Praise — Mrs. Neal "damns with faint praise" as the saying goes. Rather than laud the *Potter* books as edifying and challenging books, she says a Christian can read them without risking their salvation — and really clever Christians can use them as missionary tools to witness to the un-churched. This is patronizing to Ms. Rowling, and no service to the community she hopes to serve.

High Road Criticism:

8. John Granger, *The Hidden Key to Harry Potter*, Zossima Press, Port Hadlock, WA, 2002

Virtues:

(a) Single-mindedness — Mr. Granger thinks the *Potter* books have a "hidden meaning" and he is relentless in "peeling the onion" for the reader.

(b) Sympathy with Text — Mr. Granger alone tracks the principal influences on Ms. Rowling, the formula and internal structure of her series, its symbolism, and its larger meaning. This "High Road" approach demonstrates a careful consideration of the books as literature rather than pop-culture — and a greater sympathy with Ms. Rowling as writer.

(c) Depth — Mr. Granger is not afraid to challenge the reader with difficult ideas and passages from the best writers.

Burckhardt, Eliade, Cavernos, Cutsinger, Aristotle, Schuon, and friends are all here — and they aren't slowing down so everyone can keep up.

Deficiencies:

(a) Organization — *Hidden Key* was written as four lectures, and it remains in this original organization. Mr. Granger's readers would have been better served if he'd re-worked the material for his different audience; what works as a lecture sometimes fails on the printed page.

(b) Projection — Though Mr. Granger comes to his conclusion after a thorough examination of the themes, structure, and symbolism of the *Potter* novels, is it remarkable that an Orthodox Christian finds himself arguing that *Harry Potter* is about or for Orthodox Christians? Of course, it should be said that only a Christian could see Christian meaning if it is in fact there — but one has to wonder if *Key* isn't also what Ms. Rowling meant when she commented about criticism from fundamentalists: "People tend to find in my books what they want to find." *(Today Show*, **October 20, 2000)**

(c) Depth — Mr. Granger really expects his readers to learn some alchemical theory in this book, and forces the reader through some pretty long passages that could have been omitted.

Other:

Here's a list of other *Potter* guidebooks that I have not studied or which were not in print as this book goes to press.

- Jack Zipes, ***Sticks and Stones: The Troublesome Success of Children's Literature from Slovenly Peter to Harry Potter***, Routledge, New York, 2002

- Andrew Blake, ***The Irresistible Rise of Harry Potter: Kid-Literature in a Globalised World***, W. W. Norton, September, 2002

- Francis Bridger, *A Charmed Life: The Spirituality of Potter World*, Image Books, September, 2002

- Elizabeth Heilman (editor), *Harry Potter's World: Multidisciplinary Critical Perspectives*, Routledge, January, 2003

Appendix C

Reference List

Recommended Further Reading

Inklings:

* Humphrey Carpenter, *The Inklings*, HarperCollins, London, 1997

* Kathryn Lindskoog, *The Lion of Judah in Never-Never Land: God, Man & Nature in C. S. Lewis' Narnia Tales*, Eerdmans, Grand Rapids, MI, 1979.

* Paul Ford, *Companion to Narnia: A Complete Guide to the Enchanting World of C. S. Lewis's The Chronicles of Narnia*, HarperSanFrancisco, New York, 1994.

* Tom Shippey, *J.R. R. Tolkien: Author of the Century*, Houghton Mifflin, Boston, 2001.

* James Cutsinger, "C. S. Lewis as Apologist and Mystic", Lecture delivered for the Narnia Clubs of New York, December 1998. Available on the internet at *www.cutsinger.net/publications*.

* C. S. Lewis, *The Abolition of Man, or Reflections on Education with Special Reference to the Teaching of English in the Upper Forms of Schools*, Collier, New York, 1955.

* C. S. Lewis, *The Discarded Image: An Introduction to Medieval and Renaissance Literature*, Cambridge University Press (Canto), Cambridge, 1994.

* C. S. Lewis (edited by Walter Hooper), *On Stories and Other Essays on Literature*, Harcourt Brace Jovanovich, New York, 1982.

* C. S. Lewis (editor*)*, *Essays Presented to Charles Williams*, Eerdmans, Grand Rapids, MI, 1966.

* C. S. Lewis, *A Preface to Paradise Lost*, Oxford University Press, London, 1974.

* J. R. R. Tolkien, *The Tolkien Reader*, Ballantine, New York, 1966.

Traditionalist:

* Martin Lings, *Symbol and Archetype: A Study of the Meaning of Existence*, Quinta Essentia, Longsmead, 1991.

* Martin Lings, *Ancient Beliefs and Modern Superstitions*, Quinta Essentia, Cambridge, 1991.

* Martin Lings, *The Eleventh Hour: The Spiritual Crisis of the Modern World in the Light of Tradition and Prophecy*, Quinta Essentia, Cambridge, 1987.

* Martin Lings, *The Secret of Shakespeare*, Inner Traditions International, New York, 1984.

* Jean Paris (translated by Richard Seaver), *Shakespeare*, Grove Press, New York, 1960.

* E. M. W. Tillyard, *The Elizabethan World Picture*, Vintage, New York, (1942).

* Arthur Lovejoy, *The Great Chain of Being: A Study of the History of an Idea*, Harvard University Press, Cambridge, MA, 1978

* James Cutsinger, *The Form of Transformed Vision: Coleridge and the Knowledge of God*, Mercer University Press, Macon, GA, 1987.

* James Cutsinger, *Advice to the Serious Seeker: Meditations on the Teaching of Frithjof Schuon*, State University of New York Press, Albany, NY, 1997.

* Mircea Eliade, *The Sacred and the Profane: The Nature of Religion*, Harcourt, Brace, and World, New York, 1959.

* Mircea Eliade, *Images and Symbols: Studies in Religious Symbolism*, Sheed and Ward, New York, 1969.

* Titus Burckhardt, *Alchemy: Science of the Cosmos, Science of the Soul*, Penguin Books, Baltimore, MD, 1972.

* Phillip Johnson, *Reason in the Balance: The Case Against Naturalism in Science, Law, and Education*, InterVarsity Press, Downers Grove, IL, 1995.

* J. E. Cirlot, *A Dictionary of Symbols*, Dorset Press, New York, 1991.

* Rene Guenon (translated by Alvin Moore, Jr.), *Fundamental Symbols: The Universal Language of Sacred Science*, Quinta Essentia, Cambridge, 1995.

* Rene Guenon (translated by Lord Northbourne), *The Reign of Quantity & The Signs of the Times*, Sophia Perrenis et Universalis, Ghent, NY, 1995.

* Rene Guenon (translated by A. Osborne), *Crisis of the Modern World*, Luzac, London, 1975.

* Rene Guenon (translated by Joscelyn Godwin), *The Multiple States of Being*, Larson, Burdett, NY, 1984.

* Huston Smith, *Why Religion Matters: The Fate of the Human Spirit in an Age of Disbelief*, HarperSanFrancisco, New York, 2000

* Huston Smith, *Forgotten Truth: The Primordial Tradition*, Harper Colophon, New York, 1977.

* Seyyed Hossein Nasr (editor), *The Essential Writings of Frithjof Schuon*, Element, Rockport, MA, 1986.

The Church and Masculinity:

* Leon Podles, *The Church Impotent: The Feminization of Christianity*, Spense Publishing, Dallas, 1999.

* John Miller, *Calling God "Father": Essays on the Bible, Fatherhood, and Culture*, Paulist Press, New York, 1999.
* Weldon Hardenbrook, *Missing from Action: Vanishing Manhood in America*, Thomas Nelson, Nashville, 1997
King Arthur:
* Howard Pyle, *The Story of King Arthur and His Knights*, Dover, New York, 1965.
* Howard Pyle, *The Story of the Champions of the Round Table*, Dover, New York, 1965.
* Howard Pyle, *The Story of Sir Launcelot and his Companions*, Dover, New York, 1991.
* Howard Pyle, *The Story of the Grail and the Passing of Arthur*, Dover, New York, 1992.

Classical and Traditional Christian Philosophy:

* Edith Hamilton and Huntington Cairns (editors), *The Collected Dialogues of Plato*, Princeton University Press, Princeton, 1978.
* Allan Bloom (translator), *The Republic of Plato*, Basic Books, New York, 1968.
* Constantine Cavarnos, *Plato's View of Man*, Institute for Byzantine and Modern Greek Studies, Belmont, MA, 1982.
* Hippocrates Apostle and Lloyd Gerson (translators), *Aristotle: Selected Works*, The Peripatic Press, Grinnell, IO, 1991.
* William Wallace, *The Elements of Philosophy: A Compendium for Philosophers and Theologians*, Alba House, New York, 1977.

Traditional Christianity:

* St. Nikodimos and St. Makarios (compilers), G. E. H. Palmer, Philip Sherrard, and Kallistos Ware (translators), *The Philokalia: Volume One*, Faber and Faber, Boston, 1990.
* Dr. Alexandre Kalomiros, *The River of Fire*, The Monastery Press, Montreal, 1981.

Appendix D

Resources Available from the Author

Lectures:

John Granger delivers a one-hour program on "The Secret of Harry Potter" to Groups (Library, School, and Homeschool), Literary Societies, and Churches that is a guaranteed crowd-pleaser. Combining humor with insights from the Great Books, John explains the meaning and genius behind Pottermania. Call today to schedule John to speak before your group or to receive a free listing of his various programs.

Videos:

The Hidden Key to Harry Potter was originally a lecture series, and the lectures are available for purchase on videocassette at $20.00 each. John's talks are a hoot, as well as a sure bet to jumpstart discussion in Harry Potter Fan clubs, the classroom, and church groups. Videos are all approximately an hour and ten minutes in length, running in parallel with the Parts of this book with matching titles.

Video 1: "Taking Harry Seriously"

Video 2: "The Secret of Harry Potter"

Video 3: "The Meaning of Harry Potter"

Video 4: "What Will Happen With Harry?"

Cassettes:

Audio cassette packages of ***The Hidden Key*** are still in production. Call today for information about their pricing and availability.

Cassette Package 1: "Taking Harry Seriously"

Cassette Package 2: "The Secret of Harry Potter"

Cassette Package 3: "The Meaning of Harry Potter"

Cassette Package 4: "What Will Happen With Harry?"

Zossima Press

231 S. 7th Street

Port Hadlock, WA 98339

john@zossima.com